MW01063202

The Crops Look Good

The Crops
Look Good

News from a Midwestern
Family Farm

Sara DeLuca

MINNESOTA
HISTORICAL
SOCIETY PRESS

©2015 by Sara DeLuca. All rights reserved. No part of this book may be used or reproduced in any manner whatsoever without written permission except in the case of brief quotations embodied in critical articles and reviews. For information, write to the Minnesota Historical Society Press, 345 Kellogg Blvd. W., St. Paul, MN 55102-1906.

www.mnhspress.org

The Minnesota Historical Society Press is a member of the Association of American University Presses.

Manufactured in the United States of America

10 9 8 7 6 5 4 3 2 1

∞ The paper used in this publication meets the minimum requirements of the American National Standard for Information Sciences—Permanence for Printed Library Materials, ANSI Z39.48-1984.

International Standard Book Number
ISBN: 978-0-87351-975-5 (paper)
ISBN: 978-0-87351-976-2 (e-book)

Library of Congress Cataloging-in-Publication Data
De Luca, Sara, 1943–
    The crops look good : news from a Midwestern family farm / Sara DeLuca.
      pages cm
    Includes bibliographical references and index.
    ISBN 978-0-87351-975-5 (pbk. : alk. paper) — ISBN 978-0-87351-976-2 (ebook)
    1. Farm life—Wisconsin—History—20th century. 2. Farm life—Middle West—History—20th century. 3. Country life—Wisconsin—History—20th century. 4. Country life—Middle West—History—20th century. 5. Rural families—Wisconsin—History—20th century. 6. Family farms—Wisconsin—History—20th century. 7. Farms, Small—Wisconsin—History—20th century. I. Title.
    S521.5.W6D45 2015
    636.0977—dc23

                                   2014038089

This and other Minnesota Historical Society Press books are available from popular e-book vendors.

For the letter writers,
past, present, and future.

Contents

Andreas Vilhelm Vilhelmson 1851–1881   Ole Olsen Rolstad 1845–1875
Kristi Kristiansdatter 1852–1934   Maria Arnesdatter Lee (Lie) 1853–1950
| |
Fredrick 1875–1958   Clara 1874–1912
Karoline 1876–1900   **Olava 1875–1966**
William Andreas 1879–1975
Adeline 1882–1960

|

Raymond 1903–1944
Margaret 1904–2000
Adele 1906–1982
Leland 1908–1995
Clarence 1910–2006
Wilmar 1912–2006
Donald 1914–2002
Helen 1915–2010
Alice 1917–2000

|

Harvey Hellerud 1913–1992

|

Margaret 1940
Susan 1943
Sara 1943
Theodore 1946
Priscilla 1950

The Aunts, Uncles, and Cousins

RAYMOND. m. Ethel Michaelson: sons, Robert and John

MARGARET. m. Melvin Gorder: son, Charles

ADELE. m. Maurice Fleming: son, Robert (Bobby)

LELAND. m. Violet Jensen: daughter, LeeAnn; sons, Raymond and Carl

CLARENCE. m. Louise Holcomb: son, William (Billy); daughter, Joyce

WILMAR. m. Gladys Larson; sons, Gary, Alan, and Vern

DONALD. m. Vera Bengston Nelson: daughters, Renee and Kay; son, Steven
(Vera's sons from a previous marriage: Elroy, Murrell, Gary, and Rodney)

ALICE. m. Eyvind "Pud" Rostad: sons, James (Jimmy), Donald, and Dean;
daughters, Carole and Jeanne

Polk County, Wisconsin

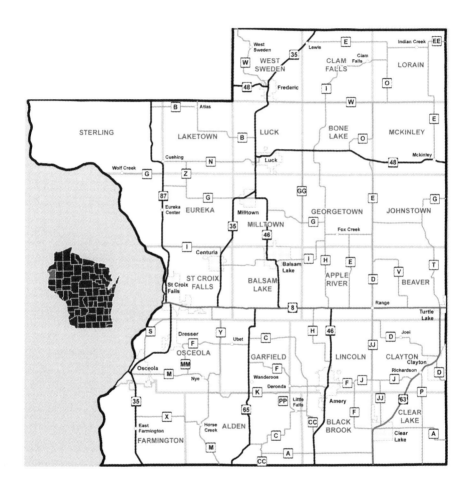

Courtesy Polk County (Wisconsin) Department of Land Information/
Division of Geographic Information Systems.

The Crops Look Good

Prologue

History is a pact between the dead,
the living, and the yet unborn.
EDMUND BURKE

MY MOTHER CAME from a family of storytellers. I didn't know they were writers, too, until one autumn day in 1995 when I was visiting my elderly aunt Margaret in Mesa, Arizona. The goal of my visit was to help her prepare for a long-overdue sorting and dispersing of her household goods and memorabilia.

"I've saved a lot of letters over the years," she said, "and because you are so keen on family history, I want you to have them. You'll know how to put them to some good purpose."

I read all night—letters from my grandmother Olava Williamson, from Aunt Adele, Uncle Raymond, and my mother, Helen, all to "Dear Margaret," the daughter who had moved away in 1923 to Minneapolis and in 1935 to Los Angeles. I read letters from Margaret to her husband, Mel, detailing her summer visits to "the homeplace" in Wisconsin. I met my elders, including my own mother, as they were in the mysterious years before I was born. I saw my own childhood through the eyes of those who had nourished and supported me.

Then I put the letters away, for nearly twenty years. They were a burdensome gift. I had been given an assignment I could not fulfill. The farming culture described in these letters has passed into history. I wanted to bear witness to that time. But any book I might create from these writings would require skillful narration, and I did not feel up to the task. My work would not be equal to that of the letter writers, whose words fell from their pens—or pencils—so freely, so directly, without artifice.

All the writers are gone, but their words remain. Now, as a family elder, I feel compelled to share them. My reasons are best described in this excerpt from *Soul Mates* by Thomas Moore:

> The culture of a family is not only a shaping influence—it is also a resource into which a person may dip throughout her life for direction, meaning and style. People living the modern life often complain about a loss of traditional values or about feeling aimless, rootless and adrift. If we were to see the family as a wealthy source of traditions, stories, characters and values, we might not feel so alone and abandoned to a life that has to be manufactured every day.
>
> We can't make a life out of nothing. Our families, even though they rarely seem to be perfect models for us, offer plenty of raw material that we can shape into a life in our own creative fashion.

Here is the raw material that was given to me. It is presented chronologically, taking the reader through the Roaring Twenties, the Great Depression, World War II, and a period of relative calm and prosperity at midcentury. The location is dairy farming country, Polk County, Wisconsin.

As compelling as an individual's private hopes and struggles, triumphs and tragedies may be, it is the setting—time and place— that deserves a starring role in this family drama, written by those who lived it.

In working with such a wealth of words, my challenge has been primarily one of omission. I have eliminated many letters and sections of letters that lack relevance to the larger story. I have used ellipses wherever sentences have been omitted or condensed. Oral narratives, recorded over a period of many years, as well as material from newspapers, magazines, and various history sources, have been included to complete a picture of the Upper Midwest family-farming culture as my elders knew it.

Directly as a Stone

1923–24

When a writer has something to say, it falls from the pen
as directly as a stone falls to the ground.
HENRY DAVID THOREAU

HELEN WILLIAMSON, age seven, is seated at the kitchen table, writing by kerosene lamplight on a cold winter evening, January 28, 1923. Gripping a stubby pencil, she addresses an envelope to her eldest sister: Miss Margaret Williamson, Dunwoody Hall, 52 South Tenth Street, Minneapolis, Minnesota. Helen adds her return address to the upper left corner—H. Williamson, Rural Route 1, Centuria, Wisconsin—and affixes a two-cent postage stamp to the upper right.

Dear Margaret,
I received your letter last Friday and haven't ansered you yet so I think I had better get busy. Now I begin as follows:
   Last night the furnace explowded over at the schoolhouse. Glen Kelly was sapposed to go home with the teacher and she kept him waiting outside for quite a while. She was in a hurry and she dumped 4 or 5 buckets of coal in the furnace and shut everything up so no air could get in. At half past five after school was let out Donald Jorgensen went over after his arithmetic book and when he stepped inside of the door the smoke just rolled out. He called his dad over there and when he got there

the pipes were blowed out of their places, the furnace door was open and the cover of the water pan was blowed off.

When Jorgensen was putting the pipes back it explowded right in his face. The basement floor was all black and the walls of the hall-way were all black with soot and when we came to school and wawked across the floor there was a bunch of footprints. So they cleaned house today at school. Everyone helped.

I got to tell you what I got for marks: History 65, Geog. 70, Spelling 100. My average is 78½. Awful for me, aint it?

I'd like to write more but it is cold and I am tired.

Your sister, Helen Williamson

Helen's mother, Olava, encloses this note:

That was some excitement at the schoolhouse. It was a mess all right, but could have been a real tragedy. Doesn't Helen write the cutest little letters? Pretty good for 7 years old, I say.

Pretty good for seven years old, any time and place. Helen's penmanship and vocabulary are surprisingly advanced, considering there is no preschool or kindergarten education provided at this time. Some early home schooling by her older sisters may help to explain it.

Helen is a second-grade student at the South Milltown Rural School, District No. 3, one of the countless country schools operating in Wisconsin in the 1920s. Since most children walk to school, even in subzero winter temperatures, rural schoolhouses are spaced only a few miles apart.

Eighth-grade commencement will mark the end of formal education for the majority of students. In addition to the academic subjects—reading, writing, arithmetic, history, geography, and science—the curriculum includes life skills, such as health and hygiene, moral conduct, and citizenship. The rural schoolhouse also serves as a center for public life—a place to gather for picnics, town meetings, patriotic celebrations, and cultural programs.

The 1923 census lists thirty-four students in the one-room school, representing seventeen families from surrounding farms, south of Milltown village. The teacher, Hazel Benton, is paid one hundred dollars per month during the nine-month school year, instructing children in grades one through eight. The students help with routine cleaning, washing blackboards, dusting erasers, raking leaves, shoveling snow, pumping and carrying water, and assisting with the younger children. Parents pitch in for major cleaning and repairs before school commences each September.

The fall 1923 school census lists four students from the Willie Williamson family: Clarence, thirteen; Wilmar, eleven; Donald, nine; Helen, seven. (Alice, age five, will begin first grade the following year.)

Four older siblings—Raymond, Margaret, Adele, and Leland—have also attended the South Milltown School. Raymond, a recent high school graduate, is a banker in Downing, Wisconsin. Adele attends high school in Milltown. Leland, who happily left school after completing the eighth grade, is farming with Willie. Margaret has recently moved sixty-five miles away, to Minneapolis, where she works as a bookkeeper for Walman Optical Company.

This is dairy farming country, settled primarily by Scandinavian and German immigrants. Much of the gently rolling land has been logged off, the stumps blasted from the ground with dynamite, the fields and meadows divided into neat rectangles bordered by gravel roads. Tidy farmsteads with soaring red barns, silos, and sheds, protected by windbreaks of oak and elm and pine, dot the landscape. An abundance of glacial lakes and streams provides essential water for livestock, as well as recreation and scenic beauty. The soil that once nurtured hardwood forests is rich and loamy. But the climate is extreme and unforgiving, ranging from one hundred degrees in midsummer to minus thirty in the deep of winter.

This is the world that Helen knows, the world her eldest sister Margaret misses keenly. Margaret has been a second mother to the little girls, Helen and Alice. She writes often, and Helen replies.

JULY 15, 1923
Dear Margaret,
I love summer vacashun and right now the weather is just perfect. I rode on Fanny this morning when we put the cows out to

Olava Williamson (center) with (left to right) Adele, Alice, Helen, and Margaret, 1922

pasture. Alice and Donald and Wilmar rode to and I was at the rear end. I just about fell off.

It's Sunday and the men are haying today. Papa says he can't afford to rest on Sunday.

Last night I saw the cutest little rabbit with brown fur and blue eyes. That's all I can think of to write for now so I will close. Piles and piles of love from sister Helen

P.S. Mama is going to write to you now and she will put her letter in this same envelope.

JULY 15, 1923
Dear Margaret,
Received your card and see that you are comfortably located and I hope you will like it there in Minneapolis. I was so lone-

some for you all last week, but am sort of getting over it now. Plenty of work and a bunch of youngsters around help to overcome a great deal of troubles. I wrote a few words to Raymond on Monday and told him you have gone. I got an answer from him yesterday. He likes his job at the Bank of Downing and expects to be promoted to Cashier before the year is through. He didn't say anything about coming home this week. It is pretty far to come up here from Downing—more than 50 miles I think—and perhaps he is unable to borrow a car. Even when he does manage to come up he spends most of his time in Milltown courting Ethel Michaelson and we hardly see him at all. I guess the old home isn't good enough for him anymore. Well, if those two decide to get married soon they will never know what it is to be young and have fun.

Papa wants to finish haying before he ships livestock to South St. Paul next week so he and the boys are working hard, putting up hay. They have hauled in fifteen loads and will put up that field in front of the house today.

Alice, Helen, Donny, and Wilmar on Fanny, about 1923

Next week I am going to try my luck at getting some berries in Korsan's pasture. I have been busy canning gooseberries. I also made some jelly from the currents I picked on the back 40. Yesterday I washed clothes all day long and my back hurts today . . .

Papa and I went up town Wednesday evening. I had to get some groceries. I heard some terrible news. You remember H. E. Perrin that sold us the strawberries and watermelons. His eleven year old girl met with an accident on Wednesday. She picked up a dynamite cap in the yard and stuck it into her pocket and in some way it blowed off and killed her in a little while. They started off with her to get to a doctor but she died on the way, bled to death from the torn blood vessels. I surely feel sorry for the poor parents. I believe I could never stand a shock like that. We have been more than lucky raising a bunch like we have and never losing any. How thankful we should be.

Well, I must close now as I have work waiting and a bunch of hungry boys wanting dinner. I am going to make a shortcake for them. I hope you are getting lots of sleep so you will stay rested and if you do that you will get along all right.

We miss you. Your loving Mother

Olava Williamson is not quite forty-eight years old when she writes this fretful, hopeful, sorrowful, thankful letter. She writes of routine tasks on a busy summer day: haymaking, berry-picking, jelly, laundry, and a trip to town. Then, a horrific accident.

Most farmers keep explosives on hand for blasting stumps, clearing the land. Farming is a dangerous business—right up there with logging and mining. Tragedies occur, nearly every season. Sometimes they involve a child.

Olava is grateful for nine healthy children. She thinks she could never stand the shock of losing one.

JULY 26, 1923
Dear Margaret,
Well, I don't feel so very good tonight, but I must write you a few lines anyway.

I have wondered if anyone let you know the sad news about Alva's passing. You went to see Alva on Sunday, I believe, after she had her second operation. Did you get a chance to see her any more after that? You were her dearest friend, I know.

We have witnessed the largest funeral today that has ever been held in the North Valley Lutheran church. They picked out twelve girls to carry flowers and then the casket was loaded besides. The flowers were so beautiful I can't describe it.

Alva was buried in her wedding dress and her casket was a bluish gray brocaded plush. Rev. Hanson made a very impressive sermon and Bakke also spoke. The choir sang several songs. I have never seen a time when everybody felt so sorry. Rev. Hanson almost broke down too.

Poor, poor Oscar, he told me he has nothing to go home for now. He caressed her before they closed the casket and they just had to take him away. Pretty hard to see him.

Alva's mother has been crying so much. I could see she was really sick and she may have to go to bed too.

Wasn't it strange how fast Alva went, and she was in such high hopes of getting well and coming home soon. How uncertain this life is when we think of it. How necessary it is to look into the future and have those things in mind at all times.

Alva was a good example for any girl and I wish more were like her. She was simple in her ways and always had a smile for everyone, nothing put on.

The business places in Milltown closed up for the afternoon. North Valley church was too small today, completely filled, and I think there were just as many outside. Alva had so many friends and of course many were there on Oscar's account too. Oscar belongs to the Oddfellows and they will have a meeting tonight to see if they can hire someone to go out there and keep house for Oscar until he sort of recovers a little.

I am going to bed now and will try to write to you again soon.
Your loving Mama
P.S. Enclosed flower that I picked off Alva's grave.

*

Olava's letter expresses a collective grief, raw and real as yesterday.

The bereaved family, the Langkoses, lives a quarter mile away. The Williamson and Langkos girls have walked to the South Milltown schoolhouse together, shared buggy rides to church, picnicked and partied together in that tight-knit neighborhood. Now, as a new bride in the fullness of youth and beauty, Alva is gone. A burst appendix. The doctor's attempt to save her has failed. So has a chorus of prayers.

This is a community of Christians, who believe in a loving and protective God. Many farmers, including the Williamsons, do not attend church regularly, due to work, snow-clogged or muddy roads, and inclement weather. Theirs is a straightforward and unchallenged faith, requiring little discussion. Private prayers are heard as well as those raised in a church. Good works will be rewarded, in heaven if not on earth.

And yet, the earthly suffering can be hard to reconcile. Why must the most faithful, honorable families be burdened by such grief? God moves in some mysterious ways.

The death of a young person like Alva brings many past losses to Olava's mind. Her beloved sister, Clara, died in 1912, at the age of thirty-eight, from a bowel obstruction. A half-sister, Bella, died of "brain fever" in 1903, at thirteen. Another half-sister, Agnes, died of a ruptured appendix in 1897, at the age of six. The nearest doctor at that time was twenty miles away, in Taylors Falls, Minnesota, and he was not easily summoned. Most rural homes were without telephones, and if someone was dispatched to bring the doctor, it could be hours—even days—before he arrived at the bedside. Often it was too late.

Olava doesn't know her future losses, which must be taken one day at a time. She worries, though. She understands how precarious is the health and welfare of her family. *How uncertain this life is when we think of it.* And she does think of it, daily. In this time before antibiotics, serious illness and death are very present possibilities, even for the young and strong and beautiful. Along with the sorrow of that funeral, every parent must struggle with a guilty relief: "Thank God, not in my family, not yet. Please God, not now. Not ever."

Every tragedy is felt throughout the countryside. Every loss is shared. Yet, no matter what news the day has delivered, the work must go on. Cows must be fed and milked morning and evening, the barn must be cleaned, fields plowed and planted, crops cultivated and gathered in.

A few details to set the stage: Throughout Wisconsin's dairy country, small settlements are located five to six miles apart, on average. Milk has to be hauled to the creamery in town by horse and wagon on a daily basis. Extreme summer heat, or subzero winter weather, adds to the challenge of getting the milk to market without spoilage.

The Williamson farm is located midway between the villages of Milltown and Centuria, and Willie Williamson trades in both of them. These pioneer villages have developed with a system of bartering; the term *trade* persists long after most transactions are conducted with cash. Established around the turn of the century, the settlements are growing and thriving by 1923. Polk County, which consists of 956 square miles (425 of those water), now boasts nearly twenty-seven thousand residents. There are eleven villages, twenty-six unincorporated hamlets, and hundreds of family farms throughout the fertile countryside.

Village streets are not yet paved. They are muddy when it rains, dusty when it doesn't, and nearly impassable during winter snows. But there are creameries, feed mills, grocery and dry goods stores, slaughterhouses, butcher shops, lumberyards, livery stables, blacksmiths, banks, post offices, railroad stations, schools, churches, and cemeteries. Populations are expanding—already five hundred or so in each village.

The Soo Line Railroad has become a major factor in the region's development. Freight and passenger service through northern Polk County villages (beginning in 1901) connects the area with Twin Cities markets, the Duluth/Superior ports, and beyond. Everything comes in and goes out of town by rail, including livestock, commodities, merchandise, mail, and money. While the Milltown Telephone Company has been operating since 1913, most farmhouses are not yet equipped with telephones. Mail is the primary means of communication; urgent messages are telegraphed to the railroad depot and delivered by the depot agent, who holds a highly respected position in the community.

By the early twenties, many farms and rural villages have installed Delco systems, which provide a new source of illumination and mechanical power to areas not yet connected to the electrical grid. Delco technology utilizes a combination of gasoline engine generators and batteries. Power fluctuates; motors burn out. Yet this is a major improvement over the dim and dangerous kerosene lanterns of the early days.

An excerpt from "Centuria's Fiftieth Anniversary," published by the Centuria Commercial Club in 1950, describes the progress of that village:

> The first street lights were kerosene lamps. Each evening, Jim Howard, who was dray man, would light them. The kerosene lights were replaced by Albert Lea gas lights, six or eight on the Main Street. They had to be pumped up for pressure and Mr. Jim Walsh had the honor of tending them. In 1916 or '18 came battery powered electric lights, which were even better. In 1937 "White Way" lights were installed up and down Main Street. Each big round globe put out an unbelievable amount of light and the town seemed to be literally lit up like a Christmas tree.

The 1920s are an optimistic decade, a time of unprecedented industrial growth. National unemployment is measured at 2.4 percent. Electricity, modern plumbing, telephone service, and improved transportation are changing the face of America. Radios (called "radio sets" or "radio music boxes") are appearing in family parlors, providing a new form of entertainment as well as timely news from the wider world.

General health and life expectancy are improving nationwide. Vaccines for tetanus and whooping cough are developed in 1923. Tuberculosis ("consumption" or "white plague") remains a major health concern, with fresh air, rest, and patient isolation providing the only treatment options. Other worrisome diseases include poliomyelitis, diphtheria, measles, mumps, scarlet fever, pneumonia, and influenza.

Prohibition, that "great social and economic experiment, noble in motive" (in President Herbert Hoover's words), has been failing in rural American as well as in urban areas since its enactment in 1920. American ingenuity finds numerous ways to outwit the federal agents charged with enforcing the unenforceable. The Temperance Leagues despair; the profiteers rejoice.

Urban areas are experiencing an alarming rise in graft, corruption, and violent crime. But it will be a long time before most country folks will feel a need to install locks on their doors.

The height of hair fashion for women in 1923 is a boyish bob, shingle cut, close to the head, but it may take a year or more before such daring styles reach the rural population.

Cloche hats are beginning to appear. Shiny rayon stocking are replacing silk hose. A fast fox-trot, called the Charleston, is becoming the rage across America. Churches are reacting with fiery sermons against the dangers of lewd dancing. Free-spirited young women, known as "flappers," are scandalizing their parents and elders. Women have had the vote for three years, and where is this new freedom leading? Will it upset the order of a civilized society?

Time, the nation's first weekly news magazine, publishes its first issue on March 3, 1923. A new monthly called the *Readers Digest* is gaining popularity.

Warren G. Harding, the first president ever heard over the radio, dies in office on August 2. Vice president Calvin Coolidge is sworn in.

Auto sales are booming. Over four million new cars are produced in the United States in 1923, a 50 percent increase over the previous year. One out of every two cars sold in America is a Ford. The basic Model T touring car can be purchased for three hundred dollars, representing about 30 percent of the average household's annual income.

This is a time of general prosperity across the country, yet farm incomes are falling—a precursor to a looming financial crisis that will sweep across the continent and beyond.

A massive earthquake rocks Tokyo and Yokohama, Japan, killing an estimated 140,000 people. Such a distant disaster is barely noted in Polk County, Wisconsin. There are silos to be filled, cattle to be fed and milked, school clothes to be sewn and washed and ironed, preparations for another winter season that is coming on fast, too fast. There is never enough time for it all.

Olava Williamson writes to her daughter on Monday morning, August 27, 1923.

Dear Margaret,
Just a few lines before the mail carrier comes. You must be wondering by now why I haven't written more often of late but I have been unusually busy. You know we are done threshing and I have done considerable canning, which takes time. I am not through yet, as I have lots of pickles to put up . . .

Raymond said he wasn't planning to come home from Downing this last Sunday, as he was home a week ago, but when we drove to town, he was there. He did not come home to the farm at all this time, so I don't know what to think of it. It surely does cause us a lot of worry. He must be spending all his time with Ethel Michaelson and you know her mother has the tuberculosis, and it is contagious. Mrs. Michaelson is not expected to live very long now. The doctor has told them about two or three weeks is all she has left. I wonder if Raymond stops to think what the outcome may be if he continues this way. I have warned him and that is about all I can do . . .

Papa has decided to drive Adele to high school in Milltown this fall. Uncle Fred's kids too. Maybe he can trade driving with Fred so he won't have to make all those trips into town.

By the mid-twenties, approximately 45 percent of the nation's youth are attending high school, but the percentage is much lower in rural areas. High school education for country students often requires considerable effort and sacrifice. Since schools provide no transportation, parents must make two daily trips with their high school students or arrange for room and board in town. Tuition and book fees are often paid by the families, putting a high school education out of reach for many young people.

Because the Williamson farm is located only three miles from the village of Milltown, the trip is not impossible, but it is difficult on snowy or icy roads and during the spring melt. Sometimes neighbors will take turns with transportation, as Willie plans to do with his neighbor (and brother) Fred.

When the roads are passable, Willie Williamson enjoys motoring to town. He has owned an automobile for nearly six years, and has received his share of criticism. "Can you believe that Willie wasted his money that way?" the neighbors exclaim, shaking their heads. "Mark my words, those contraptions will never replace the horse, not on these narrow muddy roads, not out here in the country!"

In the case of that first car Willie bought, the critics were probably right, as he described decades later.

Now you take that Buick I bought in the summer of '17. That was a case of ignoring my common sense. Nice car—leather upholstery. But it was a mistake. It didn't add a thing to my income, nothing whatsoever. The only thing it did was add to expenses. I paid $119 for two hind tires on the damned thing. I don't believe I ran it 5,000 miles as long as I had it. That was George Moreland, the banker in Centuria, who recommended a car with a self-starter, and Buick was putting out a model like that. So he came out here to the farm with Martin Korsan, the car dealer in Centuria. They said I ought to have some entertainment for my family. I told 'em we had all the entertainment we needed right to home. But Korsan says, "I'll sell you that car for $715." I supposed that was a pretty good deal and I thought Olava was a little in favor of it . . . maybe she needed a little enjoyment. So due to that fact . . . Well, it was one of the worst mistakes I ever made. Damned car! It was big and clumsy, hard on gas. I paid fifty dollars for the battery. Had to store the battery every winter, and paid $10 for that, too.

Korsan, he gave me a driving lesson. Took me out back toward the pig house, on the hills. He wanted to show me how powerful the damned thing was. When it went uphill you had to pump air into the gas tank and force air into the carburetor. Korsan spent half a day with me on those hills and hollows and then I was on my own. No such thing as a license in those days, you know.

Willie's skeptical neighbors will be buying their own motorcars before long. By the mid-twenties, many farmers are tired of long trips by horse-drawn wagon and feel ready to give the horseless carriage a try. The car's engine can also be used to grind feed, pump water, cut wood, and power various farm implements.

Olava writes to Margaret on September 8, 1923.

Dear Margaret,
Received your letter and see you have been a busy girl. It is so good to get those letters from you. They brighten up my day considerably.

I didn't do any extra work after you left on Sunday morning. I felt so blue, and tired too. I finished cleaning up the house and then I slept awhile in the afternoon. I guess Papa would have liked to say good-bye to you, but I didn't call him. The minute he woke up he asked if you had gone. He thinks the world of you, don't you forget that. He would be a far different man if he didn't have so much to do, but he is sort of nervous and fretful from too much responsibility. We just have to overlook those things. Some day things will take a turn over and we will get rid of some of this worry.

We are going to leave the silo filling until next week because the corn is pretty green and Papa needs more time to clean up around the silo.

I am going to sew this afternoon. The little girls need some school dresses and I got them some gingham. I think I can manage that. I have a horrible spell of rheumatism so I just have a time of it getting around. It works in one leg and thigh so I can scarcely stoop down or get up.

We had a hard rain here a couple of days ago. I was washing clothes outside and had to quit and finish yesterday.

I haven't heard from Raymond all week. I hope he isn't sore at me for mentioning how he spends all his time at the Michaelsons and can't find a chance to visit here at home. Adele said she saw Ethel in front of her dad's blacksmith shop in town one day, looking all forlorn. I believe Mrs. Michaelson must be really sick by now.

Hulda Jasperson and Floyd Hansen are married. They got married young enough. They will never know what it is to be young and carefree. Foolish kids.

Foolish kids, Olava writes of the newlyweds.

Her own life is so lacking in recreation. Her days are filled with heavy work: pumping, hauling, and heating water; cooking and baking with a wood-fired range; gardening and preserving fruits and vegetables; cleaning the house; maintaining the yard; sewing, knitting, patching, scrubbing, and ironing clothes; looking after a large family in a small house with two bedrooms and no plumbing, central heating, or electricity.

Like most of her neighbors, Olava was a daughter of Norwegian immigrant farmers. Her father, Ole Rolstad, suffered ill health and died at the age of thirty on July 2, 1875. Olava was born four months later. She grew up knowing two very different worlds. Her primary home was the humble pioneer farm of her maternal grandparents in Eureka Township, Polk County. Olava also witnessed the luxurious life of the wealthy Charles A. Pillsbury family in their Minneapolis mansion, where her widowed mother was employed as a housemaid.

During her many visits to the mansion at 2200 Stevens Avenue South, Olava played with the Pillsburys' twin sons, Charles and John, marveling at their wealth of toys and games. (The boys, who were three years younger than Olava, kept in touch with her throughout their lives, pleasing her immensely.) Olava admired everything she saw—fine clothing, china, artwork, tapestries, expensive furnishings, fresh flowers—things that existed for the sake of beauty, not for utility, not because they could help a person get something done. The Pillsbury family enjoyed books and music, elegant foods, formal parties, and refined conversation. Olava would never lose her yearning for culture and elegance, in whatever form she could find it.

Following her eighth-grade graduation, Olava attended the Polk County Normal School in St. Croix Falls. She received additional teacher training in River Falls, Wisconsin, and taught in several rural schools before she married Willie Williamson in August 1902. As a teacher, she enjoyed respect and a degree of independence, though she was expected to follow a code of modest dress and deportment. During the school year she boarded at her students' homes, including with Willie's family.

Marriage, at the age of twenty-seven, ended Olava's teaching career. Raymond was born five months later. Eight children followed, spaced approximately two years apart.

The wedding was a quiet event, as circumstances dictated. There were no wedding photographs, but petite, fine-featured young Olava was surely a lovely bride.

William Andreas Williamson was also born to a Norwegian immigrant family. The family name, Vilhelmsen, was anglicized soon after they had settled in Wisconsin, the summer of 1881. Willie was two years old when his father was killed in a train accident five months later, leaving his mother responsible for three young children, with a fourth on the way. Willie remembers being tethered to chairs or trees while his mother worked in the barn and fields. Somehow the family survived, with the help of neighboring farmers and the good people of the Norwegian Lutheran church.

Willie's schooling was limited to five partial years in a country school, which was common at that time. A boy's labor was needed on the farm, making school attendance sporadic at best.

Willie grew tall and strong, and he was born to farm. He loved everything about it. Before marrying Olava in 1902, he dismantled the cabin he had grown up in, numbered the logs, and rebuilt it on eighty acres he had purchased between Milltown and Centuria.

Olava Rolstad, schoolteacher, about 1900

All nine children were born in that small cabin. In 1918, the family moved half a mile up the road to a slightly larger home with one hundred acres of tillable land and a deep well with an ample supply of water. Now they could really forge ahead.

Daughter Margaret recalls that as she and her siblings grew up, "Papa" counseled them about choosing mates who were capable and ambitious. "That's why I chose your mother," he would say. "I knew her family and I saw how she conducted herself. I knew she would work hard with me. Without that kind of help and cooperation, a man would just be finished."

William A. "Willie" Williamson, about 1900

There was never any mention of love—certainly not passion—figuring into the bargain. But of course there was more to the story than Willie and Olava were going to share, and Margaret learned it from a thoughtless friend.

When I was sixteen or seventeen, a young man I was out with for an evening of fun gave me what I took then to be terrible news. His father had been Papa's best friend and confidante when they had been young, and my young boyfriend said that he knew for a fact that my parents "had to get married." Papa had apparently confided in this boy's father at the time. I guess my friend thought this was funny, but I cried all night and was upset about it for days afterward. I knew it was probably true. Getting married at such an awkward time, before he was ready to move onto his own land, wasn't something Papa would normally do. And of course they had a very private wedding ceremony, which they never discussed.

Mama was always so tolerant of anyone who got "in the family way" ahead of schedule. And it wasn't so uncommon in those days as you might think. I remember her saying, "There's a new little baby just down the road. He's a little early, but he'll be loved just as much as if he had come at the proper time."

I realized later, of course, that none of this was important.

When Olava writes to her eldest daughter on September 8, 1923, she is nearing her forty-eighth birthday. The farm has expanded during the twenty-one years she and Willie have been married. His time and energy is consumed by crops and cattle. He is often irritable, too tired for conversation.

The years have spun by so quickly. Two of the nine children are already grown and gone. Olava misses Raymond and Margaret with an ache she can feel in her bones. But the letters help a little.

NOVEMBER 2, 1923

Dear Margaret,

Well, it seems that we are getting more careless every day, here it is a whole week gone and no one has written a word to you. I'm ashamed of the whole bunch but when Sunday rolls around I'll see if someone will take enough time to write.

You know I have been down with that sciatica. But I have actually done quite a bit of work this week and accomplished a little sewing too. I think I can tackle the washing tomorrow. It is taking a long time for that leg to get well. I sit down to wash dishes and almost everything. I made over a winter coat for Helen and patched up the balance of the overalls—8 or 10 pair. Tonight I gave the range a good polish so it shines like sixty.*

---

*This expression—"like sixty"—was used to emphasize excellence, or top performance. It's a good guess that it originated from the idea that a fine automobile might achieve sixty miles per hour.

We bought 6 bu. of apples from the Equity Co-op rail car so next week I will try to can them. We used a lot of canned stuff while I was in bed.

I got a letter from Raymond today. He sounds fine, didn't mention any girl affairs this time. Wait till he gets to another party, he will write and tell us about all the pretty girls in Downing.

Write again when you have time. Letters from you and Ray are the best for me. You see, I am here by myself all day and never get out. I hope I will be able to get to the dentist before it gets cold.

Love from us all, including little Helen and Alice and of course Donny boy, and last but not least, your dear Mother.

THURSDAY MORNING, NOVEMBER 15, 1923

Dear Margaret,

I want to write and thank you for the birthday present you sent me, Margaret. I feel that you should not sacrifice so much because you need your money for yourself, but I know you like to give. We will wait for a chance to make some things up to you. The tablecloth is something we need and it is a good one. I am saving all the new things until we get the house fixed up better. Ray gave me a pair of pillow cases with crocheting on. He bought them on a sale by the Ladies Aid Society of Downing . . .

I must drop Ray a few words today. He was so tired when he was here Sunday night and I felt worried about him. It is a long way to drive from Downing and he made the trip three times last week. I'm sure it is at least fifty miles one way because it takes a couple of hours to make the trip, in good weather. He had all kinds of car trouble last Sat., including a blown-out tire, but our neighbor Johnnie Kjer was with him and I was glad of that.

You know that Mrs. Michaelson has died. Ethel called me yesterday, which was her birthday, and she talked a long time. I think she knows that we are scared of the disease. She talked so much about that and told me they were cleaning up good and fumigating the house. I wanted Papa to go to the funeral but Papa had four rail cars of hogs and cattle to figure out for Equity Co-op and he said he couldn't go. Ray went, of course.

Well, I must close, hoping you are well and getting along all right. Eat well and try to build yourself up because anemia can be serious you know. Dress warm and be careful in this damp weather. Love from us all, Mother

Raymond Williamson graduated from Milltown High School as class valedictorian at the age of fifteen, having skipped two grades in elementary and another in high school. Following graduation, he took a few months of training at Minneapolis Business College and went to work at Milltown State Bank. After a year or so, he found higher-paid employment at the Bank of Downing.

There would be no farming for Raymond, not if he could help it. No milking cows, slopping hogs, shoveling manure. No barn boots and overalls. He would carry a briefcase, dress in low-cut shoes, white shirts, and ties.

Raymond's letters from Downing are quite formal in tone, sometimes a bit boastful. He is not yet twenty-one, but eager to prove himself in the world of business. His sister Margaret is earning as much as—or more than—Raymond in her city job, and it rankles. He will advance, in salary and status, of that he has no doubt.

On September 18, he writes to Margaret.

Coolidge is going to promote me to Cashier next month, when Ericson leaves. Just think of it—being cashier at my age! Won't that make people sit up and take notice, though. He said my work had been so satisfactory that he feels I can handle the job and it means more salary too. I am to get $90 per month after October first and $100 as soon as I am of age.

OCTOBER 3, 1923

The new job suits me just fine. I know I can handle the Cashier position and if I can just keep it up I will be sitting pretty in a few years.

NOVEMBER 15, 1923

Dear Sis,

Mother was feeling better when I visited Sunday and I believe she is going to recover entirely after a while. Her birthday was yesterday—same day as Ethel's. Mother is now 48 years old.

Ethel is 19. Poor girl, she couldn't enjoy her birthday much this year, I'm afraid. It is really surprising how well she kept control of herself Sunday. I think it helped that I was with her all the time. She always braces up when I am around. Her mother told me that, a few days before she died.

I believe it was the largest funeral there has ever been in Milltown. Such a collection of flowers I have never seen before. The weather was ideal and everything went just as Mrs. Michaelson herself had planned it. She had chosen the text for the minister, the songs for the choir, the pall bearers, and even the eight boys who carried the flowers.

Now that she is gone I think it is better, for she suffered a lot and was such a care toward the last. She was a wonderful woman though, as I have good reasons to know.

Well, my head aches and I am tired, so I think I shall say good night. I am sorry to have neglected writing, but time never seemed to permit it.

Love from Ray

NOVEMBER 18, 1923

Dear Sis,

I haven't much time to write you, but suppose I had better write something or you will be wondering what is the matter with me. It is funny, isn't it, how we gradually become accustomed and grow into new ways and acquaintances when we move to a new place. It is a good thing, or otherwise we should die of lonesomeness . . .

My friend Arnold is out of a job. The bank that he worked in has been closed. By this time I expect he is in Minneapolis. Dakota is sure going on the rocks fast. Palm told me that there were five banks closed in one county in one week that he was out there this fall. The bank he used to work in is closed too.

Some Sunday I think I shall jump on the train and take a run to Minneapolis and look over the city again. It is seven and one half months since I left there. Time sure does fly. The first thing we know we will be getting old . . .

I am going out to play some cards now. That is all the excitement a person can find most nights in Downing. I believe it is the dullest little town on earth.

Love, Brother Ray

Dakota is sure going on the rocks fast . . . Although most Americans are enjoying relative prosperity, the American farming economy has been depressed since the end of World War I. Farmers, as well as business people in the small towns that support them, are facing tough times. The Roaring Twenties are, for much of rural America, a continual cycle of debt stemming from decreased demand, falling farm prices, and the need to purchase expensive machinery to increase efficiency. Well-intentioned government programs seem only to exacerbate the problem. The warning signs are there for those who are paying attention, but few can imagine the disastrous years that lie ahead.

NOVEMBER 27, 1923

Dear Sister,

It is about time that I was writing you a line, isn't it? I was up to Milltown Sunday. Johnnie and I left Downing Sunday morning about 7:30 and came back the same evening. I didn't spend much of the time at home, however. We did not have any battery in the car and so were without lights.

Ethel's dad said that he would fix the lights by connecting them direct to the magneto so that we would not have to go home so early in the afternoon. When we were about half way the lights burned out and we had to drive 30 miles without any lights. Some drive, believe me!

. . . As for my coming to the city, I am afraid that will not happen before 1924 rolls around. We are too busy now to permit me to take a few days off. I will have to get fitted out with glasses and I am afraid that will take two days at least. Maybe you can advise me about the process.

Some day when I have more time I will write you a longer letter.

Big Brother Ray

Helen, who is now eight years old and a third-grade student at South Milltown School, finishes the year with this letter, dated December 7, 1923.

Dear Margaret,

We are going to have a Christmas program over at school on Friday night. I am in a Dialogue and have to speak a peece.

The boys went to school this morning on horseback. Wilmar took Beauty and Clarence took Fanny. Then they let the horses go home by thereself.

Papa is in bed. Mama says he has a cold and we should stay away. Mama just came in from the barn, ten minutes after 8, looking pretty tired. I did all the dishes by myself. It took me nearly two hours. Mama said she was proud of me.

Goodbye from your sister Helen

The next year, 1924, brings some surprising developments and achievements.

— Ellis Island is closed as an immigrant port of entry.
— U.S. citizenship is granted to all Native Americans born in the United States.
— The Pulitzer Prize is awarded to poet Robert Frost.
— George Gershwin's *Rhapsody in Blue* premiers at Carnegie Hall.
— The nation now has coast-to-coast radio broadcasting capability.
— The first regular air-mail service is established in the United States.

— The first successful round-the-world flight is completed, in a total of 175 days.

— The ten millionth Model T is manufactured by Ford Motor Company.

— King Tutankhamun's sarcophagus is discovered in Egypt.

It is doubtful the Williamsons of rural Centuria are aware of all this news. But Olava and the girls, who love music and enjoy playing the piano, know some Gershwin tunes. Robert Frost's poetry is performed as a "choral reading" in the South Milltown School. The students talk excitedly about King Tut's tomb. The youngest Williamson daughter, Alice, age seven, is fascinated by that discovery, and she makes up little songs about it. Her endless chants about *King Tut-ANK-hammen* earn her the nickname *Anky,* which sticks throughout her life.

On February 7, 1924, Olava writes of news closer to home.

Dear Margaret,
Received your letter and see that you are well but busy, doing the work for two people. How do you manage? Isn't old man Walman going to pay you something extra for all that extra work? Gee, I think he ought to.

We got a letter from Ray today. He complains of not getting enough salary. I wrote to him and told him that he ought to enjoy a few years of single life, as I always think a person gets more burdens to carry when one gets married. It is not all roses, believe me. He doesn't need to be in a hurry anyway, only 21 yet. And he should look around a little more . . .

You know it makes me feel as though Ray will be gone from us once he gets married. And I almost feel as if he is a child yet. I don't know where the time has gone and still, look at what we have been through. It is surprising that a body can stand so much abuse. I wish Papa would get out of that creamery business. There is so much bookkeeping that comes with it. It is just too much, on top of all the farm work.

Papa is still shipping cattle and hogs for Equity Co-op too. He goes down on the train to South St. Paul with the livestock because he has to try to get the best price for these farmers. I think he likes the trips, but there is a lot of work to it, including more bookkeeping. He made over $700 at it last year. I wouldn't care if we were off the farm, because it is too hard to keep going this way. And hard on the boys. They don't seem to take the interest that they should. Except for Wilmar. We can always count on him . . .

The first farm cooperatives in the Midwest, originating from informal work exchanges, have evolved into a system of neighborhood cooperation. Wisconsin counts several hundred cooperative creameries and cheese factories by the 1920s. Farmers are investing in these local enterprises and sharing in the profits. Livestock shipping associations have also flourished since the end of World War I.

Olava's letter continues with more details about work accomplished, work to be done. She takes comfort from writing these letters to her eldest daughter, sharing her concerns and the details of her day. She has discovered something that Lord Byron described a century earlier: "Letter writing is the only device combining solitude and good company."

Helen writes this short letter on February 23, 1924.

Dear Margaret,
You know, the puppy is kind of mean now. When I put on my coat he hangs on to it with his big white teeth. I tell you they stick right through the cloth. Papa says we have to put the puppy out when he acts like that but it's so cold and I feel sorry for him.

Oh gosh, the phonograph works swell now. We listen every night and dance around the room. That is so much fun! I wish we had a radio set like the Larsons but Papa says we can't afford that yet and we have the phonograph so no complaining.

When Alice and I play with our dishes I pretend that my doll is my baby and then I come over to Alice's house and we have lunch. We are stylish. We call dinner our lunch and we call supper our dinner. We play that we are from the city. Sometimes Alice plays Old Maid with me. Once Mama played with us and we made her the Old Maid. She said, fine, she thinks that being an Old Maid would be an easy life.

Raymond is writing to Margaret nearly every week, sharing news from the Bank of Downing, along with some brotherly opinions and advice.

MARCH 6, 1924
Dear Margaret,
It pleases me greatly to learn that you are going to have a new listing machine and regular Burroughs system of keeping your books. System is the whole thing as you have undoubtedly learned already. The methods used in keeping books makes a world of difference.

I installed our Burroughs posting machine the first of the month. They intended to have someone come down from the Burroughs office and put it in for us but I told them they were foolish to do anything like that, for I could do it just as well. I got the job and did it up in fine shape.

You sure will be qualified to work in a bank after you have been down there at Walman's awhile. Maybe someday we can have a bank of our own and then you sure will get the first chance to work for me. To tell you the truth, you have a better job where you are than you could have gotten in any bank. Just think—you are getting only $5.00 less than I am now and I have a high school education and three years actual experience . . .

MARCH 13, 1924
Dear Margaret
. . . You seem to be having about all the work that you can manage these days. Just stick to the ship and if Mr. Walman is the

right sort you will not regret it in the future. I am beginning to get afraid that you will be earning more than I am soon. Coolidge is tighter than heck when it comes to wages but leave it to me, I'll get a raise or quit the first of April.

DON'T bob your hair. It will be no end of disappointment to you if you do. Remember that it will soon go out of style too. Besides that about 99% of the men just detest bobbed hair. If you don't believe that just ask a few of them and you'll find out.

Every time I see a young girl who has chopped off her locks I know that she is lacking in good sense. There are a few girls here who haven't bobbed their hair and when one gets to know them you find that they are the pick of the crowd . . .

Raymond Williamson might have agreed with the witty analysis of Winthrop Sargeant in his article "Fifty Years of American Women," published in the January 2, 1950, issue of *Life* magazine:

On the heels of the 18th and 19th Amendments to the Constitution, came chaos. The second great dark age of the 20th Century American woman was to reach a depth of psychological and physical degradation seldom matched in human history. It stretched roughly from 1923 to 1930. Women not only lost their waists, they sat on them. They not only lost their hair, they twirled what was left of it into spit curls and imbedded their scalps in a helmet-like contraption known as the cloche hat. Everything female about them, including bust and hips, was either concealed or flattened out of all recognition. The only exception to this concealment was their legs, which poked obscenely from beneath their knee-length skirts . . . Where women were concerned, it was a lost generation indeed.

Raymond writes to Margaret on May 8, 1924.

. . . I am sorry to hear that you have been on the sick list. Mother writes that Adele and two of the boys have been sick at home. Adele was out of bed for the first time in a week and planned on going to school on Monday. I know she worries about missing, with high school graduation coming up so soon. Commencement at Milltown is the 23rd of May and I am going to try to get Saturday off so I can go up Friday evening and stay over Sunday.

My friend Ed went to the city last Saturday and brought back a fine new Oldsmobile Sport touring car for himself. Dad wants to buy another car and I can save him the dealer's commission (about $140) if he will take an Olds. They are a dandy car and I hope he decides to buy one . . .

Willie buys a Ford in 1924 and keeps it until 1930. He is happy to be rid of that troublesome Buick, although he gets only fifty dollars for it, from a farmer who wants it to power some machinery. ("Later I heard the damned thing blew up!" Willie exclaims. "Good riddance!")

Helen shares some news from home on June 9, 1924.

Dear Margaret,
Papa and the boys butchered a pig today, so we will have liver tomorrow for breakfast. I like it so much, don't you? And blood-cake. That's the best!

Say, I bet you can't guess what time we got home last night. 9:30! On the way home from town we met Harry Hendrickson. Harry flagged us and we stopped. He had run a twenty-penny spike into his brand new tire on his new Maxwell car. It ripped the tire. Harry didn't have any tools with him and that's why he stopped us. It took over an hour to fix it. I tell you, Papa, Leland, and Harry almost got killed last night. A great big sedan came speeding along the road and came right for Harry's car. The men were right by the bumper fixing the tire and just then the car swung out of the way and went into the ditch on all four. He put on the brake and it made such a noise. It took time to get the sedan back on the road. That's why we got home so late.

Well it's after 10 p.m. so I am off to bed. Love from your sister Helen

P.S. Say, there are some little chicks down in the granary. Oh they are cute. Alice and I fed them breadcrumbs yesterday.

Note at bottom of the page from Olava: *Bedtime for girlie.*

*

Oh, the trouble—and the allure—of the auto! Between 1920 and 1929, the number of registered automobiles in the United States will triple. By 1930 the nation will boast over a hundred thousand miles of paved roads. Filling stations and trucking services will proliferate. Suburbs will begin to flourish. Tourist cabins and advertising will spring up along the highways like quack grass. The Williamson family cannot yet imagine all of this, since Wisconsin Highway 35 is still a narrow gravel road, designed for horses and wagons. There are no shoulders, no ditches, no safe escapes for contraptions with blown tires or other mechanical failures.

Olava shares family news with Margaret on September 15, 1924.

I have been so lonesome today I haven't eaten a meal all day. I always get the blues so bad when any of you kids go. I get all upset, but I just have to get used to being alone again. You see Adele has been here with me until now while the other kids went to school, but today I was all alone. It was nice when she was here and she was such a big help too. But now she is down there at the Normal School in River Falls and she will not come home for over two months. She will get four days off for Thanksgiving and plans to come home then.

We all drove down to River Falls with her yesterday. We wanted the boys to stay home and attend to chores in case it would get late for us but they are never willing to stay home. Wilmar was the only one that was willing, but we wouldn't leave him alone. Ray and Ethel were up here and they had started milking when we got home about 9 p.m. We don't have so many cows milking now since a lot of them are dry but of course some milking still has to be done.

I could hardly recognize River Falls, it had grown so much. And the two new school buildings are swell. I don't know just what Adele thought when she saw the Normal School. She didn't say a word, poor kid. She was the most serious that I ever saw her when she realized she was really leaving home. It will be different from high school. She got a place to room and board where a lady keeps only girls for $6.50 a week . . . I hope she is not too homesick but I am a little afraid that she is. It will help when she gets it all lined up and gets her studies to work at.

I sewed her a twill dress and made her some new bloomers. I think she will need a good winter dress after a while. She got two new hats, one cheap one for school and another for best. I didn't like the hat but Adele picked it out for herself. It is one of those close fitting ones that are the new style. I suppose one has to get used to it. She got beads and stockings too—two pair of dark stockings and a silk pair for dress up. She can wash her things at the house there, right in the kitchen. I hope you can go to River Falls some weekend on the bus to see Adele . . .

We had threshers for five meals this week. I was good and tired, I tell you. We threshed out about 3,000 bushels. Papa bought a bunch of livestock and we are going to sell off some of our good-for-nothing cows.

Well I must close now. I wrote to Adele this afternoon too, because I got so blamed lonesome I couldn't work.

Love from Mother

"A mother who is really a mother is never free": these words from the French novelist Honoré de Balzac have been true in every time and place.

In the fall of 1924, the second Williamson daughter, Adele, has left for teachers college in River Falls, about sixty miles south of the Williamson farm. That is a long, difficult trip, mostly on narrow country roads, and Adele's visits home will be few. Yet Olava is glad they can provide this opportunity for Adele, who is small in stature and was born with crippled hands—five stubby fingers on one hand, four on the other, and no opposing thumbs. She is an unusually bright, creative student, and Olava feels she will be able to earn a living if she gets an education. It isn't so important for the boys, who can farm or do other physical labor. But a girl should have something to fall back on. This is good, clean work. And there will always be employment.

Adele's passion for teaching has been evident since her elementary school years, when she would line up the little kids in rows of chairs on the porch or in the parlor, wave a big ruler, and give them all kinds of lessons. They begged to be excused from the game, but Olava encouraged it. It kept them occupied.

Now that both eldest daughters have left home and the young ones are in school, Olava is alone in the house on weekdays. She doesn't drive and wouldn't find time or energy for social outings if she did. Letters continue to be her solace. She writes her loved ones often and waits impatiently for the mail, looking out the window several times each afternoon to see if the telltale red flag is still raised on the mailbox. A lowered flag means the mailman has come and gone, possibly leaving her a first-class letter. Anything is welcome, of course, even a bill or some local advertising. Anything is better than an empty box, a wasted walk to the end of the long gravel driveway.

Helen writes to her sister on September 23, 1924.

Dear Margaret,
I wish I could be down there in the city with you. We would have fun!

Say, one of the cows—Daisy—got some twin calves. One of them is mine.

Pretty soon it will be my doll's birthday and I am going to celebrate it with her. And you know Oct. 6 will be MY birthday. Nine years old!

Tonight John Cosgrove is here trying to sell Papa a radio. Papa always says no, we don't have money for that kind of thing.

By 1924, the radio business is booming. Sales will rise from less than two million in 1920 to sixty million by the end of the decade. For now, Willie Williamson resists this frivolous and costly temptation.

Now, electricity—that's a mighty fine thing. By this time the Williamson house and barn have been fitted with some kind of electric service (probably a Delco battery system), and Willie is in favor of this new source of energy. It saves a lot of labor and contributes to profits.

But a radio? A fellow has enough trouble getting the kids away from the phonograph. A radio in the house would only make it harder to keep them on task with housework, field work, and barn chores. Sure, it's a connection to the wider world, but there is a world of work right at home. No, Willie can see little use for a radio.

Bread and Butter

🐔

1925–29

*The History of the World is the record of a man
in quest of his daily bread and butter.*
HENDRIK WILLEM VAN LOON

THE ROARING TWENTIES bring something less than a roar to rural Polk County, Wisconsin, where national and global events are slow to intrude upon daily life.

Rural residents are paying little attention to the John Scopes "monkey trials"—passionate arguments by Clarence Darrow and William Jennings Bryan regarding the teaching of Darwin's evolution theories.

Few farmers realize that New York City has become the largest city in the world, taking the lead from London. Few have access to the new chain stores, latest consumer goods, and installment buying that is helping fuel corporate production and profit. But those with radios in their parlors may have heard President Coolidge declare that "the business of the American people is business!"

Olava's business continues to be cooking, baking, cleaning, sewing, laundry, and more laundry. Her poultry business is expanding; the leghorn hens are beginning to produce a modest income that will be hers to manage. Several of Olava's letters to Margaret mention the egg money and how it will be spent—on stockings and slippers, gingham for the little girls, other household items previously beyond the budget.

*

Olava writes to Margaret on Monday morning, January 21, 1925.

Dear Margaret,

I am sure you are wondering why we haven't written but one day goes after another and it seems there is so much to do. But we are all right so don't worry. I have quite a backache but I think I got it from washing clothes so it will disappear when I get rested. I am not much good when it comes to doing a big wash by hand. It is such a headache to try to dry everything in the winter too. I have to string it up all over the house. It takes me days some times.

Tomorrow is Ray's birthday. Twenty-two years old. He didn't come home this weekend. He wrote to tell us that his boss's son, Dana Coolidge, shot himself. He has probably written to you too. The boy wasn't even 18, had his whole life ahead of him. It was all on account of his failure in school. It certainly is too bad that he should take his life for that when he could have gone to his father and told him all about it and something could have been done. He could have done easier work of some kind and still made something from his life. Poor boy, he was quiet and brooded so much about everything, Ray said, and he just thought he was a total failure and there was no future for him. He left a letter for his dad saying that he felt he was such a disappointment and he had been praying about it and reading his Bible every day. Ray said that Mr. Coolidge was all broke up after the funeral. I am sure sorry for him. Just think how he must feel.

I don't know much news from around here. We are busy with our own work all the time and don't get anywhere. Milking 22 cows and picking eggs, etc. I get about 3 dozen per day. Papa takes them to town for me. The pullets are starting now so watch for an increase.

We have installed a motor for pumping water in the barn. It is a dandy outfit.

Well this is a short little pencil I am working with and I sure hope you can read it. And I hope you will bundle up warm when you go out in this awful weather and take something for that cough.

Love from Mother

That motor for pumping water in the barn will save untold hours of labor. The Williamsons are milking twenty-two cows, an average-size herd for a family dairy operation. Milking is done by hand, at twelve-hour intervals or as close to that schedule as possible, to maximize production. The milk is stored in heavy metal cans, submerged in a tank of cold water until they can be hauled to the creamery. Bedding, feeding, and watering the cattle are major chores, especially in winter, when animals must be housed in the barn and let out for short periods of exercise. The ponds and streams are frozen solid; water is pumped from the well and carried in buckets to the livestock. Most of the work is done by muscle power. A farmer who wants to electrify on a small scale, as Willie Williamson has done, can generate his own power using a water wheel, windmill, or gasoline-driven dynamo.

Willie waters, feeds, and beds eight Percheron horses—two teams of four. He and his boys are farming with horses, and will be for another twenty years. There is a shed full of hogs, and Olava's flock of chickens, all needing attention. Gutters and pens have to be mucked out, manure pitched into wheelbarrows and pitched out again, forming a frozen mountain in the barnyard. Following the spring thaw, it will fertilize acres of corn and oats and hay, as well as Olava's garden.

By 1925, advances in science and technology are making life easier and healthier for many Americans. Death rates from infectious diseases such as typhoid fever and diphtheria have been greatly reduced, thanks to improved sanitation as well as increased use of vaccines and antitoxin serums.

— The first motel (motorists' hotel) has opened in California.
— The Maxwell Motor Company has been absorbed by the growing Chrysler Corporation.

— The price of a Model T has dropped to $260. Ford has ten thousand dealers selling the Model T.

— An employee of the 3M Company has invented a new adhesive tape for use in painting automobiles, not anticipating that Scotch Tape will soon find many uses and become a household word.

— F. Scott Fitzgerald has published a new novel, *The Great Gatsby*.

— In Germany, Adolf Hitler has published his personal manifesto, *Mein Kampf*.

When Helen writes to Margaret on April 17, 1925, spring has arrived on the farm, bringing gifts of baby pigs in the shed and some new apparel for the youngest daughters.

Dear Margaret,

Adele has gone back to normal school in River Falls after her Easter vacation. Mama is glad that Adele is going to be a teacher and says she doesn't mind helping to pay for something like that. I think most of the egg money is going to Adele these days.

I am so lonesome around here now with both you and Adele gone. It feels kind of empty. Alice and I still have fun though. The boys are always outside working and Donny is such a tease. He hides our dollies and books and we have to look for days sometimes.

Yesterday Mama went to town with Papa and she bought Alice and me some new stockings. They are ribbed, black cotton. Mama paid 25 cents for Alice's and 30 cents for mine. Mama is going to get us some new slippers too. Today Mama sent more cases of eggs to town. She gets 24 cents a dozen now. Pretty good, don't you think?

There is a whole bunch of little pink piggies in the shed now. They go "uff, uff, uff." Can't you just hear them saying it? "Uff, uff, uff."

Papa is going to drive all the way to the city tomorrow. He

really loves that Ford! He said he was going to get me a hat because there is no hat in the Montgomery Ward catalog that will fit my head. My head is 23½ inches around, almost as big as Papa's!

Last week when Papa shipped cattle to the city he brought home ten pairs of shoes. Most of them fit somebody and the rest will be saved for growing into. Papa got Alice and me each a pair—blue leather trimmed with tan. We wear white stockings with them and they look awful cute. Mine pinch but I wear them anyway.

Mama is making Alice and me new dresses for the last day of school. Mine is yellow and Alice's is kind of a burnt orange color. Mama is trimming both dresses with black ribbon.

Bushels and sacks full of hugs and kisses from your sister Helen

Willie has made another trip to the South St. Paul Stockyards, something he does almost weekly now, for the Equity Co-operative in Centuria. Most towns on the rail line have local stockyards where the animals are herded up and loaded into freight cars. Willie rides down with the cattle, negotiates prices with the buyers in St. Paul, and settles up with the farmers when he gets back home. He is able to make the overnight trip since he has four boys at home to feed the livestock and manage morning and evening milking. He enjoys the company of other men, swapping news and jokes, playing cards, and sleeping in the caboose. Sometimes there is a free cot in the stockyards commission building. If he can hitch a ride to nearby shops he can buy shoes, clothing, or other merchandise, with a wider variety and better prices than he finds at home.

Willie takes pride and pleasure from these business dealings. There is considerable bookkeeping involved in the shipping of livestock. Margaret helped with that during her teen years at home. She remembers it well, some sixty years later.

I got only a couple years of high school you know. When I was fourteen, I had to stay home from school and help for the next few years because there was so much to be done. Ray was gone by

then, working at the bank in Milltown, and the other kids were too young to manage the heavy work. I worked like a hired man. I remember standing in the window and crying when I saw the neighbor kids go off to school in the morning.

But I always enjoyed the bookkeeping and I helped Papa with his Equity Co-op Shipping ledgers, writing checks, running the adding machine. I helped with the creamery ledgers too—Papa was on the co-operative creamery board at Centuria—and it involved a lot of paperwork.

I got my first job on the basis of that experience. I completed a few months of business training in Minneapolis when I was nineteen. Mr. Walman interviewed other classmates of mine in the business school. When my turn came, I sashayed into his office and he pulled up a chair for me and asked if I had ever done any bookkeeping. I said, "Oh yes, I helped my father with the creamery work."

He sat back in his chair and asked, "What's creamery work?"

I launched into an enthusiastic description of how I had helped

Papa bought a car! Helen and Alice on hood, Donny looking in window, 1924

keep records of the pounds of milk the farmers brought in each day, multiplying these figures by the butterfat content . . .

He was enjoying all this. Then he asked me about the livestock shipping and the recordkeeping that entailed. So I filled him in on that, in great detail. And he hired me.

Helen knows these stories and greatly admires her eldest sister. Someday she hopes to have her own city job. She will make some weekend trips home on the train or bus, wearing business suits with matching hats and stylish shoes. She will carry long, thin pencils in her handbag, like Margaret does, sharpened by a machine, not with a butcher knife, the way her papa's are.

JULY 24, 1925
Dear Margaret,
We are not getting any more strawberries now but we have been picking rasberrys for quite a while. Some of the rasberrys in the middle of the bushes are so ripe they are pretty near purple and they are so nice and big. Mama has canned 25 quarts of rasberrys and she has canned 12 quarts of peas.

I milked 3 cows last night and washed all the supper and lunch dishes.

They finished haying yesterday afternoon and soon they are going to cut the last field of peas. Mama is washing clothes today and I have to find my new stockings so she can wash them.

Good-bye for now and love from sister Helen

Brother Raymond's letter to Margaret, dated September 2, 1925, is handwritten on ornate letterhead stationery.

Master Radio Shop
32 N. MAIN STREET • FOND DU LAC, WISCONSIN

Distributors for
RECEIVERS—Erla, Thorola, Magnavox, Crosley, Airo-Master
REPRODUCERS—Burns, Thorola, Dictogrand, Musette

BATTERIES—Ray-O-Vac, Burgess, Marathon, Philco, U.S.I.

TUBES—Cunningham, Radiotrom, Magnavox

Dear Sis,
Meet the new Radio Shark from the Master Radio Shop. We opened up last night and prospects look good. Gosh! But I have sure worked hard this week. Have hardly had time to eat or sleep until today. You should see our store. It sure is a pretty nifty layout and gets plenty of good comments . . .

More news from Raymond on September 29, 1925:

Dear Sister,
It is raining tonight with the result that the radio business is rotten. People stay at home on evenings like this.

Thursday you will be another year older, won't you? You must excuse me for limiting my birthday greetings to a letter this time but I am pretty hard up. Going into business takes a lot of money.

I had a letter from Mother today and of course she jumped me because Ethel isn't going to Minneapolis to work but is moving down to Fond du Lac. I am afraid there is going to be hell to pay when I get married and I can assure you that time is not very far off. Don't mention this to anyone, will you? I'll tell the folks before I do it, don't worry about that.

We need help here in the store and Ethel can just as well do that with the result that we can be married and live together.

Well, Sister Dear, I wish you the happiest of birthdays. I am sitting here listening to a musical program from Chicago. Radio sure is interesting . . .

What an amazing thing—to have a world of music, news, and entertainment in your own home, right at your fingertips. Some are frightened of the invention. It is rumored that exposure to radio waves can cause cancer and other dreaded diseases. Who really knows? But of all the new products put on the market during this decade, none will meet with more spectacular success than the radio.

*

Margaret Williamson, 1923

Olava writes to Margaret on September 30, 1925.

Dear Tootsie,
You remember, I'm sure, how everyone called you Tootsie until you went to school. It is your birthday tomorrow. Just think, twenty-one. Can it be possible? I wish I could send you a cake. Maybe you can come home by bus on the weekend and then we will have a cake for you at home. I hope you can spend a pleasant day tomorrow and think of Mother once in a while. Wear your sweater and feel comfortable.

Oh how I do cherish the days when you were all small and it was Mama here and Mama there all day long. I must admit I was far more happy then than now. But that is the way of this wicked world. I am glad nevertheless that none of you are farther away but you can come home at any time.

I was so tired after silo filling that I couldn't sleep. I ached all over. Yesterday and today I have canned ripe tomatoes, pickles and apples. I think I will wash clothes tomorrow. Silo filling is finally done around here and it is always good to see the silos filled for the winter.

Wilmar likes school real well. He is so interested in his studies. Clarence has to stay home from school this week to work with Papa. Tomorrow they will load stock for Equity Co-op. I don't like the boys to miss so much school but Papa never cares.

Well, I must go to bed because I have to be up at 5:30 in the morning. Write often, even if it is just a few words, because I am awfully lonesome. It helps wonders.

Love from us all, Mama

OCTOBER 8, 1925
Dear Margaret,
The little girls have written to you to express their many thanks for the good warm nighties you sent and I also want to add my thanks.

I want to try to get to River Falls some weekend soon, if

Nine "Willie kids," Easter Sunday, 1925. Left to right: Alice, Helen, Donald, Wilmar, Clarence, Leland, Adele, Margaret, Raymond

possible, with Adele's winter clothes. A trip like that would really help.

I feel rather blue and can't shake it off. You have perhaps heard from Ray. Ray and Ethel took out a marriage license on the sixth and intend to get married soon. He has gone into a radio business with Fritz Spickerman, you know, all the way down in Fond du Lac. Fritz is engaged to Ethel's sister Violet and I think they are planning a double wedding down there and it will be soon. Ray did not sound so happy when he wrote that to us. I think he feels that he is going a little too fast, not having the finances. We will try to help him as much as we can. I hope everything will be all right, but it seems so hard to think of him being gone from us for good. I have cried until I am sick, but what is the use. He preferred to stay in town at the Michaelsons when he came up to Milltown anyway. Oh, if he knew how I felt about it I believe he would have come home more often.

The letter continues with more fretting. Now Ray is in Fond du Lac, three hundred miles away. He is too immature for marriage, especially to a town girl who will expect fine things. And these home radio sets he plans to sell are priced at fifty to one hundred dollars; surely that will be out of reach for most families. This is a risky venture. If only Ray had been patient enough to stay in banking, at least he would be guaranteed a steady paycheck. Olava knows this young man and his thirst for success. He is impulsive. Impatient. And vulnerable.

SUNDAY EVENING, OCTOBER 18, 1925

Dear Margaret,

I received your letter Tuesday and have not had time to answer sooner as we got a letter from Ray asking us to come down to his wedding which was Thursday at 5 o'clock.

Spickermans gave a wedding for Fritz and Violet, and Ray and Ethel joined in to make it a double ceremony.

Papa didn't think we should both go and leave the kids alone as it would take the best part of three days and he wouldn't enjoy the trip because he would worry too much. Besides, it was shipping day too. I went with Martin Michaelson and his new wife in her car. We started from here at 1:30 Wed. and didn't get there until 1:30 Thursday. We stayed at a small town (Colby) overnight. Had a little trouble twice on the way down, like a puncture, etc.

Ray was so glad I came and I am satisfied that I made the trip for his sake. He didn't hardly expect it because he thought, I presume, that we were sore at him and we wouldn't care to go. I have not exactly felt sore but have had a terrible streak of the blues. I think it set him thinking all right. We gave him that $1,000 as a present because we felt he earned something when he was home. Poor boy, how he used to work and always did it cheerfully. We have not forgotten it. We felt we ought to give it to him now rather than later because he needs it now, badly.

They had a very nice wedding, just the Spickerman family and their relatives, Martin and his wife, and me. They were so glad that I came. It is too bad that Ray should go down there and get married. If they had it up here all our relatives could have been there.

I gave Violet and Fritz $10 to buy dishes with. Ray said Spickermans gave him $10, so I did it to sort of square things up. They are all living together so they will all use the dishes anyway. They have rented an apartment, 6 rooms, and will all live together this winter to save on fuel, rent, lights, etc. They pay $40 per month rent. The rooms are fine and the building is new so it is not papered yet. Fritz furnished the kitchen, living room and his own bedroom and Ray furnished the front room and his own room. Ray had bought a swell davenport and chair to match and another pretty rocker, center table and rug, and Ethel has the piano from home. They bought a swell bedroom suite.

Believe me, it costs to get married, they'll find it out.

I like Fond du Lac real well. It sure is a pretty place. It is located on the south end of Lake Winnebago. The lake, they said, is 40 miles long. You can't see across anywhere. It is like an ocean. I would like to live on a body of water like that. You must try to make a trip down there. I guess the fare is about $8 from St. Paul but you could watch for an excursion some time.

Fritz is not of age yet so he had to get his parents' consent. His father thought it would be best to consent as his boys are sort of wild, you know, and he thought this would make him sort of settle down to business. Ethel is going to help the boys in the store when they are out on business, so Violet will be doing most of the housework. She seems so kiddish. She bobbed her hair but Ethel didn't. Ray is so against it you know. When Adele got her hair bobbed last spring Ray told her that she looked like a floozy, and it really hurt her feelings.

Well, I have told a little but there would be more to talk about if we could get together.

Ray said he worked until eleven o'clock most nights so he hadn't had time to write much. We'll have to excuse him I guess. I did feel real sorry for him because I could see he looked worried . . .

We left Fond du Lac on Friday morning 8 o'clock and got home here 11:30 midnight. Made a mistake and drove almost 100 miles out of our way. Drove 425 miles and it should have been about 330.

It was a fine trip. I never was so far from home before. Write soon. I must go to bed.

Love from all, Mama

Despite her misgivings, Olava hopes for the best. Maybe Raymond is right. This radio shop could be a case of good timing. The venture could result in a better living than farming—or even banking—could provide.

All hopes are dashed the following year. The timing is right, but Ray and Ethel Williamson will not benefit from the soaring demand for home entertainment. In December 1926, the young couple make a Christmas trip to the homeplace with a fine-looking Magnavox radio set for the family. They return to Fond du Lac to find that Fritz Spickerman has sold out most of the inventory and absconded with the cash. Willie and Olava's generous wedding gift is gone. The Master Radio Shop is out of business.

All family letters written during 1926 have been lost. But details of daily life during this time were recorded by the youngest Williamson daughter, Alice.

Helen and I were only two years apart in age, and we did everything together. I remember that when it rained we would hurry to the machine shed and sit out the storm under the tin roof. There were three large grain bins and when they were partly empty we played house in them. We had our older sisters' high heeled shoes and we put our own little shoes inside them so they would stay on our feet. Then we went visiting back and forth from one grain bin to the other with our dolls and had the best fun.

Our oldest sister Margaret was our Lady Bountiful when she came home from the city on weekends. She brought us doll dishes, little kettles, even a tiny stove that we could actually cook on. We caught bullfrogs with our brother Donny in a swampy place down the cattle lane, then cut off their legs and skinned them and fried them in butter on that little stove. We set up our kitchen under a willow tree in the back yard.

Mama baked eight loaves of bread twice a week and we carried our lunches in two-quart Karo Syrup pails. Lunches consisted of homemade bread, butter, cheese, cake or cookies and a piece of fruit or vegetables from the garden. We didn't drink much milk because it couldn't be kept cold. Mama used a lot of it in cooking and baking instead. If an animal had been butchered recently we would eat cooked liver, maybe three times a day. And Mama's bloodcake (made from the blood of a butchered animal) was equivalent to a blood transfusion for nutrition. It was never very appealing to me, but Papa loved it.

When we got home from school we usually had a huge piece of molasses cake that we could smell as we were coming up the driveway. We heaped on the butter until it dripped down our wrists.

We ate well and had everything we needed for a healthy diet except citrus fruits. Oranges were a special treat, usually bought only at Christmas time.

It was considered a sin to use "store-bought" food when you could garden and put food by and make do with what you raised at home. Sugar, coffee, and salt were the only foods regularly bought in town. We even ground our own wheat for flour.

Throughout my childhood we pumped water by hand into the wooden cattle tank and the milk cans were put into it for cooling. The water was not changed each time the cattle drank, but would usually get freshened after the cans were hauled to the creamery. In summer the cream would be far from cold by the time it reached its destination. (Cream was separated from the skim milk before hauling; the skim was fed to the calves and hogs.) No one thought of taking a bacteria count in those days.

We all worked hard and did whatever we could to make life easier for our parents. In those days you did your chores without complaint and without question—the way you said the Pledge of Allegiance at school or the Apostles Creed in Church or the way you ate every morsel that was put on your plate. Everyone had to pull his own weight and there was pride in that.

Helen and I dusted and swept and helped clean the dishes from about the age of seven. We were as close as a pair of twins. Our house was small for such a large family, with only two bedrooms, so Helen and I slept together in the living room on a leather folding davenport. Occasionally the folding mechanism would get out of kilter and we would get folded up in it.

We were fortunate to have a Chickering square parlor grand in the house—a gift to Mama from her maternal grandparents. Mama had played that piano when she was a girl and she encouraged us "little girls" to take lessons. We rode into town with Papa when he hauled milk and took our lessons from Mrs. Mueller while Papa did his errands. Mama loved to hear us play and she would offer to do the dishes if we would go into the living room and play duets. She paid for our lessons with her egg money. That was a dandy trade. Music has enriched both our lives beyond measure.

The youngest Williamson son, Donald, adds his memories to the picture of family life during the mid-twenties:

I was two years older than Helen and four years older than Alice, and I teased them pretty bad. I wasn't mean, exactly, but I loved getting a rise out of them. They got so excited about the funniest little things. I used to hide their dollies and once I poked the eyes out, just trying to figure out that mechanism that made the eyes go open and shut. I didn't really mean to damage the dolls but after I figured out that eye-gizmo I couldn't fix it again and my sisters were pretty sore at me. I felt a little sorry but of course I couldn't tell them that.

When Helen and Alice got to be about twelve or thirteen Margaret gave them little lipsticks and boxes of powder she had bought in the city and I would hide that stuff and laugh while they went looking in every corner of the house. I'd hide it real good, like down in the pants-leg of an old suit of clothes back in the storeroom closet, and they would have a devil of a time finding it. When I thought they were lazy, sleeping too late in the morning, I would think of all kinds of punishments for them. Once on butchering day I put a pig's head on their dresser and I sure had a laugh over that. I made sure it was good and bloody too—put it on a baking sheet, though, so it wouldn't make too big a mess. I remember thinking I would really teach those slug-a-beds a lesson. I got into some trouble with Pop over that but it was worth it.

Clarence and I got in to all kinds of mischief. We liked to drill holes in the end of dried corncobs and stuff dynamite in there and use them as toys. That was a risky game, but the folks didn't have time to supervise us like parents do today. Makes me laugh the way I see these young parents hovering over their kids these days.

Well, I got some tricks pulled on me too. We had a hired man who was a terrible tease. He told me and Clarence and Wilmar, when we were just little kids, that if you held your finger tight over a gun barrel the bullet wouldn't come out. We believed that and Clarence shot the ends of his fingers off. Same guy told me that if you held a skunk by its tail it couldn't squirt you and I tried this when I was about nine years old. I was trapping skunks in those days. Got a bounty of $2.50 for every skunk hide and $10 for a mink. That was pretty good money—but I didn't get a lot of minks in my traps, mostly skunks. Well I got this big skunk by the tail and I held it right in front of my eyes and it got me good. The stink was streaming down my face. I couldn't see, couldn't even breathe. I put wet snow on my face and for a while I thought I was going blind. Anyway, I recovered from that and it seems to me I could see better than ever. I think it actually helped. I have been able to see perfectly all my life and everyone else in the family had to get glasses. I have recommended this to people a few times but no one takes me seriously.

I'll tell you what I loved the most back in those days—the butchering. I loved the excitement of it, everyone working fast, working together, you see. Hogs especially. When I got old enough I got the job of sticking the knife in the brisket, real deep, and the blood would just pour out. You had to have the water just the right temperature to scald the hair off, but not too hot or it would set the hair even tighter. We built a fire under a fifty-gallon drum and *dipped the pig in from one end, then the other. After the scalding you had to scrape it clean and that took some doing. After we got the animal cut up, we would hang the hams in the granary and paint them with Smokene. Mom would can the rest of the meat because we didn't have refrigeration. We butchered lots of chickens and cattle too, the old cows that couldn't produce any more.*

I was never very interested in school. How could sitting inside a schoolhouse compete with the great outdoors and all the things going on at home? I couldn't see much use for reading until later when I got interested in those western novels by Zane Grey. Then I was glad I got a little schooling. But you know, I was never one to sit around indoors. Not at home, or school or church. I always said I took my religion in the woods. That is the best place to be if you want to do some big thinking.

With literacy rates and leisure time increasing throughout the twenties, newspaper circulation is booming, reaching an estimated forty million by the end of the decade. Mass-market publications, such as the *Saturday Evening Post, Life, Colliers, National Geographic,* and *Literary Digest* are also seeing a dramatic increase in readership.

Radio is a luxury that has reached the masses nationwide. And the airwaves, originally considered a public trust, are now becoming a medium for commercial advertising. Popular regional radio programs are becoming firmly identified with sponsors' products, and no one seems to be objecting. Listeners are regularly turning to the *Philco Hour,* the *General Motors Family Party,* the *Dutch Masters Minstrels,* the *Lucky Strike Orchestra.* On New Year's Day 1927, Americans tune in to the first nationally broadcast radio program: the Rose Bowl football game, followed by a New York Symphony Orchestra concert. The nation is shrinking.

Average salaries in the United States have climbed to $2,312.

Henry Ford has announced an eight-hour day, five-day work week for employees. Farmers, of course, continue to work from dawn to dark, seven days a week.

A canning plant, Fame Canning Company (to be bought by

Stokely's in 1929), has been established in the village of Milltown, Wisconsin, providing a new source of income to local farmers who can raise and sell cash crops of peas and beans and corn. Local workers are glad to have a new source of seasonal employment.

Milltown's Co-operatives Services are expanding. The cooperative now operates a grocery and dry goods store and full-service feed mill. Plans are being made for a gas station. The Milltown Co-operative Creamery produced 614,000 pounds of butter during the previous year, with about 93 percent of it shipped to the Twin Cities and distant markets, the remainder consumed by patrons or sold in local communities.

Milltown Mutual Telephone Company is growing rapidly. Subscribers include nearly all businesses in the village and the majority of private households. Area farmers are also gaining access to telephone service. Rural multiparty service can be purchased for four dollars per quarter. Rules, printed in the annual telephone directory, instruct subscribers to reach Central with one short ring and give the three- or four-digit number of the party being called. Callers must talk directly into the transmitter, keep conversations brief, and signal with one short ring when finished. Children are not to play with the telephone, and no one should listen to their neighbors' conversations. Business hours are 6 AM to 11 PM; calls made outside these hours are subject to a ten-cent charge.

Willie and Olava Williamson are listed as subscribers in the 1927 directory, with a four-digit number: 52–31. Their party line ring is two shorts and a long.

Olava writes to Margaret on February 6, 1927.

Dear Margaret,
Today we were quite surprised when Nels Simonson from St. Croix Falls called up to talk to Ray about working for him at Kingsdale, Minnesota. He is running a crew up there cutting timber and sawing lumber. He needs another man to help with the books so Ray is going up there Tuesday to work until spring. After that Nels may put Ray at St. Cloud where he has a

big lumber business. I hope Ray will like this and I believe there is a future in this lumber business, if only he will pick up and forget about the blunders he has made. He is only 24 years old and it sure is ridiculous for him to take the stand he has been doing. He is not a bit strong to do hard work. He gets so played out when he is out in the woods cutting wood or hauling pea silage, so I think he ought to take a chance like this.

This week Papa goes down to St. Paul for the Central Shipping Association. He will probably go tomorrow and come back Thursday night or Friday. I would like to go with him sometime but this will be a train trip and I'll wait until spring when he can use the car. I figured on getting a dress similar to your black one, but wonder if you could get one if you see a good sale. I am so much thinner now that I can wear about the same size as you do, but to be safe it can be one size bigger. Papa wants me to get one. I am going to make my old suit over so I will have that for spring. We will see how the weather stays and hope I can come down before too long.

Adele wrote and told us about her A's and all her work. She is too busy for her own good. It will seem good when she gets done with this schooling. Adele wants to come home some weekend and hopes to come when you do so you kids will have to plan between yourselves.

I know we will miss Ray when he leaves but of course that can't be helped. Clarence is home too so we really should be able to get along here. Just think—last winter we were milking as many as 26 cows and Lee and I often were alone. This winter we are milking 15 cows. So many are dry right now.

I must close as I have rattled quite a while now. I hope you are feeling well and not working too hard.

Love from us all, your dear Mother

The "dry" cows Olava refers to are those that are not producing milk. A cow "freshens," or begins producing milk, after a calf has been born; she will continue to produce as long as she is being milked. Most cows produce a calf every year, but they need a vacation now and then, so dairymen will allow cows to go dry for weeks or months—often during the winter—before having them bred again. The farmer, however, does not get a vacation.

The summer of 1927 is an exciting, if chaotic, time for the Williamsons. The house is plumbed for hot and cold running water and wired for electricity. A second story is added, with four bedrooms and a bathroom, complete with flush toilet, wall-hung sink, and claw-footed tub. No more doubling and tripling up in narrow beds; no more folding cots in the dining room. No more chamber pots beneath the beds. The old lean-to kitchen is torn off and given new purpose as a woodshed. A new and larger kitchen is added to the lower level, as well as glassed-in porches, front and back. Willie builds a new granary, expands the chicken coop and barn.

The enlarged home is ready in time for Willie and Olava's twenty-fifth wedding anniversary party on a Sunday afternoon in August. Three hundred relatives, friends, and neighbors arrive at the farm to help them celebrate. This community is wide and deep, though a stranger wouldn't know that, passing through. A city dweller might not recognize a neighborhood that has little to do with geographic proximity and everything to do with interdependence. The rituals of work exchange, informal trading and sharing, and celebration of life events are as strong and stable as any written contract.

Helen celebrates her twelfth birthday on October 6, 1927. She is beginning to sound like a young lady, and she is frugal as her mother, impressed by a bargain.

NOVEMBER 14, 1927

Dear Margaret,

We arrived home from the city safe and sound around 4:30 this afternoon. After we left you off we went to the ten cent store and bought some little things, then we drove to M.W. Savage & Co. Papa bought two $12.00 suits that were marked down to $4.98 for Clarence and Wilmar. They have only one pair of

Willie and Olava's farm on Highway 35 between Milltown and Centuria

trousers but they were very good material. Donny bought a gun too—a Stevens single shot. He paid $4.50.

We left Minneapolis at 12:45 and drove as far as White Bear Lake and then we had a lunch. The roads were terribly slippery and we had to stop about five times to clean off the windshield even though we have got an electric windshield wiper. We also stopped at Centuria to get the mail.

I was going to take a bath tonight but it is too blame cold. I am sitting over the register now writing on my knees and it sure looks like it don't it Margaret?

Mama bought herself a hat on a sale. She paid $3.95 for it and it is a pretty good fit too.

Well I must close because it is 8:15 and I have to get to bed because I was up so early this morning. It sure was an exciting trip.

Love, your sister Helen

JANUARY 2, 1928
Dear Margaret,
How are you managing to keep yourself alive in all this cold weather? It was 32 degrees below zero yesterday but there

wasn't much wind. There was more wind today but it wasn't quite as cold. There was a little horse over at Johnson's yesterday. He had to stay outside all night and today Papa sent Lee and Donny over to help him get in the barn but he wouldn't go in so they brought him over here. He is a bay horse with a little white mark on his head. I wish we could keep him.

We have seven little calves now and will have more in a few days. That will mean a lot of fresh cows and more milking. Mama picked 123 eggs today but she has had as many as 153.

We went to Literary last Friday night at the school house. There were 49 people there counting kids and grownups. Not so good because of the cold weather. Adele and cousin Agnes were on the program. Adele sang One Fleeting Hour and When I'm With You.

Papa loaded stock today. He got one heavy load and might go to South St. Paul tomorrow if the weather is better. Goodnight from Sister Helen W.

Another year, with many milestones, has come and gone.

— The Food and Drug Administration has been established.
— Charles Lindbergh has made the first solo nonstop transatlantic flight from New York City to Paris, in his single-engine aircraft, the *Spirit of St. Louis.*
— The Great Mississippi Flood of 1927, affecting nearly one million people, has been declared America's greatest natural disaster to date.
— The first "talkie," *The Jazz Singer*, starring Al Jolson, has been packing movie houses coast to coast.
— Ford Motor Company has unveiled its new Model A. Gas stations are springing up, and ribbons of new and improved roadways are unwinding across the United States, expanding markets and bringing city and country closer together.
— Locally, in Polk County, plans are being made to pave and widen Highway 35, which will result in faster travel by motorcar, the year around.

On February 18, 1928, a son, Robert, is born to Ray and Ethel Williamson. While Willie and Olava worry about their eldest son's financial struggles, they are delighted about the birth of their first grandchild.

Helen writes to Margaret on July 24, 1928.

Dear Margaret,
While watching the egg I will write to you. I am helping Mama with breakfast this morning.

We are very busy haying today and will have ten men for dinner. They started yesterday.

Bad news—our dog Brownie has mange, a common disease among dogs where the hair falls off. It starts usually in the ear as it did with him and spreads to all parts of the body. It will spread by contagion to human beings. I hear there is a cure for it by clipping the hair off and washing with soap and water but Brownie won't stand for it. His mouth is all raw from it so if he bites you, you would get it too. I guess we will have to kill him but we hate to do that because he is such a good cattle dog.

Ray and Ethel were home last Sunday from that lumber camp in Minnesota. They said they would come again next week and hope you can come home too.

The raspberries are ripe now too, so you better think about it.

Well, I must get this mailed and take the cows over to pasture. Try to come next weekend if you can.

Love from your sister Helen

Poor Brownie. There are no more letters that mention him, and it's likely Willie has to shoot him and find a new cattle dog. A well-trained dog can be a great help herding cattle, guiding skittish beasts through pasture gates, through barn doors, and into designated stalls. Dogs, like every other living being on the farm, must earn their keep. There are no *pets*. You can spoil a working dog by showing too much affection. To some extent that goes for children, too. Too much praise and attention can go to their heads.

Their labor is crucial to the success of the farming operation; that will not be changing any time soon.

Laborsaving technology is coming very gradually to rural America, while in the nation's thoroughly electrified towns and urban areas, citizens are seeing the results of mass production, innovation, mechanization. Leisure time is expanding; standards of living are rising. At the same time, wealth and power are growing more concentrated due to the rise of large corporations.

President Coolidge decides not to seek reelection. The Republican candidate, Herbert Hoover, defeats his Democratic opponent, Al Smith, by a wide margin on November 6, 1928. Hoover predicts that "America is nearer to the final triumph over poverty than ever before."

Helen to Margaret, July 29, 1929:

Dear Margaret,
Mama and I just finished a big washing and feel rather relieved so I thought I would settle down and write some letters. Adele and Alice did all the other house work so we got done in good season. It's so hot out that the clothes dry real good.

The boys are haying today. It surely is hot work. These are days when a person feels like swimming but no time for that. Donny was out at Rice Lake about 4 o'clock this morning and caught three nice pickerel. We ate them for dinner.

Adele has been sewing today. You remember that little flowered dress you brought home for Mama? It was a little too small for Mama and she busted it out in the arms but Adele ripped it all apart and fixed it over for me. We starched and ironed it and it looks awfully nice. And out of that pink and tan striped goods we had laying around here she made me a two-piece dress. Then she sewed a pink rayon dress for Alice and trimmed it with white rayon and white lace and it surely is cute. She fixed over a green rayon dress for Alice and trimmed it with tan pongee. She's a real seamstress.

Lee is working in Centuria at Archie Wells' garage for $60 a month. He also gets a free room at the hotel and a special price on meals for being a steady boarder (21 meals for $7.) He likes the work fine and Mama is happy to see him settled in a job.

Love from sister Helen

What a surprising decade this has been. Sixty-eight percent of American homes—but only ten percent of farm homes—are now electrified. The country has over a hundred thousand miles of hard surfaced roads. Route 66 is under construction, cutting a 2,400-mile arc through eight states and three time zones. By 1929, there is nearly one automobile for every U.S. family. The Ford plant in Detroit is paying six dollars per day and workers are putting in only forty hours per week. With the automobile industry leading the way, American factories are mastering the techniques of mass production.

Large merchandisers like A & P, Sears and Roebuck, and F. W. Woolworth are bringing an abundance of goods to the masses. Inventions proliferate. Bakelite, "the miracle material of a thousand uses," is showing up in the kitchen in the form of pot handles, art deco flatware, radios, even fashion jewelry. Rural families have access to much of this merchandise thanks to mail-order catalogs. But they are cautious in their purchases. This tendency is due in part to fiscal conservatism, but also because they do not want to appear frivolous or pretentious. An interdependent farming community is stabilized by practicality, humility, and a fairly even distribution of wealth—or lack of it. A family's most important asset is their own good name.

The nation as a whole surely appears to be gaining in wealth and productivity. Americans are producing more than half the world's iron and steel, nearly half the coal, and two-thirds of the petroleum. They are manufacturing four-fifths of the motor vehicles, twice the number at the start of the decade. Business is booming and investors are driving up stock prices in a frenzy of buying and selling. There seems to be no end in sight.

*

While mass marketing is transforming the American economy, farmers are not buying many of the new gizmos. Most are struggling with problems of overproduction, falling prices, rising debts. They keep hoping that supply and demand can somehow be brought into balance.

Few realize the dangers posed by largely unregulated banking and investment systems, or the widening inequality across the nation. The top one percent of Americans now own more than a third of all the nation's wealth, while the poorest 20 percent own only four percent of it. High profits gained from mass production have been paid to investors rather than workers. Eighty percent of Americans have no savings at all.

Helen to Margaret, October 14, 1929:

Dear Margaret,
Just a little note to you before I hop into bed.

I may be coming down to the city with Papa next week or the week after to get my eyes tested and get glasses. My eyes are an awful handicap to me at school because I can't see the writing on the blackboard. I tried Mama's glasses on and I can see twice as far with them but they are too strong for me because her eyes are even worse than mine.

I am going to send for some music from Jack Mills & Co. If I send for 20 pieces or more I can get them for 5 cents each. Otherwise the regular rate is 10 cents. There are so many songs I want to play. Tiptoe Through the Tulips. With a Song in my Heart. Those are two of my favorites.

How is your boyfriend Mel? Tell him hello from me! Love, Helen

The stock market crashes ten days after Helen writes this letter. Black Tuesday, October 24, 1929, and its anguishing aftermath will be long remembered by all who live through it.

Leland Williamson soon loses his new job at the garage in Centuria. He returns home to farm with Willie and the boys, but a shrinking milk check makes it difficult to support the family.

Later that winter, scarlet fever strikes the Williamson household. Helen is the sickest of all, missing many weeks of school. She studies at home when she is able, preparing for stringent eighth-grade examinations in the spring. When everyone has recovered, the house is fumigated, top to bottom.

Decades later, Margaret gives an account of that tough time.

That scarlet fever siege in the winter of 1929 was really serious. We figured that Ethel brought the disease home to us because she had been up at the Kingsdale lumber camp with Ray, and they had an epidemic there. Helen was thirteen at the time, in eighth grade, and she missed months of school. She worried about passing eighth grade, but of course she was so bright she was able to do it. I remember the folks had to pay for her school books after the scarlet fever because they couldn't be re-used. She was terribly ill, worse than anyone. Her throat was red hot and she couldn't swallow her own saliva. A red rash covered her whole body. She peeled from head to toe.

Mama took care of everyone and somehow didn't get sick, which was a miracle. Helen, Alice and Mama and one of the boys were quarantined in the house. Papa and a couple of the boys stayed in the old summer kitchen, away from the house, so they could carry on with the necessary chores. Mama made food for everyone and passed it out through the window to the men out there.

Well, I had been seeing Mel Gorder in Minneapolis—I met him through some mutual friends—and our relationship was getting quite serious. I had already been out to Dakota, to Bottineau, to meet his family and it was time for him to meet the Williamsons. Mel suggested that we drive up to the farm one Saturday and we got there about five o'clock in the afternoon. Mama had been too busy to write any letters so we didn't know about the scarlet fever. When we got to the farm we saw a big quarantine sign on the door. Papa came out of the summer kitchen and there we were with Mel's shiny Buick car. Papa and Mel shook hands and Mama and the younger kids just waved at us through the window. Then we turned around and drove all the way back to the city. That was Mel's introduction to the family.

What One Has to Do

1930–35

What one has to do can usually be done.
ELEANOR ROOSEVELT

MARGARET WILLIAMSON and Melvin Gorder marry in 1930, in a small private ceremony. Not wanting to spend their modest savings on a wedding or impose a burden on the many guests they would like to have invited, they keep it as quiet and simple as possible.

Margaret describes her mother's reaction to news of the upcoming marriage:

Mama smiled and said, "That's good. He has clean work." I suppose she was so tired of washing dirty overalls and she didn't want that life for me. She liked the idea that I had found a man with a city job and professional appearance. She asked me how I felt about him and I remember saying "I sit in the car with him and I just want to climb into his coat pocket." That seemed to satisfy her. I could never use a word like LOVE with Mama, but I guess she knew what I meant. That was the extent of our talk. She must have felt that whatever facts young people needed to have about marriage they could figure out on their own. And of course we did.

The newlyweds rent a small house in Minneapolis. Mel is employed as an accountant with a downtown business; Margaret is a bookkeeper at Walman Optical Company, located in the Medical Arts Building, Ninth Street and Nicollet Avenue, a job she has held since 1925. She prepares a budget for 1930, their first year together, with monthly rent of $37.50 and grocery expenses of $20, allowing total monthly living expenses of $120.50.

Early in the marriage, Mel's widowed mother moves in with them. Mother Gorder's health problems and financial dependency put additional strain on the young couple's careful household budget.

Although the economic crisis had been many years in the making, it seems that the country has suddenly gone from the best of times to the worst of times. The nation's gross national product will fall from $104 billion in 1929 to $58 billion in 1932. More than fourteen hundred banks will fail in that year alone. By 1932, one in four farms will be sold to meet financial obligations. There will be little work for the displaced.

Willie Williamson recalls these trying times:

So many small businesses went bust, including the cheese cooperative I helped to establish in 1904. The business flourished for several years and we joined with the creamery in Centuria, where they were making butter. I served as secretary and treasurer. We all shared in the profits. In the early twenties the bank started insisting that we should buy government bonds. I didn't have any money, so the bank volunteered to pay for the bonds. They wouldn't take the bonds as security. They wanted my note. I was on the bank board at the time and I told them it made more sense to keep our investments at home with local mortgages and cattle so we could help develop the area. That didn't seem to influence them any. When the bank closed, we lost all our capital and earnings of $65,000 and bonds worth $60,000. We lost a total of $125,000, all taken out of the community.

I think our Co-operative could have survived if it hadn't been for all those bonds because we lost only $3,000 in local obligations. We could have stood that. Agents had come out to solicit us to buy that crap. That is something that sits in my craw to this day—the injustice that was done to the rural community.

And of course prices were so depressed in the thirties that we couldn't make a living on our own place. It cost more to produce and harvest a crop than what you could sell it for. Many farms were lost to foreclosure, and we came mighty close.

It was Raymond who picked up on a deal he saw in a Twin Cities newspaper that he thought could get us through until things turned around. The owners of a large farm near Houston, Minnesota, were advertising for farm managers, and Raymond wrote to inquire. The place was called Money Creek—that was the nearest creamery—but by God, there sure wasn't any money in it for us. I went down there on the twenty-sixth day of February, 1930. Olava and three of the boys [Wilmar, Clarence, and Leland] *came down on the tenth of March. Donald and Helen and Alice stayed home with Raymond and his wife so they could finish out the school year. Then they joined us when school was out in the spring—all but Raymond. He was unemployed, so he stayed back to manage the place up home.*

Helen and Alice had two years of high school there in Houston. We couldn't transport them into town every day so they lived in a rented room in town. We got them home most weekends and Mama would send groceries and baked goods and clean clothes back with them on Sunday nights. They were pretty young to be on their own that way, but education was important to the girls. Donald, of course, quit school after eighth grade and was happy to be done with it.

Well, we worked like the dickens, all of us. The farm was 1,116 acres, with steep hills and bluffs. Lots of big rattlesnakes there near the river. The boys always carried a revolver when we were working the fields. We had twenty-four work horses and one tractor. Those horses knew when there was a rattlesnake nearby and they would stop in their tracks and snort and whinny. It was dangerous hauling high loads of hay down those steep hills, too, but the horses were used to that.

We ran that farm until the twenty-fifth day of June, 1932. It ended when I got into a misunderstanding with the owners, and I was right. Their attorneys told them to give me a release because *they had violated their contract. It called for $3,000 per year, $250 per month. That was for five men working every day of the week, not counting Olava and the girls, who helped plenty too. The contract obligated me for half of the personal property—machinery, feed on hand, cattle and all equipment. They didn't take inventory at the beginning, as they should have, and when they took inventory at the end of the year their judgment was so entirely unreasonable that I called their attention to it.*

The second year it got even worse. I knew we had made a good profit that year, but the way they figured it, we ended up owing THEM money. So many ways they tried to cheat us. For example, they inventoried the silage in the silos as if they were full when we started, and any damn fool knows a silo isn't full of silage on the first day of March, not after you've been feeding out of it all winter! But you couldn't build a case in court on that. They made a big mistake, though. They inventoried the silage at more than the CAPACITY of the silo, and that's where we had 'em.

It was such a bad time, and Raymond felt responsible for it because it was his idea in the first place. I think it preyed on his mind for a long time. We had worked like demons and it was a near disaster. A couple of bankers from Winona had threatened to foreclose on our property up home. We could so easily have been wiped out. Well, with some legal help I was able to get it straightened out and we moved out of there in June of '32, back to our own place.

Of course our troubles weren't over. Prices fell so hard after the crash. A bushel of wheat that sold for three dollars in 1920 was worth thirty cents by 1932. I recall we sent some pigs to market and got three cents a pound for them. We started butchering them after that because we couldn't afford to feed them. The cattle depreciated about seventy percent in one year. They stayed depressed like that, right through the thirties, right up until the war. But we held on to our land. With land prices as low as they were, we were able to acquire more acreage. I bought another place east of Milltown in 1934 and got Clarence and his wife set up on that. Later on I bought another dandy farm a mile west of Milltown and set Leland up on *that one when he got married. Paid only $3,800 for it. If only I had been able to help Raymond that way, but he never wanted to farm, you know, and the timing was never quite right for him. Timing is so important. So is hard work and common sense. You have to have all three to make a go of things. A little luck helps too.*

Luck is in short supply for the nation's farmers throughout the thirties, and for wage earners as well.

The Smoot-Hawley Tariff Act of 1930, originally intended to preserve American jobs and protect farmers against agricultural imports, has a catastrophic impact on international trade. When U.S. tariffs are raised to historically high levels, foreign governments retaliate with high tariffs on American products, crippling international commerce and expanding the depression worldwide.

American wages are cut drastically as the Depression wears on. A quarter of the nation's work force is unemployed by 1932. There is little relief, except whatever help can be obtained from churches, private charities, relatives, and neighbors. Hourly wages have dropped 60 percent since before the crash of 1929; white-collar salaries are down 40 percent. Suicide rates have risen 30 percent over the past three years.

The fourth Williamson son, Wilmar, speaks of the Depression years:
I suppose if I hadn't come out of high school during the Depression I might not have become a farmer at all. I had a notion to study electrical engineering, but there was no money for school by that time, no jobs to be had either. So farming was my only choice and it suited me in some respects. I liked the field work best. Always did. I loved being out there with the horses—and later on the tractor—from sunrise to sunset.

I never felt completely comfortable working with animals. Had to kill too many of them as a boy, maybe that had something to do with it. I remember killing all those little Jersey calves when I was a kid. There was awhile there during the Depression when the new calves—bull calves especially—weren't worth the feed you put into 'em. I had to hit 'em on the head with a hammer as soon as they were born. They had those big wet eyes and the way they'd look at you and follow you around . . . I didn't care for it much. I had to wring the necks of those young rooster chicks too. That was a kid's job and I was the kid that got to do it. Wait till they start growing little combs, Mom said, that's the only way to be sure it's a rooster. Then I'd catch 'em and twist their necks, like this. I don't think I could do that now.

Pop made a good decision, you know, going into Holsteins. I think that's what saved us. They are certainly a superior breed when it comes to financial return. Big hardy calves. High volume milkers, lower fat content. And that became important. In the old days when creameries paid for butterfat, which went mostly into butter and cheese, you fed the milk to the pigs. But as you know, that's changed. These days you sell the milk, and a good first-calf heifer can milk a hundred pounds a day, the way we feed 'em now. I'll bet we've more than doubled the production.

Cows used to be much smaller—even the Holsteins—before the days of artificial insemination. And of course we couldn't always feed 'em the way we wanted to. God, I'll never forget those Depression years. What an awful thing not to be able to feed your animals. We tried to pasture them at least five months a year, but some of those dry years there wasn't any decent grass. Some of the farmers went up to Grantsburg to cut grass out there in that area they call Crex Meadow now, but it wasn't good feed.

Donald and I went to work on the road crew that was paving Highway 35 so we could buy some real hay. It was backbreaking work, but of course we were used to that. We'd been lifting eighty pound milk cans out of the stock tank and we were hard as nails. The road work paid pretty well too—forty cents an hour. I wasn't always so keen on all those government programs—some of them seemed to do more harm than good—but I'll tell you, that rural electrification and the road construction projects—that improved our lives considerably in the long run.

In November of 1932, after three years of hardship, the American public elects a new president. While Herbert Hoover tried to preserve the spirit of self-reliance, practicing a hands-off approach toward business, Franklin D. Roosevelt believes in expanding the role of government to relieve economic hardship and protect the public. Roosevelt's New Deal will include a wide range of acts and agencies—the Civilian Conservation Corps, Agricultural Adjustment Act, National Industrial Recovery Act, National Recovery Administration, Public Works Administration, Civil Works Administration, and more. The varying success of Roosevelt's "alphabet soup" programs will be praised, maligned, and debated for decades to come.

By 1933, over 150,000 U.S. farms are being lost to foreclosure every year.

Adolf Hitler has risen to power in Germany. Europe is suffering from the global economic depression. German people hope that a bold and charismatic new leader can return the country to prosperity.

On March 4, 1933, President Roosevelt's first inaugural address is broadcast coast to coast, heard by millions of Americans. The most memorable line: "The only thing we have to fear is fear itself."

Congress passes the Emergency Banking Relief Act on March 9, closing the banks for four days; banks reopen on March 13, their deposits insured by the newly created Federal Reserve Board.

The Agricultural Adjustment Act goes into effect on May 12, attempting to restrict agricultural production by paying farmers to reduce crop area and kill livestock.

In May 1933, the Century of Progress World's Fair opens in Chicago, Illinois. It is a successful event, both in financial and attendance terms, taking advantage of cheap labor to keep costs low. The fair draws over thirty-nine thousand visitors during two seasons. Popular exhibits include the American Dream Cars displayed by Cadillac, Nash, Lincoln Pierce Arrow, and Packard; the 1933 Homes of Tomorrow, showing modern conveniences and creative new building materials and techniques; and the sleek new passenger trains from Burlington Route and Union Pacific Railroad. The Burlington Zephyr has recently completed a record-breaking run from Denver to Chicago in a mere thirteen hours and five minutes. Such speed is difficult to comprehend.

Life is gaining momentum for Miss Adele Williamson, who has completed a bachelor of education degree and is ready to resume her teaching career.

MAY 22, 1933
Mr. J. E. Adams, Principal,
Grantsburg High School,
Grantsburg, Wisconsin.

Dear Mr. Adams,
I wish to make formal application for the English-History vacancy in the Grantsburg High School.

I graduated from the Milltown High School in 1924. In June 1927, I graduated from the three year English-History-Social Science course at the River Falls State Teachers College, being an honor roll student during my training. I have spent this year in River Falls earning my B.E. degree, which will be conferred June seventh.

I have had five years of teaching experience in Wisconsin high schools, having taught one year at Centuria and four years at Red Granite. I am prepared to teach English, history, botany, and the social sciences. I possess a state library license, which qualifies me to manage a library. I have spent my summer vacations traveling, an experience which should lend interest to my teaching.

I am also prepared to manage vocal music and chorus work, all forms of forensics, debate, drama and operettas. I have had training and five years of coaching experience in the above activities. Each year I have had one or two winning representatives at the league and district forensics and dramatics contests. I have managed Girl Scouts, YWCA and all school publications. I have had no difficulty with discipline and I thoroughly enjoy my work.

I am twenty-seven years of age; my health is excellent. In fact, I have never lost a day of school due to illness. I am five feet three inches tall and weigh 112 pounds. I am a member of the Lutheran Church at Milltown, Wisconsin. During my teaching year I work in the Sunday School and sing in the choir.

I will send letters of recommendation and arrange to interview with you at your soonest convenience if you are able to consider me for this position. If appointed to your faculty, I assure you I will do everything I can to cooperate with the teaching staff, supervision and townspeople.

With me, salary is of secondary consideration in the face of present conditions. Each year I taught I received a $10 per month raise, receiving $155 per month at Red Granite last year. I am more interested in securing an advantageous position than I am concerned about salary. Whatever consideration you may give me will be much appreciated, I assure you.

Yours very respectfully,

(Miss) Adele Williamson

Adele Williamson may be an ideal candidate, but competition for any job is fierce. And in this case, she is too late. The letter is returned with a note penciled across the top: *Vacancy filled the day your application arrived. Thank you for your interest.*

Being a day late can change the course of an entire life. So much depends on timing.

Adele will find work for the coming school year, at the high school in Pepin, Wisconsin, a small town on the Mississippi River, one hundred miles to the south. By November 1933, she has fallen in love.

PEPIN WISCONSIN. NOVEMBER 2, 1933

Dear Margaret,

It is in love that I am, I know! And what an elevating thing it can be! It makes me feel that I want to do good for everyone in the world and makes me glad when every new day arrives. Then there are times when there is a sort of mixture of Heaven and

Hell—Heaven when you get what you want and Hell when you don't. Damnable economic situations ruin more happiness! If it weren't for the uncertainty of Maurice's position, we would be married when school is out. As it is, who knows?

Gee, I'm crazy about him and this must be something of a mutuality or he wouldn't do or say the things he does. Every night we talk over the marriage possibilities, but always come back to the first point of difficulty—economics! Of course there are many fellows who are supporting families on less than he is getting. With his post office job, the commission from his sales at the store, and his income for helping at the funeral home, he always averages well above $130 each month. He likes to do things for people though, so he isn't satisfied with that salary when he puts a wife into the budget. Then there is his family, partially dependent upon him.

When the Post Office changes hands after the holidays, if he doesn't get the Postmaster's job (he wrote the test) he plans to take further studies in undertaking so he can operate a service of his own. If he gets this training, he will look for work in Minneapolis. There is money in undertaking. Maurice says that one can live well on just one funeral per month.

Margaret, you will love him! Some Friday evening we will leave here when Maurice is through at the Post Office and we'll descend upon you for approval. He is so eager to favorably impress you and the family. What are your Thanksgiving plans? I have time off from teaching from Wed. eve through Sunday night. What to do? I can't decide. I hate to spend the money traveling alone and Maurice has just Sundays off, unless he asks for a special favor of more time. He is so conscientious.

We have winter in dead earnest now, but that will be lots of fun because there will soon be grand evenings of bridge. And this town goes in for winter sports because we have the water and the hills. I am going to learn to ski and skate before the winter is over.

Isn't it funny how everything favors me? I hardly deserve all these breaks—coming here, tumbling into the Schindlers—

such great landlords—and finding the greatest chap in all Christendom. That is more than my share for two short months! It makes me afraid that it won't last.

I wrote to Vern P. recently and let him know that I am seeing someone else. This new happiness is so complete and enveloping. I find myself damn near unconscious regarding everything else except Maurice. I have lost another pound—110# now, down from 117#—and I have never felt better or been happier. Maurice is the first man that I have ever been able to visualize myself married to. He brings out all of my best traits. I have no bad temper left, and am not even spunky or stubborn. And I don't swear any more, if you can imagine that. There isn't a thing in the world that I wouldn't do for him—and do it because I WANTED TO! That's what I mean when I say that I am dangerously in love!

Next to being born, this is the greatest thing that has ever happened to me, and when I'm the happiest I am afraid that something will ruin what could be absolute perfection. I'd enjoy so much being able to see you and talk to you. Meantime I have to write to you about all these grand things that are happening to me. I know you will understand. I am feeling a little guilty about giving Vern the bum's rush, but he won't mind so much when the first big hurt is over. He is so terribly sensible. In fact, all that sense was one of the problems, I think. A person has to feel excited about the prospect of marriage, don't you think? And as you can tell, I AM EXCITED!

Thanks for your grand letter. I'll write again soon, with the next installment of this drama.

Love to you—Adele

Adele has always been the emotional, excitable sister, but this is excessive, even for her. As she puts it herself, she is *dangerously in love.*

Love is something that Adele has long been craving. She will remember that well, some fifty years later.

You know, I was always envious of Margaret, though of course I loved her dearly. She was tall and sweet and pretty, with that thick, curly hair, and she got praised, mostly I think for her even temperament. I used to watch for signs of favoritism toward Margaret, even counting the dumplings in the soup, feeling devastated if I came up short. If I had even one less dumpling I was sure Mama had doled them out that way on purpose. Now, if I had an extra one, I was sure there was some mistake—that bowl had been meant for Margaret.

Then there was the problem with these paws of mine. Mama said that a cow stepped on her right hand when she was milking out in the barn, during her pregnancy with me, and that's why I was born with this deformity. Mama had been a schoolteacher too, you know, but in those days women weren't taught a thing about reproduction. Not a thing! I've got Mama's old Normal School textbooks, published in 1894. Every single body system was reviewed in pretty good detail, except the "naughty parts"—and not one word about sex or how babies came into the world. So you had all these old wives tales.

Well anyway, Mama seemed ashamed of my handicap and I sure picked up on that. "Poor Adele has these crippled hands," Mama would say, whenever we had visitors. "We're going to be sure she gets an education because she won't be able to work like the others." And they did do more for me, sent me to teachers college at great sacrifice. Margaret didn't even get to complete high school, you know. But I only took that as a further sign that I had serious flaws and needed special treatment. I got to thinking no one would ever want me. As it turned out, I had plenty of fellows coming around . . . but most of them seemed so dull, so short-sighted. It was like they wanted to live in monotone. And I wanted a full spectrum. Technicolor! Fresh scenery, wide horizons.

I think I saw the danger signs with Maurice before we ever married. The flashes of temper that seemed to come out of nowhere. The moods swings, the sarcastic and arrogant remarks. But I chose to ignore them.

With 1933 drawing to a close, the Twenty-first Amendment to the Constitution is ratified by the states, putting an end to Prohibition. Citizens have had enough of the unenforceable law; alcoholic beverages return legally to American life, subject only to the jurisdiction of individual states.

A new term—*Dust Bowl*—is being heard around the country. The early thirties have been hot and dry in many regions, particularly in the Great Plains of the West. Due to the economic depression, farmers have stopped cultivating huge areas of land, leaving it idle, stripped of its protective cover of grass, turning it into a virtual desert. Dust storms have been blowing away whatever valuable soil is left. Countless farmers who have been "dusted out" are taking to the road to seek whatever work they might find in California and elsewhere. Route 66 becomes the major route west for those fleeing the Dust Bowl.

The Upper Midwest has been experiencing a lesser degree of drought; crops of oats and corn and hay are still holding most of the loamy soil. But prices are not holding up so well.

Margaret receives this letter from her mother on January 10, 1934.

Dear Margaret,
Today Papa and the boys have butchered three hogs and tomorrow they will kill the other two—that finishes the hogs. We will share one with Ray and Ethel and keep the rest for ourselves. We need that many for the whole year. We will dress two beef this week too, so when you come up to the farm we will fix you up for a while.

The market is down on eggs and butterfat. We got 19 cents for butterfat today. One man up here paid me only 15 cents per dozen for number one eggs last week. O. B. Jensen at the Milltown Mercantile paid 17 cents in trade. We sold some of our layers for only 5 cents per pound.

We had a letter from Wilmar. He is still out in Dakota, you know, but wants to come home again. It's been so hot and dry out there, with dust storms and all the top soil blowing away. Wisconsin probably looks good to him now. Maybe Wilmar can get on the road crew when they start paving this spring.

Ray had to take an awful cut—from $36 to $24 per week. It will be hard for them to make it on that, but he is glad to have work.

I got my hair bobbed and everyone says they like it, even Papa. He says I should have had it done years ago. It feels good to have the stringy hair out of my neck.

Be sure to eat well now Margaret, and get rested. That is especially important during these cold winter months.

Love from us all, Mother

January 1934. Helen is in her last year of high school in Milltown. Alice, having skipped a year of high school, is one year behind her. Raymond has found office employment in nearby St. Croix Falls but has recently taken a drastic cut in salary. Clarence, Leland, and Donald are farming with Willie, picking up odd jobs where they can—hunting, trapping, cutting and splitting firewood—for extra cash. Wilmar is in North Dakota, working temporarily as a farmer's hired hand.

Adele marries Maurice Fleming early in March 1934 without much ceremony. An unplanned pregnancy is the reason for such haste, but Adele makes no direct mention of this in her next letter to Margaret. She expresses no regrets about foregoing a festive wedding. Nor is she fretting about finances or the need to keep her marriage quiet until the end of her teaching term. Love and passion have, for now, blown all her worries away.

PEPIN WISCONSIN. MARCH 9, 1934

Dear Margaret and Mel,

I received your letter this morning and Maurice and I have both read it at the Post Office. I was so afraid that you were cross with me and I don't want you to be because I am so happy! I have never before known how perfect one's life could be if she were really in love and then married to that someone! I think I have the grandest man in the whole wide world and nothing can change my mind. He is everything I have ever wanted in a man: a combination of Vern's gentleness and breeding, Ed's conservative nature, Mel's honesty, character and kindness. To make the thing almost unbelievably good, he is easy on the eyes and has interests that check with mine perfectly. His disposition and patience are more than I deserve and I am still stunned by my good fortune.

I always felt that any marriage I would make would come as a result of a whirlwind courtship. This one has, but we feel so thoroughly acquainted and so sure that we have done the right thing that we can't seem to remember the time when we haven't known one another . . .

I can't help but believe that there is a Divine Providence guiding us. Why should I have come to this town—just hating to—unless there was a reason? At least the Williamson girls are happily married, and two greater and grander men were never born than your Melvin and my Maurice.

Maurice and I are anxiously awaiting the day when we can begin housekeeping. That will be a delight. I have been hungry for a long, long time. I want Maurice to call "Waffles!" on a Sunday morning. I will come running, too. He inspires me with thoughts to be good and unselfish and I want always to keep him as happy as he is now.

Perhaps for my birthday we can come to Minneapolis. That falls on a Sunday, so I'm hoping we could come on a Saturday evening because it would almost double our visiting time. We shall let you know, though.

I told my landlady that Maurice and I are married and she is an old peach! I had to let her know because she might question his staying with me until so late otherwise. She has given me the studio couch downstairs and she and her husband use my room, you see. No one else suspects a thing—that's how slippery we have been. It will be grand fun when we DO announce it.

Maurice has been buying furniture and you should see the exquisite taste he has! His folks gave us a washing machine. They are real peaches. All his younger brothers and sisters have the measles now, so last night I packed a box of goodies and reading materials for them. They were happy.

I just live my days through knowing I will see Maurice at night. I have a class coming so must go.

Love to you both, Mrs. Maurice Fleming (I like that name!)

Margaret writes to her husband, Mel, on August 24, 1934, addressing the airmail envelope to Mr. Melvin Gorder, 2503 West 7th Street, Los Angeles, California.

Mel has lost his job in Minneapolis and, with help from a friend in Los Angeles, has secured an accounting position with Buzza-Cardozo, a greeting card company. Margaret plans to join him there as soon as possible. She begins the letter with details about her work at Walman Optical, then turns to family news.

Helen came back to the city with me on Sunday. Today we went over to the Minneapolis Business College to get her enrolled. Mr. Mosher was very obliging about arranging a special accelerated course for her and her supplies cost only $5.50. Mine cost about $20.00 when I started ten years ago. Helen can live in the apartment with me for these first few months until I make the move to L.A. Then I'll help her get established in a girls' club, wherever we can find an opening. Mosher says she should be ready to go to work by the first of the year. He is sure she can do it because he knows the Williamsons are hard workers. He still remembers Ray, and me too, of course . . .

SEPTEMBER 11, 1934

Dear Mel,

Hurray! Soon I won't have to worry about this business any longer. It will be California and you, and to the devil with all these collection letters.

Now for some sad news: Helen and I spent the weekend in Pepin. Adele had a rather bad time and nearly lost her baby. He was born at seven months, very small and fragile. Adele had washed windows and strained herself and began flowing

last Tuesday. By Friday she was in serious condition. She had
gone about the house for four days after the water broke and
the flowing started. The baby, of course, was losing all his nour-
ishment, and was so nearly dead when born that they had to
give him hypo's in the hip to keep him alive. That wasn't all,
either, because the saddest part of it all is that he has crippled
hands just like Adele's and one very short twisted little arm,
and the kids feel just terrible about it. He is getting good care at
the hospital and he was still living Sunday night so he may pull
through. In addition to all the rest, they found it necessary to
perform an operation on his lower bowel. All in all, he will be
a pretty exceptional baby if he lives. They say he is very pretty
and bright looking, even tiny as he is. Adele didn't realize her
condition because the baby wasn't expected until the latter part
of October.

Adele is coming along fine now . . . I have told the folks only
some of the details about the baby—nothing about his hands
because Mama will be just beside herself with grief when she
hears it. I have cried about it all—at least I did Sunday night
when I got back—but I'm not going to let it worry me anymore.
If he lives, he will get along just as well as Adele did and if he
passes away, that could be a blessing too. The most pathetic part
of it all is that Adele won't ever dare to have another baby for
fear that it will not be normal.

Maurice is a darling. He says that he wants the baby to live
because he is sure that he will be a swell little fellow. Don't write
to them for a few days yet, Mel, because I'll let you know about
the baby each day. If he is coming along all right, it will be easier for you to write and if not, you will be able to write just the
correct thing . . .

Goodnight, Dear. Please take care of yourself until I can get
there.

I love you. Sunshine

One week later, Margaret and Helen receive this surprisingly
cheery letter from Adele.

PEPIN, WISCONSIN. TUESDAY NOON, SEPTEMBER 18, 1934

Dear Margaret and Helen,

I am up and dressed today. I bathed the baby for the first time this morning and had no trouble at all. They kept him in the hospital until Friday forenoon, so he came home on his one week birthday. He is getting along just fine now, even though he has had a tough time. He cries a lot at night, but his days are well spent. He has a hard time nursing and whenever tea-time comes I have a fight on my hands because he just roots around and won't clamp down.

He is the best-looking kid I've ever seen, a pocket edition of his handsome daddy, and has just as winsome ways . . . His eyes are the bluest blue. He has the most kissable mouth and his ears lay down like mine. He has a short, fat body and broad, short feet . . . His hands aren't so bad and I can look upon it sensibly. He could be so much worse off and the doctors speak encouragingly of what can be done for him. I should be glad we live near such a miracle center as Rochester [home to the Mayo Clinic].

I wrote home and, as mild as I could, told them about his operation and his hands. I thought I had best do that before they come down so they can get used to the idea and enjoy their visit more. They may come this weekend. I hope you will be able to come again before long too.

Maurice is assisting at the Pepin funeral home. He had two funerals since you and Helen were here, so has been too busy to write and wishes to apologize. He's so darn sweet to me. I'm crazy about him. Everyone here has been grand. There are 11 huge bouquets in the house, food enough for a big family and so many sweaters for Bobby he will have to wear two at a time to wear them out.

Don't worry about me, Margaret. I feel good, even though I am still weak.

Love, The Flemings

Margaret writes many letters to Mel during the last months of 1934, when she is finishing her work in Minneapolis, selling their household goods, preparing for the move to California. The very sound of it—*California*—carries a measure of magic and adventure. California means warmth and sunshine, movie making, oranges growing on the trees. And Melvin Gorder. But as she prepares to leave her job, her friends and family, and her girlhood home, Margaret struggles with mixed emotions.

SEPTEMBER 19, 1934

I sold a few more items last night, including that little lamp, a small rug, the kitchen stool and icebox. Just think, a month of separation is gone already, and in about three more months I will be on my way. So many people envy us this opportunity. It sounds as if business is good out there, isn't it? Adding people in times like this is something most business houses can't do. I have $132 in the bank now and the rent and all bills paid to the end of the month. I'm taking care of Helen's expenses for now too, but soon she will be earning her own way.

SEPTEMBER 24, 1934

I now have $350 in the bank, which includes $225 from furniture sales. I hope to increase that to $400 when I sell the rest of our things. I am dreaming every night of California and YOU.

OCTOBER 1, 1934

Grandma Knutson [Willie Williamson's mother, widowed for the second time] is very sick with heart trouble. She is at the Frederic Hospital and I hope to see her later in the week, as she may not live much longer. Last time I visited she patted my face and in her own way said good-bye. I hope her suffering will soon be over. We will all miss her, such a dear old soul. Everyone at home sends greetings and love to you. Dad is thinking of buying a 32 Ford so he and mother can drive out to California to visit us after we are settled there. Wouldn't that be fun?

OCTOBER 5, 1934

Dear Mel,

This is Friday evening and it is six weeks since you left. I am lonesome for you, Honey. Last night after I went to bed I could hear the music from the Pla-More Dance Hall, which is just down the street a bit. I enjoyed the faint strains of music until I heard them play "My Wild Irish Rose." That almost did me in. I didn't cry though—just picked up something to read, then went to sleep and dreamed about you. It made me think of the last Saturday evening we danced at the Coliseum. I said good-bye to you when we danced that waltz together . . .

This separation is so hard. Another six weeks and it will be all behind us. We will look back on it in a year and be glad of the circumstances that prompted us to make this move.

Dad called me today to tell me that Grandma Knutson passed away yesterday. The funeral will be Sunday and your mother, Helen and I will go up home to attend. We will try to get a ride with friends and if that doesn't work out we will take the bus. I am grateful that Grandma had so many happy and comfortable years and I only hope to do as well someday.

OCTOBER 8, 1934

I am all nerved up and wish you were here to hug me and help me get over all this. Funerals are terrible things, don't you think? Good-byes are so hard and that kind of good-bye is the worst of all.

NOVEMBER 4, 1934

Sweetheart, you know I have been gaining weight and should be strong enough to do justice to a baby within a year or so. As for providing the kind of home we want for our little one— Honey, you are going a long ways in business and the home is going to be all we hope for, I know. I will always try to make our income buy value received and together we will LIVE and also put away for the future. I believe in LIVING as well as saving, because we are only young once and should get some pleasure while we are able to enjoy it. Too many people wait too long to live. I love you for the way you feel about all these things and I am confident that we have many, many happy years ahead. This is an adventure to look forward to.

When you tell me about California it seems like a fairyland and I imagine that is at least partly true. Think of all the places to go and things to do! I will take the ocean for my first date, and please order a big moon for our special benefit. I'll be on deck for every date you arrange.

NOVEMBER 30, 1934

I get so painfully lonesome for you. On the other hand, I realize that it is going to be hard to leave the family at home and my friends here in the office and I have such a mixture of feelings that I am happy and sad at the same time.

Walman is having a grand dinner party at the Buckingham Hotel on December 15. I am to sit at his right hand as a guest of honor. It is a Christmas party, but from things he tells me, I guess it's going to be a farewell for me, too. The St. Paul and Minneapolis office forces will be here. It will be grand, I think, and Honey, I have a nice new dress to wear—black velvet! I can't wait to wear it on a date with you.

I am so glad to hear that you are busy and like your work. I hope I am not going to miss my work too much. I'm going to do something about it if I do, because I must be contented in order to be a good wife. Oh, I know! That is where the baby comes in. You see there is another good reason why we should think about a little fellow coming to our house to live. I could keep awfully busy that way. He will be a rascal I'm sure and he could keep me as busy as a set of accounting books and collection letters! What do you think?

DECEMBER 14, 1934

Good news, Mel! Mr. Walman has hired Helen to fill some of my responsibilities! He says he knows he can count on another

Williamson girl to do a first rate job. Helen is almost finished with her course at Minneapolis Business College. She will come in every day after school for now, until she is through, and then will be on a full time schedule. She will keep up the collection records and take care of retail accounts without supervision, then take Walman's dictation on wholesale accounts. She is a crackerjack typist and is doing very well with her shorthand and bookkeeping so I have no worries regarding her ability. I will be proud to turn her over to Mr. Walman. Helen will have a good job and earn $15 a week to start. Before I leave Minneapolis I will see that she gets located at the Mabeth Paige Club.

Honey, it is exactly 20 days—480 hours—28,800 minutes—until we will be together.

Helen has been living with Margaret and Mel for the past several months. She will relocate to the Mabeth Paige Club at 272 Fifth Avenue South, one of several low-cost housing facilities for working women run by the Women's Christian Association.

DECEMBER 25, 1934, 11 P.M.
Helen and I just returned from a trip home to the farm. There is a lot of snow piled everywhere and the roads have been plowed out just enough to make driving possible. We took the bus from Milltown to Minneapolis, leaving at 6 p.m., and were comfortable all the way in spite of zero degree weather and snowdrifts.

Helen Williamson, age twenty

Dad and Wilmar came to the city to get us on Saturday and we got home after 7 p.m. Everything went fine until we tried to get into the yard. The car slipped off the beaten path and had to be shoveled out the next day. Mama had a big kettle of home-made soup for us and we felt fine after warming up with that. The boys and Dad and I played poker all evening and I lost my little store of pennies. We put the Christmas tree up on Sunday morning and then played more poker into the evening.

Your Sunshine was so excited opening the California package! Such beautiful underthings—a complete trousseau! Wait until I show them off for you. That will be the evening of Saturday, the fifth of January. I'll thank you properly then.

I saw Grandma Lomo [Olava's mother, widowed for the second time] on Monday and when I said goodbye to her she said she felt it was the last time. It was hard to see her cry. Poor little old grandma. She is so sweet and nice.

I told them all today to pretend I was just going back to Minneapolis. I made a hurry-up job of leaving. I am going to come home next summer for a visit and that is only six or seven months, a comforting thought. Helen is back here in the apartment with me now and that will help until I go.

I am tired and full of pent-up emotions. This may be the last Christmas I will ever spend at home. I am not sorry about our plans but just wish I was already there with you so I could have your shoulder to cry on. Write to me soon, Honey.

Love from your Sunshine

Margaret arrives in California on January 5, 1935, and starts settling into the bungalow that Mel has rented at 962 South Parkview Street, Los Angeles. Letters from home begin arriving within a couple of weeks.

Sister Adele's letter is dated January 15, 1935.

Dearest Margaret,
Because I haven't written sooner is no sign I haven't been thinking about you. It must be a grand and glorious feeling to really relax and have no "office hours." It is still so hard to realize that you are so far away—California! I am happy that you are having

what you so much deserve, but I envy you living with a man who loves you so much and finds you so necessary to his happiness. Be sure to thank Mel from us for the lovely Christmas things he sent. There was a tie for Maurice, stocking for me, and a stuffed cat for Bobby . . .

We took Bobby to Madison last week but brought him back home with us. The x-rays show one bone from the elbow to wrist in the right arm entirely lacking. There is very little they can do for him. Because he is doing so well nursing, they advised me not to wean him, but to give him severe stretching exercises in an attempt to help straighten the hand, and then in the spring we will take him back, leave him there, and have casts put on the hand and arm. They don't want to do that now because he is growing so fast they would have to be changed every week. I had hoped much could be done for him, but they can't supply something missing.

I feel so disheartened. I suppose we should feel grateful that he is as normal as he is. But this feels like a punishment for all of us. Probably Maurice and I deserve some bad luck, but it seems that Bobby is going to pay and pay because he has sinful parents, and that doesn't seem fair.

To make bad things worse, I found myself pregnant again after the New Year, but I got darn good and busy and I'm all right now. Dr. Brookie helped me. Maurice is slow to act on anything—even getting information—so Dr. B. talked to him and told him what to get, etc. Still no action from him. So I am living here as his cook would. I work days and half the night, but collect no pay. If we have to give Bobby up and leave him in Madison for some time, I'm going job hunting near there. I have laid my mental plans. I would like to be nearer Madison if Bobby has to be there for any length of time.

We have had no end of snow here and 42 degrees below zero ten days ago. Helen was here to visit two weeks ago and plans to come again soon. It is so good to see her occasionally.

I have had so many big hurts this past year that I can't feel the same. Something in me is dying fast and I am getting more bitter every day. I try to understand why things are as they are, and I try to remind myself that one can't always have just what you want. But Maurice didn't even give me a Christmas greeting card, to say nothing of a gift. Nothing. And it was our first Christmas together too. The money I spent on all the shopping and my trip home—all that came out of my retirement money, which I had worked darn hard for. I'm glad I went home, though, because it may be a long while before I get there again.

Gee, I'm sorry to sound like a complaining youngster, but it is hard to be so unhappy when one loves so well to be happy. I ask for only an occasional indication that I matter just a little bit.

Write when you have time. It is so good to hear from my family.

Love, Adele

P.S. Bobby can turn over now and laughs all the time!

As much as Margaret loves receiving news from her family, Adele's letter certainly has not lifted her spirits. Margaret is now reunited with her husband but has been torn away from everyone else, everything else she knows and loves. She is two thousand miles from home, and this new place with its incessant sunshine, skinny palm trees, modern "ranch style" homes, tiny yards, and busy streets is not her fairyland. Mel works long hours; Margaret is at home caring for her mother-in-law, who is seriously ill. Margaret is so homesick she would like to go to bed herself.

Recalling that time will bring her to tears, even at the age of ninety-two:

Mel's starting salary with Buzza Cardozo was $125 per month. We had Mother Gorder with us and doctor bills to pay out of that too. Dr. Moore took Mel in his arms and said, "Mel, I don't want you to pay me any money and I will loan you enough to bury her." I got so worn down and anemic myself, I didn't see how I could manage everything. The doctor said, "Just hang on, it won't be much longer now." And I was angry with him because I didn't want Mother Gorder to die, even though her cancer had advanced and she was really suffering.

But the financial strain was real. We knew we wouldn't be able to pay the doctor and Mel was so proud. That was the same time when he was in so much pain with his teeth. He had a major infection that was poisoning his whole system, but could not afford dental care. He finally got the uppers pulled and got a plate. That was the first good sleep he'd had in a long time. He'd been in such pain that his muscles had weakened. They put him on some kind of rack and tried to stretch his body. For a while he could work only two hours at a time. Yes, that was a bad stretch, and it lasted a while after Mother Gorder died.

I was so homesick, too. I could think of nothing but going home. I felt as if I had been yanked up by the roots. I had always been so capable, so in charge, and those first months in California I felt completely helpless. I remember hanging laundry on the line behind that little rented house and sobbing into the wet sheets. Still, you know, California turned out to be a good move for us, in spite of that bad start.

Katherine Mansfield has written: "How hard it is to escape from places! However carefully one goes they hold you—you leave little bits of yourself fluttering on the fences—like rags and shreds of your very life." Margaret feels as if she has left big chunks of herself in Minneapolis and with her family in Wisconsin.

Olava's next letter to Margaret is dated March 7, 1935. It sounds as if the family's farming prospects are improving, as least temporarily.

Dear Margaret,
We hope you are liking your new home in California and that you will gain some weight too. Don't think because we haven't written that we don't think of you early and late. We miss you, so, but I am happy when you are and want you above all to get everything you can from this life. Too many of us are just plugging along day after day and never knowing anything but work.

We do enjoy helping these boys, though and are going to try to see if they can get something for themselves someday. Papa goes back and forth from one to the other and helps here and there, wherever he is needed most.

We have just bought another team of horses for $300. We are so busy here at home on account of milking and chickens. The hatching season has started. We are gathering eggs from something over 1,000 hens on both farms. Eggs from 825 of them go to the hatchery. Eggs are down to 18 cents now. We got 30 cents per dozen in January.

Helen was home from the city last weekend. Poor kid, she is so homesick. It hurts me to see her feeling like that.

We have a real old time winter here. March has been worse than February so far. We have had colds galore here and I have been really sick—first Dad and then Lee and me. I could hardly talk above a whisper for three weeks. Why do we have these dreadful cold winters?

We received the package of dates from you and they are sure fine. How do they look when they grow? Gee it sure must be grand to see so many new places and things. The ocean I can't quite imagine.

Well, I've got a lot of eggs to clean and grade and pack and some dirty dishes waiting so I must close. Much love from Mother

Helen's letter of April 14, 1935, sent from Minneapolis, brings welcome news of home.

Dear Margaret,

I just got back from another grand weekend at home. I had planned on spending this weekend in the city when I got a telegram from Adele yesterday morning at the office, saying that she was going home and I should plan to come too. (It's the first telegram I have ever received so I'm putting it away in my special souvenir collection.) Well, you can just imagine how excited I was. I left the office a little early and took the Greyhound, which let me off on Highway 35, right at the driveway. The folks didn't know that either of us was coming so I surprised them plenty when I arrived about 4 p.m. Adele got in about 7:30 on the train and Ray went to town to pick her up. I was out in the barn practicing up on the "bossies" when she arrived. It was fun to be milking again, but I found that my arms were sore after the first cow and my legs shook like leaves after the pail got about half filled. It's funny how tender a person's muscles do get when you haven't used them for a while. I even helped Lee throw down hay and feed the cows. I'll have to do this more often. I don't intend to turn into a city girl completely!

You should see Adele's little Bobby! He is getting chubby now and laughs all the time. He doesn't have much use of his crippled little right arm. Adele is still hopeful that the doctors can do more for him. Adele is much thinner, but says she is feeling fine. I hope to go down to Pepin on the train and visit them at Easter time.

Mom has been busy with her chickens. The men have been logging this winter and spring to raise some cash. Brother Donny has 86 lambs now. He is pretty proud of his flock and rightly so. Mom said that he had about 15 orphans on the bottle.

Love to you and Mel from everyone at home. I will share any letters you send my way. They will be busy with the chicks from now on and probably won't have much time to write.

Love, Helen

In August 1935, the Social Security Act is passed by Congress as part of the New Deal legislation and signed into law by President Roosevelt. It will begin payouts to retirees within two years. Workers will begin contributing into the system that same year, at a rate of two percent for the first three thousand dollars in earnings, with half paid by the employee and half paid by the employer. However, farm and domestic workers are excluded.

The U.S. population now exceeds 127 million; the unemployment rate stands at 20 percent. Farming accounts for only 21 percent of the labor force.

The Works Progress Administration, the largest and most ambitious New Deal agency, is hiring nearly three million unemployed Americans for public works projects; it also administers relief programs in cooperation with state and local government. The federal government has become the largest employer in the country.

September finds Margaret back home in Wisconsin for an extended visit with her family.

SEPTEMBER 19, 1935

Dear Mel,

It's another grand day today, sunshiny like California and just the right temperature. Helen, Alice and I have been cleaning the house for Mama and fooling around between times. I made Siamese Twins out of them by braiding their hair into one braid and tying the end of the braid so they couldn't get it apart easily. I led them downstairs and showed them to Mama and she laughed at our foolishness.

I weigh 114 now and you can almost find a double chin on me.

I was just outside shaking rugs. Mama has some pretty vines growing on the outside by the two porches. They are turning red now. The woods is pretty too, with lots of red and yellow beginning to show up. Silo filling has progressed and Dad has hopes now of getting ripe corn. He plans on picking the ears and plowing down the corn stalks on the east forty. He has plenty of feed without the stalks and plans on cracking up a lot of corn for chicken feed. He still has no pigs but plans to buy some grass calves and fatten them over winter for sale in the spring. He and the boys are milking about 45 cows now.

This afternoon I am going with Helen and Alice to the east forty to dig a sack of potatoes. We take the car. Alice drives . . .

OCTOBER 9, 1935

Dear Mel,

You will see from the envelope that I am posting this letter from Pepin, Wisconsin. Tomorrow morning I will leave for Madison with Adele and Maurice and Bobby. I just put the little guy to sleep. He is so cuddly and cute and it seems terrible that he has to go away to be hurt. Poor little darling.

Today he took his first steps alone. He walked from Adele to me and took four or five steps. We practiced him up good so we could show him off to Maurice this evening, but he couldn't do more than three. I guess we wore him out . . .

This stay here with Adele and Maurice doesn't give me much news and it won't be anything but upsetting from to-night on. It is hard already, since Bobby has gone to sleep for the last time in a long while in his little bed. The doctors have found some problems with his kidneys and possibly other organs, so we are not sure exactly what this surgery will be. The kids have had so much grief that this seems only another episode to them. Adele has aged so much and I'm hoping they can patch things up because of the little guy and because she does care a lot for Maurice. I advised her to stick it out for at least another year and then make the break if she must. Another year would see Bobby through his hospital care at least. He will be a State case, but it will be better if she has Maurice to share this thing financially, if nothing more. He is no comfort to her at all. He happens to be one of those who can turn a right-about-face and he certainly did in his feelings for her. He seems so darn likeable too, so it is hard to believe that he isn't fair and honorable. He has been grand to me—just like he always was to you and me—but he is rather short to Adele all the time. Enough of this. I don't let it get me down because I will help them all I can and then forget it. I tell Adele not to be hasty and rash because there is a long life ahead of her. She wants to leave him because it is so humiliating not to be wanted.

Adele just fixed my bed on the studio couch, so I am going to turn in now, Honey. Tomorrow will come pretty soon and we are going to leave at 7 a.m., hoping to be in Madison by about 3 p.m. Maurice is a slow driver.

Goodnight, Dear. I'll write at least a card from Madison. Your Sunshine

Margaret writes to Mel from the homeplace on November 1, reporting that the ground has frozen solid and a sheet of ice covers the entire yard. It is time to plan her return trip to California.

... I am going to try to buy a berth for at least one night, if I can do that with a coach fare. I'm sure the train will be more comfortable than the bus, even without a berth.

As the time comes closer I am thinking more and more of L.A. and you. I am satisfied to leave here now. I will mind it, of course, but there is a big thrill ahead for me too, being with you again.

It would be terrible if I didn't feel satisfied to go back out there, but it isn't so. I have gained so much in spirits—and an extra five pounds too. I was terribly irritable and wasn't fit to live with, I know. If it hadn't been for you, Honey, with your level head, I guess I might have jumped off somewhere. Isn't it terrible to get into such a frame of mind? Sick minds are as bad as sick bodies, or worse.

I haven't felt this good since I was a kid. And the headaches are gone too. I have missed you terribly, but I am glad for that too because it shows me how much we belong together. I will let you know my travel plans as soon as I get it all arranged.

Love, Sunshine

Helen closes out the year with this letter to her California sister.

MINNEAPOLIS, MINNESOTA. DECEMBER 16, 1935, 5:40 P.M.
Dear Margaret,
I just got your Christmas package wrapped and mailed and hope it reaches you on time. I have spent most of the past week shopping on my noon hours, whenever I had time. The auditor has been here and some days things piled up. I had so much dictation that I had all I could do to squeeze in some lunch.

We had a nice snowstorm last week and things are looking Christmas-y now. How does it seem out there without snow? We have had some terribly cold weather recently, and ice too, so walking on these sidewalks can be dangerous. You are missing a real old-fashioned winter, calling for mittens, overshoes and earlaps.

Pop finally blew himself to a new car—a 1935 Pontiac with only 4,000 miles on it, good as new. Pop got it for $550 plus Grandpa's old Ford. He actually bought it on an installment plan—the first thing I believe he has ever gotten that way . . . I am hoping Pop will take Mom on a California trip next summer, now that they finally have a car they can depend on. But I doubt if he will want to spend the time or money.

Well, I need to join some of the girls for supper, then turn in early.

Love to you and Mel, Helen

A School in Patience

1936–39

Life on the farm is a school in patience.
You can't hurry the crops or make an ox in two days.
HENRI ALAIN-FOURNIER

THE GREAT DEPRESSION has been well recorded, due in part to the New Deal's Works Progress Administration. The government became one of the biggest sponsors of the arts, hiring artists, actors, directors, musicians, and writers to produce new work. From 1936 through 1940, the Federal Writers' Project paid sixty-five hundred writers twenty dollars per week to go out and interview ordinary people and get their life stories. The programs of the WPA, one of the longest-lived New Deal agencies, resulted in extensive documentation of this trying period of the nation's history.

Helen and her mother and sisters continue to record their lives during these lean times, but they do not have history in mind. They are simply metabolizing their day-to-day existence, paying witness to the world around them and sharing that witness with each other.

Thomas Moore has written, "Something happens to our thoughts and emotions when we put them into a letter . . . Writing letters requires a certain level of artfulness and thoughtfulness in expression. Then they remain, to be re-read, perhaps to be stored away for another day of reading, or even to be encountered at some distant time by a future, unknown eavesdropper."

When Helen writes to Margaret on January 27, 1936, a new year is under way. The season is deep winter, bitterly cold.

Dear Margaret,
Well, here I am all greased up with a big woolen sock around my neck. We had two frightfully cold days last week when it got as cold as 33 degrees below zero here in Minneapolis. I walked to work those days and even though I did put extra clothes on, it got me. I went to bed Thursday night with a sore throat and have been here ever since. The housemother brings my meals but I haven't been able to eat much. I hurt all over. My eyes are even too sore to read but I have the radio on all day and that helps me pass the time.

Boy, as soon as I get a chance I am going to have these darned tonsils yanked out so they won't cause me any more trouble. Who would you advise me to go to? I suppose they charge about $35 for the job now. That's what my friend Mary paid. If I get it done on a Friday and stay in bed all weekend I should be able to go back to work on Monday.

I just tuned in the weather report. It has warmed up—only 8 degrees below today, and mind you we think that is mild. Several of the girls at the club froze their legs and faces walking to work last week and one girl met with quite an accident. Because of the cold wind she held her muff up to her face to protect it and hurried across the street, running right into a car on the corner of Second Avenue. She fractured her skull and broke her collar bone.

I had a letter from Alice a few days ago and it was full of news about the cold weather on the farm. She said the sink and washbowl pipes were frozen up. I suppose it is even colder up there than in the city. All I can say is I envy you when I hear that it is 76 degrees in L.A.

Love from your ailing sister, Helen

MARCH 20, 1936

Dear Margaret,

I went to Pepin over the weekend and what a trip that turned out to be! I took the bus to Wabasha where Maurice was going to meet me and when I got there the Wabasha bridge had been washed out over on the Wisconsin side, near Nelson, so Maurice had to go way around through Winona and then come up to Wabasha to get me. It was about 140 miles round trip just to go three miles across the lake! I came back by train Sunday night.

Maurice and Adele aren't getting on so well, Margaret. Adele says that she is satisfied now that they won't ever be better. I saw one or two little displays of temper from Maurice and I can see where Adele will just go on being miserable as long as she stays. It's a pretty hopeless situation when they can't get together and talk things over because things can't just mend themselves. Maurice just sits around and won't talk and Adele goes on not knowing where she is at. I think the sooner she makes a move to go, the better. It will be much harder when Bobby gets a little older. Gosh, I don't know what's to be done about it. I wish she would write you and tell you her troubles, but she says she isn't in the mood for it. You are a pretty good Dorothy Dix [a popular advice columnist of the times] and maybe you could give her some good ideas, though I believe she has tried almost every approach with Maurice. Adele wants me to go down there for Easter, but I would like to go up home too. I can't decide yet what I will do. I will let you know as soon as I have made my plans.

Love, Helen

Adele writes to Margaret on March 31, expressing cautious hopes for her troubled marriage.

. . . Things this week have been fine between Maurice and me. I could be quite happy if this continues. Our big trouble is not talking things over enough, so we are always guessing what the other is thinking and feeling. I think all marriages have trials of one sort or another and an idealist is apt to become disillusioned when he bumps up against the cold realities. That has been Maurice's experience, and in looking for a reason, he blames everything on me. Essentially there is no really great difference between us that shouldn't be surmountable.

Maurice's boss is back on the job again and now we can sleep later in the mornings. That will improve dispositions, I think. Being physically tired can be so hard on one's nerves . . .

The weather is a test of nerves for everyone this year. Wisconsin has always been known for extreme temperatures, but 1936 is breaking records. Winter's deep freeze, followed by rapid snowmelt and raging floods, has turned to punishing heat, as Helen describes in her letter of July 21, 1936.

Dear Margaret,

No doubt you have been hearing reports of this awful heat wave. The weather has moderated a little and we have been working full time in the office again the last few days. We had to quit by mid-afternoon several days when it was 107 degrees—too hot to accomplish much anyway. Lots of people passed out on the street. We had two weeks straight when it was 100 or over every day. Some people didn't mind the days as much as the evenings, but we were more fortunate at the club, having the roof to sleep on. The girls slept up there every night when it was so hot and toward the last we got tired of dragging our mattresses up and down and we just slept on blankets. We woke up stiff in the joints but at least we slept.

The folks are talking about a trip to California later this summer. They might as well go. Raymond says he and Ethel could stay on the home place and do the necessary chores. The harvest won't amount to a hang this year because the crops are burning up. They are cutting their grain to use as hay because the kernels didn't fill at all. The only grain they will have for threshing is 27 acres of winter wheat. Pop and the boys were hauling oats into the haymow last Sunday when I was home.

Pop cut with the mower and it was devilish stuff because it was so short and spindly. Some of the neighboring grain fields are too short to cut with the mower. If they don't get rain soon the corn won't amount to anything either. Then they will have to start selling cows.

I didn't get a chance to see Clarence or Donny on my last trip up home. Donny spent most of those hot days fighting brush pile fires that got away from them up in the woods. Donny was almost overcome by smoke and heat before he and the neighbors got the fire out. There have been many forest fires north of here too, around Bone Lake. It has been so dry and the hot winds have helped spread the fires.

I have seen several movies lately—most of them not very good, but I sat through them twice, just to get cooled off. I miss you as always, Margaret, but right now I am glad you are somewhere more comfortable. I will try to make my next letter more cheerful.

Love, Helen

Wisconsin is now populated by 3.2 million dairy cows and 2.9 million people. Man and beast alike are suffering through the summer of 1936. Extreme heat and drought have reached the Upper Midwest. Polk County, along with seven other northwestern Wisconsin counties, is officially declared a drought area. This status will allow for reduced freight on shipments of feed and seed, as well as cheaper loans for those who have the courage to continue.

Decades later, the youngest Williamson son, Donald, describes some hardships of the mid-thirties. He remembers cutting and splitting firewood in frigid weather, selling it for $1.50 a cord, and hitchhiking to North Dakota to work the harvest fields in blistering heat for a dollar a day. He describes the Farm Holiday protests, with farmers spilling milk onto the roadways and throwing spiked planks on the bridge near St. Croix Falls to stop truckers from getting milk to market in the Twin Cities, part of a desperate attempt to call attention to the farm crisis. He recalls the grasshopper plagues and herding the cattle onto the railroad tracks where they might find some dry stubble growing between the ties. He remembers riding the rails in empty boxcars with an empty stomach, all the way to California, turning up at Margaret's door, getting arrested for hopping a boxcar on the way back, wiring his dad for money to pay his way home.

By the end of 1936, Donald is back in Wisconsin, farming with his older brother Clarence, who is now married and the father of two children, Billy and Joyce. Willie has helped get the boys established on a farm near the village of Luck, northeast of the homeplace. Abandoned farms and devalued land enable survivors like Willie Williamson to acquire property at bargain prices.

Raymond, the only Williamson son who is not farming, is employed as a bookkeeper for the Midland Cooperative in Jackson, Minnesota. He and Ethel have a second son, John, born in 1931. With Adele's son, Bobby, and Clarence's two young ones, Willie and Olava now count five grandchildren.

The U.S. population now exceeds 128 million; fewer than 20 percent are employed in farming.

In November 1936, President Roosevelt is elected to a second term, easily defeating his Republican challenger, Alfred Landon. Roosevelt carries every state in the union except Maine and Vermont, giving him an Electoral College margin of 523 to 8 and 62 percent of the popular vote. The election ensures Roosevelt carte blanche in his goals of the New Deal.

Helen writes long, frequent letters to Margaret during this period, catching her up on office gossip and business details at Walman Optical. (Who is making payments on past-due accounts? Who is still in arrears? Who is flirting with whom?) She also reports enthusiastically on her purchase of a violin and bow and lessons at MacPhail School of Music. She writes about books, radio programs, movies, occasional concerts, and a disappointing blind date, concluding that she should be looking for a country fellow with some old-fashioned manners.

Helen and Alice (who is working at odd jobs back home, wherever she can find them) are saving every penny they can spare, planning for a trip to California next summer. They are counting the months.

Helen writes to Margaret on February 1, 1937.

Dear Margaret,
I got a letter from Adele today, postmarked from Madison. They have been taking x-rays of Bobby's kidneys and making one test after another. The x-rays showed one kidney as being turned around, and although it works properly he has poor drainage. Adele says they aren't going to operate but Bobby will have to be treated medically whenever the infection reoccurs. She hopes to be able to leave by tomorrow. It's five weeks now since they went down to Madison and it seems as though they didn't accomplish a great deal in that length of time. Adele is getting disgusted because they have been so pokey and slow. I'm sending her letter home for the folks because they are anxious to know what has developed. Bobby is learning a fine array of medical terms—temperature, thermometer, stethoscope, hypodermic, blood test, urinalysis, etc. Pretty good for a little guy who is not yet two years old. He is a decided favorite with the doctors and nurses.

Adele says he went through an awful ordeal Wednesday when the doctors at the clinic gave him a urogram—a process of filling his veins with a dye that colors the urinary tract so that a portion will show up on the x-rays. She says two doctors began prodding for veins in his arms, back of his hands, and ankles, but gave it up after two hours and called in a specialist in anesthetics . . . The specialist finally went into his jugular.

I'm glad they will soon be able to go home. It has been costly staying there so long, but at least they know the exact situation and what to expect. He'll have to go back for frequent checkups, but maybe they will have a better idea about what to do for him . . .

*

Helen and Alice Williamson travel by train to California during late summer 1937. They spend time with Margaret and Mel, swim in the Pacific Ocean, tour the movie studios, pick fruit from the trees. Alice decides to stay for a while and look for employment. Helen returns to Minnesota. Although California is as grand as Helen imagined it would be, she is rooted in the Upper Midwest. That is not going to change—especially since she has been seeing a young man from Milltown, Wisconsin. She is falling in love.

Olava to Margaret, June 14, 1938:

Dear Margaret,
I don't know how I am going to get along using a pencil today but I will make an attempt anyway. I hope you will excuse the long time with no letter from me. I have a good excuse this time—a badly cut finger. I tried to get the yard in shape three weeks ago, which is no woman's work, the way this one is. The lawn mower picked up a piece of leather strap that was hidden in the long grass and when I tried to loosen it the blade snapped back and cut my index finger off about half way into the nail, so I'll be missing part of it. I have had a dressing on it all of the time to keep the infection out. Dr. Bergstrom has dressed it five times now but he said last night I should have it bare and sit in the sun with it. If I only had time to sit. And if only the sun would shine. We have had so much rain this summer. The cellar gets so wet and I have to scoop it up. We need an eave spout on the west side, that's where it comes in.

Ray, Ethel, Bobby and John were here from Jackson, Minnesota to visit us last weekend and the boys are going to stay here for a couple of weeks. That should be a good time for them.

Poor Ray—what a life he must lead these days. He works such long hours and doesn't get much pay, only $100 a month, but the Midland Co-op is having their annual meeting in Minneapolis soon and Ray hopes to get a raise then. His boys are so big and they eat hearty. Bobby is ten years old already and John is almost seven. With Ethel's management you can imagine how far $100 goes. If I hadn't been so careful we wouldn't have had a home, I know that.

Haying should be starting soon but it rains so much that we will have to wait awhile longer. The hay crop is heavy but the weather has been too cool for corn. The country is getting full of grasshoppers again and the farmers are putting out poison. They find the mounds of young hoppers that will soon fly. That is going to be terrible.

I tried to replant the garden with one hand. It didn't come out the first time because it was too wet and cold and the ground was hard. I'll have strawberries if nothing happens to them, but we never know.

Next Sunday is Lee's birthday. Can you believe that he will be thirty? You might be surprised to hear that he takes Violet Jensen out. She is pretty nice. And Wilmar is taking Gladys Larson home from church these days. Ha-ha. Maybe we will get these boys married off yet.

Helen has been spending some time with Harvey Hellerud, son of the Soo Line Railroad depot agent in Milltown. He was a friend of Wilmar's, if you remember, a couple of years ahead of Helen in school. He's farming on a small place his dad owns, just east of town, and I believe he has been making some trips down to the city on weekends to see Helen. We'll see what happens there.

I don't hear anything from Adele lately. I wonder how things are going for her and when I don't get letters I expect that she doesn't have any good news to tell us.

I will stop writing now because it is so hard with this finger bound up. This is the first time since it happened that I have been able to hold a pencil. Don't worry about it though because I am going to be all right. It will just take a little while. I go around holding it up in the air so I won't bump it. Everyone says "well a vacation is good for you." Some vacation.

Love from us all, Mother

Some vacation, Olava writes, with wry humor.

At the age of sixty-five, she has spent one night away from home in all her years of married life (that trip to Fond du Lac to attend Raymond's wedding in 1925). And with all those men around, Olava is still doing the yard work—planting, weeding, mowing an acre of tall grass. She is bailing out the basement when it rains because no one has time to install an eave spout. She won't complain, except privately, to her daughter. On a farm, the house—and the housewife—is often the last consideration.

Olava is accustomed to all of this. The grasshopper threat is a bigger concern. The crops have been wiped out by hoppers before. It could happen again.

Most farmers are using insecticides based on arsenic. Mixtures containing sulfur, kerosene, naphthalene, nicotine sulfate, lead, copper, and mineral oil are also employed. The poisons are not highly effective. They are toxic to humans and other species, but farmers continue to use them; they have nothing else.

The June 28, 1939, issue of the *Polk County Ledger* reports that the grasshopper bait mixing station in Balsam Lake is working full speed ahead to meet the call for more poison. Up to 254 tons of poison have already been mixed and delivered to area farmers. Surrounding townships are also preparing to meet the hoppers with poison as they hatch.

Some news from the wider world of 1938:

— In March, Germany annexes the Sudetenland region of Czechoslovakia; that same month, Hitler's troops march into Austria and proclaim it part of Germany.
— By the end of the year, Nazis will have destroyed Jewish shops, homes, and synagogues throughout Germany in the Kristallnacht riots. An estimated twenty thousand Jews will be sent to concentration camps.
— In the United States, the national minimum wage is enacted within the federal legislation known as the Fair Labor Standards Act. The minimum wage is established at twenty-five

cents per hour as well as time and one-half for overtime and the prohibition of most employment for minors.

— Federal spending reaches $6.84 billion; the national unemployment rate remains painfully high at 19 percent.

— On October 30, Orson Welles broadcasts his adaptation of H. G. Wells's *War of the Worlds,* creating a nationwide panic as listeners believe that aliens have landed in New Jersey.

— A popular new three-act play, *Our Town* by Thornton Wilder, wins the Pulitzer Prize for drama. Critics praise it as a story that transcends time and place, capturing the universal experience of being alive.

In Minneapolis, Helen Williamson is feeling very much alive as she makes her wedding plans.

Helen to Margaret, January 4, 1939:

MINNEAPOLIS, MINNESOTA

Dear Margaret,

By now you know my plans for an early spring wedding. There is so much to do to prepare for the big event, besides getting ready to furnish a house. You will remember what that is like, I know!

You are going to love Harvey, Margaret! He is so good-natured and modest, but ambitious too. And he has the cutest sense of humor. It doesn't hurt that he is handsome as the dickens. I wish you could come for the big event, but maybe you will visit us this summer, after we are somewhat settled.

I went to Dayton's linen sale today and bought six sheets and pillowcases, a tablecloth, nine bath towels and washcloths, eight yards of toweling for hand towels (which I am going to make because it comes considerably cheaper that way.) I also bought a bath mat and toilet seat cover and a pad for our mattress. I got a special buy on the sheets—84 cents each. I am going to look for more bargains this weekend. Lots of fun! I wanted to look for curtain materials too, but I don't remember exactly how many windows there are in the house we will be renting near Chisago City. Harvey and I were both paying more attention to the fields and barn and outbuildings that day we looked the place over. I want to make the house look homey, though. I'll get curtains made as soon as I can but might have to try to find the yard goods locally.

I've been shopping at Woolworth's for some kitchen tools and found some essentials at a good price—a can opener and a wooden rolling pin, among other things.

I told the girls at the office my happy news yesterday. They said they had guessed as much but were surprised it was going to be so soon. I'll have to tell Mr. Walman within the next week before the word leaks out.

I'm getting pretty excited and my job may suffer for the next several weeks. My roommate has to steer me down the street when we walk to work in the morning. Usually I am re-reading one of Harvey's letters and one day I walked straight into a light pole!

The roads and weather have been tough here lately and Harvey won't be able to get into the city this week. I plan to take the bus or train to Milltown as soon as possible and again at the end of this month. Harvey and I have a date to celebrate F.D.R.'s birthday on January 30 at Paradise Lodge near Balsam Lake. (We make up all kinds of reasons to celebrate!)

Well it's past my bedtime so I'll sign off with love from your excited sister Helen

MARCH 23, 1939
CENTURIA, WISCONSIN

Dear Margaret,

I have been home on the farm since last Saturday. Harvey drove to Minneapolis to get me and my last load of equipment, shower gifts, etc. It was hard saying good-bye to Mr. Walman and so many folks at the office. Several of the girls promised to come up for the wedding.

I worked until 10 or 11 p.m. every night at the office, trying

Helen Williamson and Harvey Hellerud, March 1939

to catch things up as best I could and train various girls in my duties. No one has been hired to take over the posting machine and I hate to see the girls burdened with more work than they can manage.

Harvey and I applied for our wedding license, had our tests and saw the minister last Monday, so the preliminaries are pretty well taken care of. Think of us on Sunday the 26th (1:30 your time) and picture about 20 people all crowded into Mom and Pop's living room, breathless with excitement.

We are going to have Rev. Strom from the North Valley church to officiate and Wilmar and Adele will be our attendants.

I bought the dress for my wedding since I wrote you last. It is a dusty rose crepe, very plain, street length . . . It is a size 9 and fits perfectly. I got it on sale for only $4.98. I got a hat of almost the same shade, with a felt snap-brim, trimmed in blue grosgrain ribbon, and then found blue shoes and purse. Everything together cost me less than $15 so I am pleased with my bargain hunting. I was careful to choose things I could wear again after the wedding. Aren't we Willie kids all alike? We are practical to the hilt!

I haven't had time to think about the actual wedding these past days with Alice's baby coming early and Alice being so sick. She has a fine boy—Jimmy Lee—and we all feel so lucky that she and the baby are doing well. Doctor Bergstrom saw her last Tuesday in his Milltown office and sent her straight to the Amery hospital. Her ankles were terribly swollen and Doc found albumin in her urine. Once she got to the hospital she started having terrific headaches and had a convulsion about midnight. The nurses called Doc after that, and he and his wife came by the farm to pick up Pop and took him to Amery with them. Pop stayed right with Alice until the baby was born, about 9 a.m. in the morning. I went down that day and stayed in the room with Alice for two days, since she needed close watching and there were no special nurses available. Her pulse and blood pressure are normal now, so she should soon be coming home with little Jimmy. His head is lopsided from the forceps delivery, but Doc said it will shape itself within a few days.

I know Mom has written you, too, so you probably know most of this news about Alice, and more. I will write a longer letter when I get time, but we are going to be very busy since we must get moved to our rented farm by April 1st. My address will be simply MRS. HARVEY HELLERUD, CENTER CITY, MIN-NESOTA. The farm is right between Lindstrom and Center City, about six miles either way.

Love from all of us at home, Helen

Alice's husband (and former high school sweetheart) Eyvind "Pud" Rostad is working road construction in a distant location. He has been unable to come home for the birth of their first child. But Alice's dear papa and sister Helen have been there to help her through.

By early April 1939, Helen and Harvey are getting settled in their rented farm near Center City, Minnesota. It will be a frugal enterprise, by anyone's measure.

Harvey has been taking careful inventory of his livestock, machinery, and equipment for several years. His list of assets prior to marriage, including livestock, machinery, equipment, automobile (1937 Ford), and insurance policy total $2,141.50. He figures his profit from the previous year at $594.50.

In the spring of 1939, Harvey records renter and owner responsibilities, as discussed with his prospective landlord. As a tenant farmer, he is expected to furnish labor, machinery, livestock, and power. The owner will furnish land, some livestock (not specified), cost of building repairs, and repairs to fences and gates. They will share equally the cost of seed, commercial fertilizer, silo filling and threshing bills, twine, veterinary fees, cattle and poultry feed. All gross income will be divided equally.

APRIL 21, 1939
CENTER CITY, MINNESOTA
Dear Margaret,
We received your letter that I have intended to answer most every day during the past three weeks. I think of you dozens of times during every day while I am busy keeping house to

beat the band. But I have been so busy getting unpacked, settled
and doing necessary jobs around the house and yard and barn
that there has been time for little else. Harvey and I did take
a day off yesterday though, and drove to Minneapolis to shop
for a dining room set. It has been raining and snowing so much
lately that Harvey has been unable to start any field work, so
we decided to go while we had the chance. When it does dry
off enough so he can get into the fields there will be no let-up.
We found exactly what we were looking for—a round walnut
extension table and six chairs—used but in good condition—
for $22. Now we will be able to properly display that beautiful
tablecloth. Thank you again, Margaret and Mel.

We got a lovely table lamp as one of our wedding gifts. It has
a three-way switch with a powerful bulb. We can't use the big
bulb here on the Delco system, but we can use it with a smaller
bulb and save the big bulb for later. Some day we may be in a
place where we are connected to the high line . . .

Again we are reminded of how long it takes for electric lines to
reach rural residents. Although the Rural Electrification Act of
1935 has resulted in an expanding network of cooperative power
companies, the work is far from complete at the end of the decade.

The New York World's Fair is about to open, on April 30, 1939,
as Helen writes this letter. Albert Einstein and President Roosevelt will deliver opening speeches, broadcast by radio. NBC will
also televise the event, as a means of inaugurating regular TV
programming in New York City. The Westinghouse Corporation
sponsors a time capsule, to be opened in five thousand years. It
contains writings of Albert Einstein and Thomas Mann, a copy
of *Life* magazine, a Mickey Mouse watch, a Gillette safety razor, a
Kewpie doll, a packet of Camel cigarettes, encapsulated seeds of
common foods and commodities (wheat, corn, oats, cotton, flax,
rice, sugar beets, carrots, alfalfa, barley), and microfilmed texts—
millions of pages.

Forty-four million people will visit the fair during two summer
seasons. The World of Tomorrow exhibits many ways in which

Americans, within twenty short years, will be focusing on recreation and travel. They will become a tanned, vigorous people who care little for possessions. They will become less attached to their homes, even their hometowns, because trains, express highways, and airplanes will transport them with amazing speed and ease. Americans will enjoy two-month vacations and drive to great parklands on giant express highways. Fifty-mile-per-hour lanes will occupy the outer edges and seventy-five-mile-per-hour lanes will occupy the center. Control towers will start and stop all traffic by radio signals, preventing accidents. Vehicles costing as little as two hundred dollars will be air-conditioned, shaped like raindrops. Off the highways, drivers will be allowed to dawdle again at their own speed and risk.

The World of Tomorrow exhibits a model network of farm/factory villages that will produce one specialized industrial item as well as their own farm produce. Woodlands will be protected. Intensive and chemically cultivated farms will become smaller, more efficient. A Borden's display features 150 pedigreed cows (including the original Elsie) on a Rotolactor, which allows for bathing, drying, and milking the bovines in one highly mechanized operation.

Mechanization is the watchword of the future, for all industries. Liquid air will become a potent mobile source of power by 1960. Atomic energy will also come into use, cautiously of course. Power will be transmitted by radio beams.

Cures for cancer and infantile paralysis will lengthen lives.

Nearly everyone will graduate from high school and many will attend college. Politics and the management of emotion are aspects of life that will show little progress; both will be "matters of dwindling patience" by 1960.

The World of Tomorrow must seem light-years away to Harvey and Helen and millions like them who hear these predictions in 1939. Can such miracles be possible?

Surely not, say the skeptics. The only thing they can believe is that part about politics and the management of human emotions trying our patience for a long time to come.

Despite the naysayers, the nation is riding a wave of optimism. Scientists have learned to split the atom. The helicopter has just been invented. Pan American Airways has begun transatlantic air service with its *Dixie Clipper*. Women are stampeding to buy stockings made of a fabulous synthetic fiber called nylon: "shrink-proof, moth-proof, non-allergic, warm as wool."

The drums of war are beating in Europe, but Americans are trying not to listen. They prefer the upbeat rhythms of a surging American economy.

Hit songs from 1939 include "Over the Rainbow," "Wishing," "My Prayer," and "Heaven Can Wait."

Helen Hellerud has found her own small heaven on a farm near Chisago City, Minnesota.

APRIL 23, 1939
CENTER CITY, MINNESOTA

Dear Margaret,

We have been on the farm three weeks today and I find myself liking it first rate, as I knew I would. I have never found it so easy to get up in the morning, nor have I ever been as happy or enthusiastic over anything as I am over farming with Harvey. He is so eager and ambitious and such an early bird. He gets up at 5:00 or 5:30 and I have been rolling out at 6:00 or shortly after. I am ready to go to bed when night comes, though. When I get caught up on my housework I am going to start taking naps in the afternoon to see if I can gain back some of my lost weight . . .

We have sixteen cows, some calves, pigs (seven new little pink ones just born the other day), five horses, 165 chickens and 400 chicks coming in a couple of weeks. Harvey has made himself a tractor from an old truck and odd machinery, something like the one the boys rigged up at home. He calls it his Thunderbug and does it ever live up to the name! We painted it green one day last week. Harvey said that way he can hide in the tall grass when the other "real" tractors go by. Actually, he is pretty proud of it and it cost him only $125 in parts. It will serve his purpose very well. He hauls cream to town with it and can go along the highway about 30 miles per hour. He trucked our furniture and household stuff down here with it too, almost thirty miles. After getting some used pieces from Mom and Pop and Harvey's folks we have spent a grand total of $100 to furnish this place. We are very comfortable and like our furnishings as much as if we had spent ten times as much.

I have been scrubbing clothes by hand on a wash board and my back hurts from all that bending and rubbing and rinsing. Harvey would like to buy me a washing machine but it will have to wait because right now we need to buy seed, grain and feed for the cattle, and the money isn't going to stretch that far.

This afternoon I am going to sew a kimono for the little one you are expecting in July. Then I plan to bake four loaves of bread and a big batch of sugar cookies. Harvey's mother is a wonderful cook and baker. I have a long way to go to come up to what she turns out in the kitchen, but with Harvey's encouragement and compliments, I can't fail. He is really a honey. He is eager to meet both of you and is looking forward to your visit as much as I am.

I must get to my ironing now, then maybe take a short rest. This early rising is beginning to catch up with me, but I am happily exhausted. We will never run out of work as long as we are farming, that's for sure. Harvey loves it too, for which I am more than glad. If I don't get back to writing for a while you will know I am busy with chickens and gardening.

Love to you both, Helen and Harvey

JULY 6, 1939
CENTER CITY, MINNESOTA
Dear Margaret,
Mama called us last Saturday evening and told us the good news about your baby boy! Alice was visiting here with her little Jimmy at the time so she answered the phone and practically jerked it off the stand, she was so excited. You can't imagine

how happy Mama and Papa are over the arrival of their newest grandson!

I am enclosing a picture of our house. Look on the back and see my notes about where the kitchen, dining room and living room are located. There are two bedrooms and lots of closet space upstairs and a full basement with shower bath, wash tubs, furnace and fruit room. Also a big cistern under part of the house. It's a nice place and we like it a lot but so far we haven't made much of a showing financially. I guess we shouldn't expect to make much the first year, especially with the price of eggs at 12 cents and butterfat down in proportion. But Harvey is ambitious to get ahead and if he can do better by moving he will do it. We are milking sixteen cows but the production has dropped off considerably since the flies and heat came. I like the milking and would just as soon be in the barn as doing housework any day . . .

We have had lots and lots of rain and the crops look good. Even the garden that I didn't plant until the first of June is coming along in great style. It keeps me busy weeding and chasing the little pigs out. I picked the last of the strawberries this morning. We had fresh berries for over three weeks.

We had a new colt since I wrote you last. Also a litter of four tiny kittens in the haymow. We sold most of our roosters last week. The flock was divided—we had about 200 roosters to sell out of the 400 chicks, and we lost only six out of the total . . .

AUGUST 7, 1939

CENTER CITY, MINNESOTA

Dear Margaret,

We are so thrilled about your baby boy! Charles is a fine name. Thank you for the adorable pictures. I will sew some romper suits for the little guy as soon as I get my garden back under control.

It is exactly a year ago that I was on my way to Los Angeles to visit you and was I excited! I have been looking at those photos of us dipping our feet in the Pacific and reliving the experience. How life has changed for me since then!

We are nearly finished with the threshing. Have one field of late oats left that will have to wait another week or so. We have a second crop of hay to put in, then it will be filling silo and plowing, but there won't be the mad rush that we've had all summer. We had just finished haying and then had to start harvesting so had no breathing space at all. I rode the binder and bumped the bundles for Harvey because he used the Thunderbug. It went ever so much faster than with horses, and since he had to do all the shocking too, the time saved was a help. We had 37 acres of grain, about the same amount they had on the home place. It was better than average this year and we had an unusually good hay crop too, so will come out well with feed for winter.

I've gotten tan as an Indian and am really quite the farmer now. I thought I knew a lot about the farm before, but never realized half of the work and effort that was put forth until I had a crack at it myself. Harvey likes it first rate, for which I am more than glad. Life's too short to be doing something you don't really like.

I have a good piece of news to share with you. I'm not SURE yet, and I probably shouldn't say anything until I know it to be a fact, but I THINK we are going to have a baby of our own next March or April. I have been thinking about it so much lately that I'll be disappointed if my hunch is wrong. I've been having an upset stomach, backache and one thing and another lately. Pretty sure signs, aren't they? These long hours in the field are getting harder and harder. I'll be going to the doctor next week and if I don't have time for a letter I'll send a postcard that says YES or NO.

Love to all THREE of you, Helen

Helen's penny postcard, dated August 15, 1939, is addressed to Margaret Gorder, 4442 Farmdale Avenue, North Hollywood, California. The message side of the card contains only one word, written large and loopy: YES!

*

There are homes you run from, and homes you run to. Willie and Olava Williamson have created a home you can run to, knowing you will always be gladly received.

During the summer of 1939, Adele and five-year-old Bobby have moved back to the home farm. Adele has been hired to teach English and history at Milltown High School, where she graduated fifteen years earlier. Maurice has visited and worked for a few days with his in-laws. Adele suspects he feels humiliated by manual labor. She has heard her brothers laughing at his half-hearted efforts and the way he "works on tip-toe, with his fingertips, as if he is afraid of getting dirty." Luckily Maurice can return to his job as a time-study engineer in New Jersey.

Time study? That is a foreign concept to the Williamsons, who have never had the time to sit and study that commodity. They know only that twenty-four hours is not enough to get the day's work done.

Adele writes to her sister Margaret on October 15, 1939.

Dear Margaret,
We are all so excited about your baby boy! He is nearly four months old now, so he must be cute as can be. I suppose he laughs out loud by now and will soon be sitting up.

If you have time, please write to the folks and try to persuade them to go to California. It would do them both so much good and I know a visit from them would mean so much to you and Mel. I think Mama is ready to take off at a moment's notice because she has hardly been able to contain herself ever since little Charles arrived out there.

Strange as it may seem, it is Papa who is holding back this time. He hesitates leaving the boys with all the responsibility of running both places and he feels that his presence is necessary in a peace-making capacity, even though he may not be so active doing the heavy work. You would be surprised, though, to see how much he does do, after being so sick with blood poisoning. Hard to believe that a cut from a corn leaf could cause so much suffering. Dr. Bergstrom had about given up at one point and said "He is in God's hands now." God finally came through on something. Papa is much better, though the rheumatism and arthritis have left him a little stiff and clumsy, but then who expects to be as spry at sixty as they were at sixteen? When we consider all the hard work both the folks have been through, I think it is quite remarkable that they are both still going on high.

Truthfully, I think we can get them to spend part of the cold winter out there if we all get to work on them. It doesn't make any of us feel very good to see the folks growing older and know that they have never really had any FUN. Soon enough they will approach the time when it will be too late to have fun and we must hope that time is still off in the distance.

This week the men have had the entire herd of more than 90 head of stock tested for abortion.* The results of the tests come back tomorrow and it would seem unusual if there weren't some reactors. We kids have all decided that with the money realized from the State on the sale of the reactors, the folks should buy railroad tickets for California, but of course they don't mind us very well. The State is sponsoring a new program of compensation now, whenever the tests are made, so much more is realized by the farmer than was previously. It will be a blessing, too, to have the herd cut down somewhat, because there have been too darn many cows to pump out for any good use. Now I wish they would go a step further and have them all tested for production and weed out the slackers in the bunch.

Don't laugh now, while I tell you what I am going to do to fatten my exchequer this winter. With the price of pork going up, I am going to become a pig-woman in dead earnest! I am planning to buy a bunch of six week old pigs and feed the skim

---

*Brucellosis or Bang's disease, a contagious bacterial disease which could infect humans who ingest unpasteurized milk or undercooked meat from a sick animal. Symptoms include profuse sweating and joint and muscle pain that could become chronic and debilitating.

milk to them this winter and will I make money on them by spring! I will pay Lee and Papa a fair return for the milk, feeding them, cleaning the pens, etc.

School is going along fine. I teach four English classes, have four assembly charges, and have all the forensics, dramatics, school newspaper and yearbook besides.

The weather has been nice so far, but winter will be on top of us before we know it. I dread the winter and I suppose when the snow begins blocking the roads I will have to move to town for two or three months.

We see Helen nearly every week or two when she comes home by bus or train. Alice not so often. Alice's baby must be nice and big now. His hair is as red as fire.

Bobby is so tall and slender. He is just the image of Maurice. He has a good brain and such a friendly personality. He has five kittens and a puppy here on the farm, so does he ever have fun! I started him in Sunday School at Milltown Lutheran and he seems to enjoy it.

Our Lee is a lucky brute to get a wife as nice as Violet, so kind and the hardest worker you ever met. Clarence has a peach of a gal in Louise too. Now if we could get Donny and Wilmar interested in someone just as nice, the brothers would be all set.

I'm thinking that if I can make good money on those pigs I told you about, maybe I could have a trip to California too. At the very least, I should be able to get my tonsils out and my teeth repaired. At any rate, I don't see how I can lose.

With the war on in Europe, there is a small boom in business out east. Maurice thinks he should stay out there and I am encouraging him to do that. He is getting $35 per week now, which means more than $150 per month. I doubt he could do that well in Wisconsin, even if he found similar employment. I think some time apart will benefit both of us anyway. I am grateful that I have my job here because we are facing a big hospital bill with Bobby next summer and will need the money.

Bobby is feeling fine now, and to all outward appearances, one would never know that there is anything wrong with him at all. The fistula apparently is causing no immediate damage to his health, but before he can start school we have to have it repaired because his clothes are wet and soiled nearly always. He is such a dear, smart little chap that I hope we are able to guarantee him good health someday.

Time for bed so goodnight and love from Adele and Bobby

In later life, Adele describes health care—and lack of it—during her early years.

Imagine, with all the dangers on a farm—working with big animals, ornery bulls, pitchforks, knives and sickles, poisons, jerry-rigged machines. And dynamite. Felling trees, climbing slippery silo ladders, breathing all that chaff and dust—and Papa was brought near to death by a cut from a corn leaf. Blood poisoning, the doctor called it. His whole body was infected and there wasn't much to be done. Antibiotics were not yet available. Clean dressings, rest and prayer, that was about all the doctor had to offer.

Mama always said it was a miracle that they raised all nine of us. So many neighbors had young ones in the cemetery. All the babies were born at home, mostly with the help of midwives, though Papa did call the doctor for the later ones. Except for the scarlet fever, which was really serious, most of our ailments were common, treated at home, with steam tents, mustard plasters on the chest, hot packs on the feet, made of turpentine and goose grease. (I guess the goose grease was to keep you from getting burned by the turpentine.) She made onion collars, too—cheesecloth bags filled with cut-up onions tied around our necks. That helped open up the sinuses. You didn't call for a doctor unless something was life threatening.

It was a hard thing to get used to—after Bobby was born—when we became so dependent on doctors and hospitals. They kept finding more and more abnormalities, and there were not always clear treatment options. But we had to keep trying.

Olava writes to Margaret on Sunday, December 17, 1939, bringing her up to date with happenings back home.

Dear Margaret,

I have neglected writing to you shamefully. Of course we have had so many doings at our house this fall, one after another. Once we had the young people's meeting for church (over 70 people here!), then I entertained the Royal Neighbors (24 ladies), then the Highway 35 birthday club, and the church choir, which consists of over twenty members. They are putting on the cantata tonight. Adele, Wilmar and Clarence sing with them.

I want to thank you so much for the aprons. They are a welcome gift and you know I never sew anything for myself. I patch on the sewing machine since I cut my finger off. I can't keep a thimble on it. It is sort of square on the end, but I have gotten used to patching overalls on the machine.

Papa is feeling pretty good again, but he is so thin and doesn't have the energy he used to. Adele is here at home and will stay here with Bobby all winter I think, unless the weather gets too bad after New Years. She may have to stay in town some.

Lee and Violet want to rent or buy a farm in the spring and there are some real bargains in farms now. The federal banks own so many of them and are anxious to sell rather than rent.

Alice and Helen have both been here for visits in the last week. Alice's little Jimmy creeps all over and climbs up on chairs too. He has four teeth and his hair fairly shines, it is so red. Alice looks good and so does Helen.

I am sending you some money to get something for yourselves and the baby. You should consider this a birthday present since I didn't send anything then. We are not getting presents for the family like we used to, but I am making mittens for the kiddies. This has been a tough year with all the doctor bills. Papa's doctor bills were over $200 and would have come to much more but Dr. Bergstrom makes it cheaper when it is such a long case. Sometimes he came twice a day.

I sure wish we were on our way to California. Maybe we will make it next year.

Merry Christmas and love to you from all of us, Mama

*

As the decade comes to a close, the Depression is finally easing, with orders for war materials flooding into the United States from panicked European countries.

Germany has invaded Czechoslovakia and Poland; Britain and France have declared war on Germany. The United States continues to maintain its neutrality.

Albert Einstein, a fugitive from Nazi Germany since 1933, has alerted President Roosevelt to an atom-bomb opportunity, which will lead to the creation of the Manhattan Project.

The National Labor Relations Act of 1935, upheld by a series of Supreme Court decisions, guarantees labor the right to unionize and bargain collectively over wages, hours, and working conditions.

The Dow Jones Industrial Average stands at 150, less than half of its high point before the bubble burst, but a significant recovery from 42 points in 1932, the depths of the Depression.

President Roosevelt continues to encourage Americans with radio broadcasts called "fireside chats." A hopeful spirit is reflected in popular tunes like "Over the Rainbow," "Whistle While You Work," and "I've Got a Pocket Full of Dreams."

A quarter of Wisconsin farm homes now have central heating systems. Thirteen percent have bathtubs; 40 percent have running water. Nearly half of all Wisconsin farms have been electrified. The state's farm population is peaking, at approximately nine hundred thousand. No one can foresee that by 1970 it will be cut nearly in half.

A Thousand Thoughts

1940–42

*There are a thousand thoughts lying within a man
that he does not know till he takes up a pen to write.*
WILLIAM MAKEPEACE THACKERAY

HELEN SHARES HER THOUGHTS with Margaret on Monday,
March 18, 1940, at 6:45 PM.

Dear Margaret,
Thanks for the nice long letters and the darling pictures of little
Charles.

I have slipped terribly at letter writing. I might do better if
I had a typewriter at hand but I keep so busy with sewing for
myself and the baby and all the house and outdoor chores that
I don't have time for another thing. I have been moving like a
snail today, too, with all my 121 pounds. I hope to lose at least 21
of those pounds once baby comes. Harvey is very considerate.
He helps me a lot and doesn't mind waiting for a meal now and
then so we are getting along first rate. I haven't been working in
the barn for the last couple of months. I will really be spoiled by
the time this baby finally puts in its appearance. Only TEN more
days to go now, by the calendar. Harvey feels certain we're going to get a girl and he rather hopes he is right. When I saw the
doctor two weeks ago he said he couldn't predict that, so I guess
I'll just have to pocket my curiosity. It's almost as bad as having

a package around that you can't open until Christmas. Harvey will wire you as soon as the package is delivered.

We will name the baby Margaret Ann if we get a girl. We have decided we will wait to have her baptized until you come this summer.

We will be moved from here before you arrive. Our landlord has turned out to be crooked to deal with and tight as the devil. He has tried no end of ways to get the best of us. It reminds me of those years the folks spent in Minnesota farming on shares and nearly got wiped out. We haven't been able to locate a suitable farm in this area or in Polk County either and we can't finance any long move this spring so we will rent land from Harvey's dad instead. He has 68 acres on the edge of Milltown and wants Harvey to come home and run it for him. The farm isn't as large as we want, but maybe Harvey can rent some pasture on the side to give him additional feed for the cattle. We will live with the Helleruds for a while. Their upstairs rooms are rented out so it will be crowded downstairs, especially with a baby. But Harvey's mother is a peach and we will make this work out temporarily. This business of moving around is expensive and really gets a fellow nowhere fast.

It will be nice to be so close to the folks again, and Harvey will be able to exchange work with the boys during haying and harvest. That should make it easier all the way around.

I may not find time to write another letter for a while but you should be getting that wire soon.

Love, Helen

MARCH 29, 1940, 9:30 A.M.
SWEDISH HOSPITAL, MINNEAPOLIS, MINN.
Dear Margaret & Mel,
No doubt you have received Harvey's wire announcing our big news. Little Margaret Ann arrived about 12:45 a.m. on the 27th, just missing our first wedding anniversary by 45 minutes.

You should see our husky little farmerette. She weighed 7 pounds, 4 ounces. She has a crop of shaggy light hair on top of her round head, and a fat little face. Her eyes are spaced far apart and look like a couple little pieces of charcoal. She has the Williamson pug nose too . . .

It's going to be tricky keeping that little "farmerette" quiet during the eighteen months that Harvey and Helen live with his parents in the crowded downstairs of their Milltown home. Henry Hellerud, a man of nervous temperament, likes peace and order when he returns from his busy day at the Soo Line Railroad depot. Agnes is a kindhearted woman, but the household atmosphere is tense and somewhat formal compared with Helen's boisterous girlhood home. Helen struggles to keep little Margaret Ann ("Peggy") quiet, and herself as calm and unobtrusive as possible.

Helen and Harvey are facing financial challenges, too—paying rent on insufficient acreage to support a good-sized dairy herd. If only supply and demand for milk could be brought into balance, they might have a chance to get ahead and buy a place of their own.

An editorial published in the weekly *Milltown Herald,* December 5, 1940, expresses the concerns of many area farmers.

> Back forty years ago the farmer thought nothing of working from sun-up until sun-down, and even more. He had no tractors, he had few of the labor saving devices of the modern farm. His taxes were only a fraction of what he is assessed today because there was no ribbon of concrete road running past his farm and out into the hinterlands.
>
> About that time the agricultural colleges began to tackle the problem of "saving the farmer." Since that day his situation has steadily declined. Today even the most progressive farmer finds it hard to break even, although the government can pay him for doing this and not doing that . . . However well-intentioned the federal programs have been during the past eight years, the plight of the farmer continues. It is said that farmers are about fed up on so-called agricultural experts who have never trod the mud and manure of a cow barn nor been on the working end of a milk pail.

A proud new slogan—*America's Dairyland*—has recently been added to Wisconsin's automobile license plates. The owner-operated family farm remains the foundation of Wisconsin's dairy industry, although the tenancy rate has increased to 23 percent by 1940 due to the foreclosures of the Depression. Farms are gradually increasing in size, averaging 119 acres in 1940, a figure that will double by 1970.

Average 1940 wages, nationwide, are $1,725. A new house costs an average of $3,900; average house rental is $30 per month. A car can be purchased for $850, a radio for $17. *Life* magazine is available for ten cents. Americans are eager to buy new products and experience some convenience after many years of hardship.

Willie Williamson buys his first tractor in the fall of 1940, having resisted this mechanization longer than many of his neighbors.

I didn't buy my first tractor until the fall of 1940. I had been chasing tractor salesmen off the farm nearly every other day for five or six years. I wasn't broke all that time, like I claimed to be, but if I'd have bought a tractor, that might have finished me. I put my car up on blocks for a year because I couldn't afford gas. We had been paying some 36 or 37 cents per gallon for gas and getting only 18 cents for butterfat, so you had to milk a cow for two days and feed her besides for one gallon of gas. How in thunder was you going to make any money that way?

Sure, I knew there were some advantages to owning a tractor. You could work a tractor all day, if you could afford the gas. You had to give the horse a rest. Four hours of heavy work was about all you could expect in one day, so I always kept three teams. All that hitching and unhitching . . . You had to feed the horse too, year around, whether it was working or not.

Well, things started easing up a little by 1940, so I thought I'd better get myself a tractor. The boys and I were farming with three teams of horses, but increasing our acreage too. Land values were still pretty low and we took advantage of that. Got Leland set up on a farm just north of my own place in 1941, when he married Violet Jensen. Paid only $3,800—to Prudential Life Insurance—for that place. A foreclosure, of course. I gave Leland a team of horses and eight cows and that got him started. I helped him plant his first *crops. Good timing, you know. Good timing, common sense, hard work. You have to have all three to make it in farming.*

The national and global news is alarming in the early months of 1941, with the escalating war in Europe dominating world affairs. Franklin D. Roosevelt, who has begun his third term as president, signs the Lend-Lease Act, providing military aid to the Allies.

The nation's first peacetime military draft has been instituted, with all men aged twenty-one to thirty-five required to register with their local draft boards.

On December 7, 1941, the Empire of Japan makes a surprise air raid on Pearl Harbor. Half of the Pacific fleet is in port. Three thousand American servicemen are killed, along with fifteen hundred civilians. Countless more are wounded. Five battleships are sunk or beached, eleven smaller ships are destroyed, 177 planes are reduced to rubble. President Roosevelt declares this "a date which will live in infamy." After years of struggling to maintain neutrality, America is plunged into war.

Willie and Olava Williamson have been planning a drive to California to visit Margaret and her family. Despite ominous news headlines, they will go ahead with the trip. Gas may be rationed within a few months, and who knows when they might be able to make a long drive if they don't do it now?

Willie's account of the adventure, addressed to Williamson Bros., Milltown, Wisconsin, consists primarily of schedules and financial details.

DECEMBER 20, 1941

Dear All,
We arrived at Ray and Ethel's in Jackson, Minn. about 6 p.m. last Sat. and found them well and Happy. Left Jackson 10 a.m. Monday, drove in fog to Spencer Iowa, then it cleared up and has been bright sunshine sence. Stayed at Kansas City Monday night, Kingfisher Okla. Tuesday night, Wednesday night Roswell New Mexico, Thursday night at Phenix Arizona, and ar-

rived at Margaret and Mel's House about 4 p.m. Friday. They are well and send greetings to you all.

The mileage from Home was 2,489 miles, Southern Route. Stayed mostly in tourist cabins, cheap, and you can cook a little something for yourself too. We bought 125 gal. of gas at an average of 20 cents per gal.. The Pontiac got about 20 miles per gal. Got greased after the first 1000 miles at a cost of $2.50. Addid 4 quarts of oil on intire trip, $1.20. Total transport to L.A. $28.75.

The best time we made was when we left 575 miles behind us and a large share of that was over mountins. Mom was a little nervous and tired from the long ride but I didn't mind it atall.

We will be heading home soon by midJanuary. Hope you are all staying warm, taking care of yourselves and the livestock.

Love, Pop and Mom

Willie and Olava have traveled through some spectacular scenery, but Willie doesn't say a thing about that. While he may not be the most observant tourist, he does know, to the penny, what the trip cost him. Accounting skills and a frugal nature have served him well in farming, helping him survive the toughest times when so many have failed.

Prices for most agricultural commodities are finally rising, yet Helen and Harvey Hellerud are finding it difficult to make any money at farming when there is rent to be paid. Late in 1941 they manage to purchase their own place, approximately forty miles south of Milltown, near an unincorporated village called Cylon. The farm consists of a hundred acres of depleted, rocky soil, a small dairy barn, a couple of leaky outbuildings, and a poorly insulated house, not yet plumbed or electrified. But their names are on the deed.

Helen's letter of January 12, 1942, is addressed to Margaret, Mel, and Charles Gorder, 4442 Farmdale Avenue, North Hollywood, California. Willie and Olava—still enjoying the California sunshine—are included in the salutation.

Dear Margaret, Mel, Charles, Mom and Pop,

These have been some tough weeks getting started on our own place, so I know you will understand why my letters have been scarce.

I am so glad Mom and Pop finally got out there to visit you. They are escaping some bitter weather. We have had ten days of real winter since I last wrote. It began on New Years Day when it got down to minus thirty degrees and stayed there for almost a week. Today is milder—nearly zero—and we can actually get our car started. We haven't been able to budge it since January first when we went to our neighbors for turkey dinner.

We have shut off all the rooms except for two—the kitchen and dining room—to save on heat. We moved Peggy's bed into the dining room when it got cold and have put our mattress on the couch by the coal stove so we have been cozy in spite of the weather. Peggy loves to play in the snow and Harvey just came in to take her out for a little while. She stayed in for ten days and begged to go outside every day. She wades around in the biggest drifts she can find and takes lots of tumbles in her big overshoes but never fusses much.

Peggy had whooping cough after Christmas. She was pretty sick but now she is feeling fine, cleaning up her plate and gaining weight again. I am giving her cod liver oil every day, hoping it will keep her healthy the rest of the winter. She is nearly potty-trained now and can say sixty-five words.

Anyone who thinks winter is a time of relative ease for farmers does not understand this climate. Long months of bitter cold and frequent blizzards mean that livestock must be housed in barns and sheds, let out only for brief periods of exercise. Silage must be chipped loose and thrown down from the towering silo; hay forked down from the mow. Water must be hauled in from frozen tanks or ponds; manure scooped up and carted out. And the milking continues, morning and evening, in the dimly lit barn. The driveway must be kept clear of snow so the milk can be trucked into town.

Wood is carried in to feed the furnace, with hope that the supply will last till spring. Laundry continues as usual, but with clotheslines strung all through the house, an obstacle course of towels and shirts and underwear. Heavy overalls are hung outside and gathered in, freeze-dried, stiff as boards.

Canned meats and fruits and vegetables—"put by" at slaughter and harvest time—are brought up from the cellar. Only the fields and gardens rest.

This is an insular existence. Although Harvey and Helen's Cylon farm is located only forty-seven miles from St. Paul, Minnesota, they have neither time nor means to travel beyond their immediate area. There are few trips off the property, even before mandatory gas rationing is imposed. Harvey and Helen get no newspapers. They have no telephone, no radio. Helen does mention her hope of buying a battery-powered radio if they can manage to put aside some extra cash. They would like to keep up with national and world events.

Helen wonders how her brothers are getting by on the homeplace. They have never been much for writing letters, so Helen has to hope that all is well.

There is plenty going on back home.

Donald remembers 1942 as the year the Williamson brothers finally begin to make some real money. It all starts with a deal that he and Clarence organize while their prudent papa is gone. Donald tells it like this:

A strange situation came up that winter. We had some fall pigs—around fifty or so, as I recall—and we were planning on marketing them. They were worth $15.75 per hundred pounds. That meant a two hundred pound animal would be worth about thirty-two dollars. A grain elevator burned up in Superior. We were hauling whey to feed the pigs, getting it from the cheese factory in Milltown, sharing trips with a neighbor, and I got to talking with him one day. He asked if I'd heard about that elevator fire up there. Said he thought we could get some of that burnt grain pretty reasonable, and I said sure, let's go on up there and take a look. So I went to Superior with him and yes, you could get a carload—it wasn't damaged that bad—for about six dollars per ton.

We had a little money in the bank. Mom and Pop had driven out to California to visit Margaret and Mel, and Clarence and I had the authority to write checks, so we were right there, by God, and we decided to get a carload of that grain. Two hundred and forty bucks—all the money we had in the bank.

When the carload came into Milltown we took the horses and wagons to get that grain and stored it in the machine shed. It was pretty good stuff and we had those fall pigs and we figured why not breed those sows and get more pigs and with all that cheap grain we could probably do pretty well.

Then we decided to try to get another carload and went into the bank in Milltown to talk to the Cashier in there. We told him what we needed and he said, "Do you boys know what you're doing?"

"Well," I said, "I think we do. The stuff we can get is pretty reasonable, about 25 cents on the dollar, and it's a good deal. We have the animals we can feed it to."

He hesitated and asked, "Well, how much do you think you need?"

"Two hundred and fifty dollars."

"Well, sign your dad's name here and you boys sign your own names underneath and I'll let you have it, but make damn sure you notify your dad what you're doing."

He was right of course. We should have done that right away, but we waited until Pop got home. I was so sure of this deal, but I didn't know if I could convince Pop, especially in a long distance phone call or a letter. I had taken samples to a place in Superior and it tested out fine—a little scorched but that didn't make any difference to a pig. So now we had two carloads of that stuff. We had to breed those little sows and raise more pigs. When Pop came home he was pretty upset. But after he thought about it—realizing that we were getting that whey from the cheese factory for nothing and had that cheap grain—he guessed it was worth a try.

It turned out to be a mighty good deal all around. All those years Pop had been farming, working so damned hard, just inching ahead. He bought that Rolf place in the fall of 1918 and had a $4,000 mortgage on it. He hadn't been able to reduce that mortgage one damn dime. Had a devil of a time just paying the interest. Almost lost it in the Depression, you know. Then we got it all paid off in six months. Goes to show you—hard work and cautious management isn't always enough. In this case it was luck—and some risk-taking—that put us ahead.

January 1942 marks the end of tire sales to all but the most essential civilian users. Most of the world's supply of natural rubber comes from Southeast Asia, now occupied by the Japanese. Factories converting to military production will need every scrap of rubber they can find, and citizens are asked to turn in old tires, raincoats, gloves, garden hoses, and rubber shoes for recycling.

A new synthetic rubber industry is beginning to help meet the need.

Gasoline rationing is imposed in the eastern states in January 1942; by May it is extended nationwide. Before the year is over, a thirty-five-mile-per-hour speed limit ("Victory Speed") will be imposed throughout the country in an effort to save on tires and fuel.

Sugar is the first food to be rationed, in the spring of 1942. Many more food and consumer items will soon be joining the list. Even during the depths of the Depression, there was enough of everything, if you could only afford to buy it. Now, with more money in circulation, it is every citizen's patriotic duty to cut back on meat, coffee, canned foods, shoes, and many consumer goods in order to support the war effort.

In April 1942, Margaret travels by train to Wisconsin to spend time with her extended family. She has now lived for seven years in North Hollywood and is employed by a well-known Hollywood gossip columnist and radio personality named Jimmie Fidler. Margaret meets movie stars in this business and is privy to all the latest news from the glamour center of the nation. Heady stuff. It makes for lively conversation with the home folks, who are eager for diversion.

A letter from Margaret to her husband, Mel, provides a description of Helen's workaday life, which is anything but glamorous. Helen is now twenty-six; Margaret is thirty-seven. Their toddlers, Peggy and Charles, are two and almost three years old.

APRIL 24, 1942
CYLON, WISCONSIN

Dear Mel,

Would you like to hear about my farming operations today? Helen says she and I could farm an eighty together with the kind of cooperation we gave one another today.

I spent last night with the folks on the home place, and arrived down here at Helen's about noon. Of course Helen had already accomplished a respectable day's work by then. Just after 12 o'clock we took the car and started for the east forty through gates and pastures and took little Peggy and Charles with us. We picked up five sacks of seed—heavy too—and hauled them back—more gates closing. To be absolutely accurate, I opened

Harvey and Helen Hellerud's farm at Cylon, 1943

and closed eleven gates today, some of them heavy wooden affairs and some of them wire ones where it was a bit of a job to
pull the wire loop over the post.

Then we came in and put both kids to bed—no small job
in itself. We left them with Harvey who was sick in bed, but at
least here, and able to tell them where we were if they woke up.
We went to town to get groceries and Ex-Lax for Harvey. Got
back at 4 p.m. and made beef stew and cake for supper and fed
Harvey special stuff. Helen gave him a sponge bath too.

At 6 o'clock we washed dishes and dressed both kids for the
barn. It was starting to rain and was blowing like the dickens.
(You are missing something when you miss seeing your sweetie
with her hair in a knob on top of her head and a big cap of Harvey's and his overall jacket flapping around. It's no Hollywood,
scene, believe me!)

Well, we got cans and separator and milk cart and kids to
the barn. Harvey's beef cattle run outside as a rule in fairly nice
weather but we decided to get them into their pens, and thereby
hangs a tale, but I'll get to that in good order.

We milked the cows—there are only six that have freshened—and turned two calves loose to suck. One went right
to the cow but the other son-of-a-gun was everywhere he
shouldn't be and it was only by a miracle we saved him from
running plumb into the silo pit. The crazy fool was wild and
tried to suck two cows that were to be milked by hand. I never
wished so much that I have more strength to move heavy and
stubborn objects as I did tonight.

We separated the milk and while I was putting the handle of
the separator around in good style, puffing away like a steam engine, Charles stooped under the thing to get a cat and the handle cracked him on the downward pull. It darn near knocked
him out. Actually I can feel a dent in his head, but he never
cried a tear—just held onto his head and hollered a little.

We fed the calves, pushed hay down from the mow (Helen
had fed silage before we milked) and washed out utensils. Then
came this job of getting a beef herd divided into three groups

and getting them into three separate doors. The wind was so strong it took two of us to open a door against it. While this was going on, one crazy critter from a pen inside simply took a running jump and leaped over her pen and we couldn't even open a gate to put her back. Her pen was the "nailed shut" kind. We didn't have a hammer so I got mad and kicked it down enough to get her back. I found a rope and tied it back together enough to hold until working conditions are a little better.

Well, when we got our cattle penned and bedded and closed up in the barn and gathered our can of milk and our kids, the evening had only begun. There were a half dozen young bull calves that sleep in a shed outside that needed hay. Helen started to carry hay to them on a fork while I put the milk into the tank and all of a sudden Helen and the hay started blowing across the cow yard. The wind sort of got under her fork of hay and it was like an umbrella turning inside out in the wind. Helen was walking west and the wind was blowing north. She had to walk to the south so as to compensate for the weather and she and her fork of hay collided with a fence. Her hay got hung on the barbs and her overall cap went with the wind. She has a long bob and her hair blew all over her face so she couldn't see where to look for her cap. She doesn't see so well anyway. She ended up by retrieving her cap and making a few trips with hay in her arms.

After that we had to close the granary, check up on the little pigs (it was pouring rain by now), put the car in the garage and tend the little chicks. They needed water so we carried their six water affairs to the house for filling. The water for them has to have some pills dissolved in it. By the time we pumped the water, dissolved and filled, etc., and mopped up after the mess, it was 8:30.

Then we took inventory to see if all things were attended to. Helen thought of the cistern and went out again to hook up a spout from the cistern to the eave spout. It blew so hard her cap got lost again and she came in dripping wet without it. Anyway, the water is running into the cistern.

We heated some water on the kitchen range and washed the kids and ourselves as best we could and here we are, all worn and weary but proud of ourselves.

More tomorrow—for the morrow will bring more adventures. Harvey is some better but still feels lousy from his cold. Helen and I have laughed until we ache at everything that happened today. That shows that we can take it. I smell barn-y and I've got hayseeds in my hair.

Goodnight, Honey. Love, Margaret

P.S. I drew a check on Saturday for $10, made out to Cash. The little storekeeper in town couldn't cash a bigger one.

Margaret writes many more long letters to Mel in the spring of '42, mentioning the prolonged cold and moisture that prevents the farmers from getting started in their fields. Finally the weather moderates, and the sun breaks through and warms the soil. Margaret hasn't witnessed springtime arriving in Wisconsin for many years, and she relishes the sudden transformation.

MAY 6, 1942

Dear Mel,

I am sitting on the woodbox in Mama's kitchen so as to watch the dinner I have made. (Dinner is noon meal on the farm, you remember.) The men are unhitching the horses. I can see them from the window. Our Charles and Alice's little boys—Jimmy and Donald—are all out there, lined up in the horse barn door, watching everything. Wait a minute now while I stir the gravy. I fried a panful of beautiful pork steak, creamed carrots and peas, boiled potatoes, and my gravy is something to go poetic over. One nice thing about a wood range is you can slide your finished product here and there to suit the pan to the temperature and toast your toes at the same time. It is so cold we have the furnace going every evening when we sit around, and the little people have to be dressed complete, even mittens.

1:15 p.m. Off they go again. When they came in for dinner, I lined up all three kids, stripped off clothes, washed three faces, six hands, and they piled into their dinner. Charles had been riding the manure spreader with little Donald Rostad this morning and neither one looked or smelled very clean.

The uncles like to have Charles along on jaunts because he talks the entire time. He asks a million questions about the farming and they enjoy explaining it all to him.

4:30 p.m. Mama is out feeding the chickens. The fellows have come in for a bite. Charles is eating bread with butter and sugar on it. Donald is eating cream and bread. Something cute: Charles wanted to wee-wee in the chicken coop and Mama asked him if he didn't want to go to the toilet instead. He said, "No, it's alright to do it in here. The chickens aren't looking."

Continued May 7, 2 p.m.—Charles hauled manure with the men this morning. He hasn't smelled very clean these days but I'm getting used to sleeping with a suggestion of barn on the pillow. There is more farmer in this kid right now than in most young people raised on the farm. And don't think his grandma and grandpa and these uncles aren't enjoying it!

MAY 15, 1942
Dear Mel,
The last two mornings the ground has been white with frost and the fruit trees may be damaged because they are heavy with blossoms. This country is sure a beautiful sight in the spring. It comes on so suddenly. It starts with the faintest hint of color in the woods. A few days later you notice the woods filling in a little, and in another week the view is a solid green wall. Down along the Mississippi River the trees actually hang over the water. I could stand for hours just soaking up the fresh green fertile look of it.

Believe it or not, I just loaded a manure spreader. Papa had three horses on the spreader. A veterinarian who came to tend a sick cow needed Pop's help in the barn so I went out to see if I could watch the team. I thought I'd give Pop a surprise so I filled 'er up! Boy, I am good! All Pop had to do was level it off a little and put on a few more forkfuls. He said, "Well, now you can tell your city husband that you've shoveled shit!"

Charles and Jimmy had a fistfight down in the barnyard this evening. They both fell down and ended up rolling around in the manure. The barnyard is juicy after the recent rains. It was too cold to hose them off outside, so I was pretty grateful for the upstairs bathtub. Charles was surprised when I undressed Alice's boys, to see that "their whistles are broken." I didn't understand at first, until he explained that "the end is off!" (They aren't circumcised.)

MONDAY MORNING, MAY 18, 1942
Dear Mel,
Charles and I went to Clarence and Louise's place to stay over on Saturday night. I stayed with their little ones so Clarence and Louise could go out dancing. Brother Donny came by after his chores were through and sat up with me until 2 a.m. We got into some heavy discussions. He talked about everything that is on his mind, including how he feels about going to war. He thinks he will be called up in October. If he has a choice of camp, I sure hope he gets to the west coast so we can see him out there. Wilmar's number will come up first, I guess, but Donny has the same rating. Neither of them has plans to marry at this point. Donny says there are none of the young fellows in town on Saturday nights anymore. All gone. Makes him feel like he ought to enlist.

On Sunday I helped Donny move some hogs and hauled feed down home for them. Some squealing cargo, coming through town. I heard some sad news there. Five young folks were in an accident on Highway 35, just northeast of town. They ran off the road and tipped over in a slough by the pea cannery. Five in a coupe, and two were killed, three injured. Terrible thing.

Continued May 18, 1942, 9 p.m.—Charles rode the manure spreader again today and got so sleepy he barely made it through supper. Pop says the spreader motion fairly rocks him to sleep. It's cold and blustery, very unpleasant. Charles has avoided the bad colds so far. Maybe the smell of him these days discourages the germs. And he is breathing plenty of fresh air on those rides. Pop said today, "He's no cooky-pusher, this one." They make about twenty trips with manure every day. I have to change his clothes at least three times a day to keep him dry. He has a great satisfaction on his face as he comes toward the house, picking out the deepest puddles. Every boy should have that chance once in a lifetime.

I am going to bed now, Dear. We listened to Lux Radio and Pop is listening to Blondie with his ear at the radio. Everyone else has retired.

Love and kisses, Margaret

MAY 20, 1942
Dear Mel,
It's hard to believe this is the 20th of May. We are in another stretch of cold, damp weather.

Picture this if you can—Yesterday, while we watched the hog-butchering, I wore Pop's overalls over my slacks and my red sweater, my black and white tweed coat and brother Donny's leather jacket, plus a big cap with the earlaps down. Charles was layered up too, including tassel cap, boots and mittens.

Now you might think that hog butchering is violent entertainment for a not-quite-three-year-old, but it is routine business around here. Donald shot the pig and then stuck him. We watched the whole process, including the bleeding out, the scalding and scraping. Charles didn't mind anything they did to the pig until they cut his head off. He didn't care for that. He was really too cold the whole time to talk much. We had fresh liver last night and a fresh pork roast today is going to taste pretty darn good . . .

TUESDAY, MAY 21, 1942
Dear Mel,
I had the first good talk I have had with Wilmar on this entire trip. He says if his number comes up this fall, he will go to enlist

(if he has to go anyway) and try to get a chance at something like mechanics. He knows some fellows who are getting a good education in some branches of the service. He is such a swell fellow in so many ways—tolerant, conscientious, and a good all-around man. He is steady and sensible, not so radical like Donny. Donny is a bear for work, though, Wilmar says, and he excuses him on almost all counts because he is always there in a pinch. Wilmar is the kind of fellow who will always recognize the good qualities in any person and talk about those instead of his faults . . .

Excerpt from Margaret's last letter to Mel during her Wisconsin visit:

MAY 25, 1942

. . . I am reminded lately of how dangerous a farm can be. Yesterday, Clarence's kids, Billy and little Joyce, were walking hand in hand by the mailbox corner, not looking. A neighbor rounded the corner in his old jalopy and Joyce was hit. She got banged on the leg and flew up into the air and landed on the side of her face. She has an awful black eye today and is pretty skinned up, but no one saw the need for medical care.

Wilmar lost his footing while feeding the hammermill this morning and got his face scratched up when he landed head first into the mill. It could have been a disaster. Again, no doctoring.

Leland has put poisoned corn out in the cornfields for the blackbirds that were stripping the corn. Darn birds dig the kernel out of the ground and leave the little corn shoots lying withered. Disgusting. I hope the kids don't decide to imitate those doggone birds. It's a stout poison.

The frozen cesspool opened up at the home place, so things are a little better there. The whole family was about to resort to clothespins for noses.

It's time I started checking on our return train fares. The Challenger costs $44 for an adult one-way trip and I think the Rocket is a little more. Of course it is also faster. I'll write you again as soon as I get arrangements made.

This has been a wonderful long time with the family and I do believe I am still a farm girl through and through. Still, I could write you a long list of the things I am missing—like plumbing I can count on, a good mattress, a daily newspaper and California weather. And YOU!

Love, Margaret

Shortly after Margaret writes this letter, three of Willie's grandchildren find an empty bottle of strychnine (used for controlling the rodent population) and take turns drinking at the well pump. Clarence's five-year-old daughter Joyce goes first and gets the strongest dose of poison. She convulses violently and nearly dies, but Dr. Bergstrom in Milltown is able to save her. Joyce's brother, Billy, and their cousin Peggy escape with mild consequences—stiff jaws and necks and very long naps.

Margaret returns to California, hoping that her Wisconsin relatives will stay safe and well until she is able to visit again. In these uncertain times, she cannot guess when that might be.

By the end of 1942, the war effort involves virtually every household in the USA. The military draft now applies to most single men ages eighteen to thirty-six, and married men eighteen to twenty-six, with carefully specified exceptions for farmers, miners, and other workers needed to produce essential goods at home. Young men are plucked from every region of the country, regardless of economic status. All four of President Roosevelt's sons will serve in the war.

The Williamson brothers are not likely to face combat. Most farmers are classified II-C, as essential workers in food production, but the local draft board has discretion in determining how essential an individual might be. And many a farm boy would prefer to be marching to battle rather than plowing and planting at home. There is tremendous patriotic pressure when a fellow goes into town.

FARM WORK IS WAR WORK! That is the farmer's defensive slogan, and certainly maximum farm production is essential to the war effort. All through the Depression of the thirties, farmers were pressured to cut production in an effort to reduce supply, increase demand, and raise prices. Now they must pull out all the stops.

As the war progresses, the stigma associated with a farmer's exemption from military service begins to lessen. An ad, sponsored by the Association of American Railroads, states the farmers' case:

> Uncle Sam has 8 million men under arms, and each man eats like two. On the home front there are another 126 million people who must be fed. Then there's the 5 million dollars worth of food that goes to our allies every day. So America's farm front faces the greatest task in history—a task that only American farmers can perform. It's up to the railroads to get most of that food and other farm products where they have to go. Together, the nation's farmers—and the railroads—are doing the job!

So are six million American women who have recently entered the labor force.

The U.S. War Production Board has halted the production of civilian cars and nonessential machinery. Factories are running full tilt, producing tanks, trucks, airplanes, shells, and artillery. Farm tractors are almost impossible to find. With few new ones being built, farmers have to get along. Some rig up their own machines, using parts from old cars and whatever they can patch together.

The entire nation has gone on "war time," setting clocks ahead one hour to save energy.

The list of rationed foods and other items essential to the war effort continues to expand. Americans are growing their own vegetables and salvaging fats, scrap metals, rubber, and silk, turning it in to local collection sites.

Production of civilian automobiles has ceased. Tires are rationed and in short supply, with doctors, ministers, farmers, and truckers receiving priority.

The *Polk County Ledger Press* publishes a weekly list of persons who have received tires. The September 10, 1942, issue reports, "William A. Williamson of Centuria got one tire for his truck."

The September 26, 1942, issue of the *Ledger* advertises a "junk rally" to be held in Centuria.

BOMB 'EM WITH JUNK!
Gather scrap metal around your farm
and home and bring it to Centuria!
Complete details next week.

The following issue contains these announcements:

Turn your scrap metal in to Guy's Restaurant and Tavern!
SLAP A JAP on Saturday!

GREASE THE SKIDS UNDER THE JAPANIZES
WITH WASTE FATS FROM YOUR KITCHEN!
Turn it in to Peterson's NJC Store in Centuria
for 4 cents per pound. We turn it into glycerine
that will blow up a few of the Axis.

A popular wartime slogan is seen and heard everywhere: *Use it up—wear it out—make it do—or do without!*

This kind of frugality does not require anything Helen Hellerud would call sacrifice. Like so many women of the Depression era, she is already a master at making do—and doing without.

Helen's letters from these years are focused primarily on the work at hand. She does mention some war-related worries in a letter to Margaret, dated Friday, December 11, 1942.

Wilmar was notified that he must report to the draft board on Thursday. Papa hasn't been able to get a hired man and he won't be able to run things alone unless he sells off some stock. To make matters worse, he ran a nail through his foot recently and is hobbling around because of that. I wish there was some way we could help without letting our place go. We are just now getting established with a herd of sheep and some better dairy stock. We are getting 59 cents for butterfat now and should be able to do all right if present prices hold.

Are you being affected much by the gas rationing? It must be difficult for those who have to drive to a job every day, like Mel. We trade off making trips to town with some folks who live down the road. The rationing creates a little more neighborliness, I think. Our tires are not very good so we don't drive much anyway.

I like your idea about getting a new mattress for Papa and Mama. We can all chip in for that and order it locally. Other than that, I think it's best to be sensible and not spend much for Christmas this year. Harvey and I are buying one another things we need. I already got my Christmas present—a swell clothes rack. He ordered an oil filter for his tractor and I will also get him a jack knife and an alarm clock. Of course we will get something for Peggy. She has been looking at the Sears Roebuck and Monkey Wards catalogs and I know that she would like a baby doll. She believes in Santa Claus so it is important to put a special package under the tree and hang a stocking for her.

I haven't heard from Adele for a couple of months and wonder how things are going for her. When she does write she doesn't really say much—just generalizations—and I don't read good news into that. I hope so much that things will straighten out between her and Maurice. She has had more grief than I could bear.

We haven't been up to Milltown area to see the family for over a month. I am eager to share some news with them. I can't keep it to myself any longer, so you will be the first to know. It looks like we will be getting a brother or sister for Peggy around the middle of May!

Continued on Monday a.m.—I missed the mailman Friday afternoon so will add the latest news. I called Mom when I was in town Saturday and she said they are fighting it out with the local draft board at Balsam Lake. If the draft board won't exempt Wilmar as an essential farm worker, he will have at least a month more at home and that should give Papa time to look for help.

It was 22 degrees below zero here yesterday so we didn't venture out. The snow fairly squeaks underfoot.

My doctor said I was okay when I saw him Saturday. He also said I was gaining weight awfully fast and mentioned the possibility of TWINS, but he's a great kidder so I am not taking that too seriously. You can bet I'll let you know if this is no joke!

Love, Helen

When Sorrows Come

1943–44

When sorrows come, they come not
as single spies, but in Battalions!
WILLIAM SHAKESPEARE, *HAMLET*

ADELE WRITES to her California sister on January 10, 1943, mailing the letter from Detroit, Michigan. Adele and Maurice have reconciled, and the family has recently relocated due to Maurice's new employment in a tire manufacturing plant.

Dear Margaret,
Thanks so much for your grand letter, which arrived Friday. Congratulations to Mel on the new and more lucrative offer. He deserves all the breaks he can get, because he has had many years of being under-compensated for his conscientious work. Living costs are so terrific now that one welcomes any increases.

We have had a bad time getting dairy products and haven't seen beef in any form for months. We have nothing to complain about, though. Usually when we feel the lowest it would do us well to count our blessings, and I'm glad to be an American with a touch of tough Norwegian stock! The latter has stood me in good stead.

We took Bobby to a specialist Friday and came away with good news and light hearts. He had been in the Somerset hospital where they threw up their hands in horror and bafflement—

mostly because they haven't seen a case like his. In the interim, our local doctor had been giving him shots of pituitary gland extract which was to contract the colon muscles and induce them to function. After the second shot, the leakage has completely stopped and he has had daily normal bowel movements ever since. That in itself was encouraging because we were tortured by two fears—that he would have to have a major operation to remove the paralyzed section of the large intestine, or that he would be doomed to the life of a semi-invalid with constant and uncontrolled drainage. It is amazing how he has come back since the third shot. He is peppy and has good appetite and color and has already started to gain some weight.

The specialist assures us that no operation is necessary at this time and the sphincter muscles are sufficiently strong to assure bowel control. Bobby is on a diet to keep things going smoothly and the doctor gave me instructions for dilating the stricture—the site of the first operation. Bobby can go back to school, which is good news to him because he had been ordered to stay out for this year. I feel as if a heavy steam roller has been moved away from the region of my heart, and I'm sure you are relieved too. Bobby surely has a tough constitution because he has made some hurdles in his short life. He is a great comfort to me.

As troubles come in bunches, so do they vanish. As I kept pondering over Maurice's conduct, I thought I would try—last resort—a psychiatrist. Monday I insisted on the visit and unless you could have seen his conduct of the past two months and could see him since Tuesday of this week, you would never believe that such a transformation could take place. It is a long story, that I will share with you in more detail later, but I think with watchful care, more rest, and therapy he will come through. This week has been the closest thing to a honeymoon that I have ever known. There is so much quality in him and I believe our marriage is worth saving. Try as I have, I can't get over caring for him. There is Bobby, too, and our consideration for him should come first. Maurice says he has respect for me, and I know he has always cared as much as he is capable of caring. We don't all have the same capacity or talent for love, but he is as happy with me as he ever would be with anyone.

Some people might think it wasn't worth the chips to try to see this thing through but the fact that I still care—combined with my damned determined nature—makes me want to go on trying. Bobby loves his Daddy too and you should see how happy he is now since things are going smoothly here at home.

That's enough of my troubles and their solutions, but rest assured things are brighter here. 1943 seems hopeful. I believe in prayer, and I have prayed long and well for both my boys.

Love to all three of you, Adele

Adele is not going to give up easily on her marriage. She has been schooled in loyalty, persistence, and self-sacrifice. She also has a great talent—and appetite—for love.

Her letter of January 10, 1943, mentions the food shortage. She is shopping in grocery stores these days and misses at least one advantage of the farm—an ample food supply.

Helen shares news with Margaret on May 3, 1943. She is feeling miserable, with a weight gain of over forty pounds. Dr. Cornwall, a general practitioner in the village of Amery, fifteen miles to the north, has taken an X ray that shows two babies, ready to make their exits butt first.

Doctor says the babies can't turn in such close quarters and since he can't turn them either, he will most likely have to do a Caesarean section. I asked him if he would set a date now and he said no, he wanted me to have a "trial labor." That will give the babies the benefit of going till the last minute in case they are premature. I have a good doctor and I am not going to worry about it now that I've come along this far, but Harvey is concerned. He is so busy with lambs coming and all the spring work, he hardly knows where to turn. It wasn't very smart timing, this May baby-business. Harvey's mother is already keeping Peggy for us and that is a big help. Peggy is thrilled with the bathtub and running water at the Hellerud's and begs to take a bath every night. She has always taken her weekly bath in my washtub here and that isn't nearly as much fun, of course.

I really don't know how I will manage twins, but as Mama says, "One baby takes up all your time and two can't do any more than that." Some good news from up home: Papa's pleading with the draft board must have done some good because Wilmar has been exempted. (All this after Papa's hired man went on another "bender" and left the folks in a terrible pickle with spring plowing and planting.) And Raymond has a new job in Amery as manager of the Equity Co-op there. They are merging the general store, garage, and feed store, and Ray will have the management of the combined works. He says the job will pay about $200 a month and it will be a good challenge for him . . .

Well, it's high time I got some dinner going for Harvey. I will have him write you as soon as the twins arrive and will follow up with details when I am able.

Love, Helen

This twin birthing is one event Helen will remember clearly, all her life.

Sara and Susie came at planting time and I thought that I could wait until Harvey finished seeding oats and hay. It got to where I couldn't bend to tie my shoes or lie down in bed. My usual weight was 100 pounds at that time, and I had gained almost fifty more. My legs were swollen like tree trunks and when I finally got into town to see the doctor he said, "We've got to get those babies to-day, before they get you." He made a little joke of it but I could see he was worried. I was so ignorant, I didn't know I was in danger. I trusted everything would be all right. Sometimes not knowing can save you.

Helen writes to Harvey from the Amery hospital on May 20, 1943, five days after her twins were delivered. Although the Cylon farm is only fifteen miles away, Harvey is unable to visit more than two or three times during Helen's ten-day hospital stay, due to gas and tire rationing and spring work on the farm. It is lambing time, and he has many tricky deliveries to attend himself, all hours of the day and night.

Harvey Darling,
I'm sorry we didn't have more time to talk when you visited last night. This will have to make up for it.

I'm enclosing a list of groceries that you might get, just in case you forget what to order. Be sure to get that can opener from Irene so you can be fixing yourself some soup and beans in a hurry. If you get too hungry, go over to Irene's for your dinners. She would be glad to feed you and when you are so busy it would be better for you to get at least one warm meal a day . . .

My stitches are much less sore today but my breasts have inflated like balloons since last night and bother today. I'll be able to come home about next Tuesday or Wednesday. It can't be too soon to suit me. I suppose that could be because I miss a certain swell guy.

I hope you are getting along as well as the Twins and I are. All our love to the best husband and daddy in the world—
Helen, Susan and Sara

Helen saves her bill from Dr. Cornwall, which includes the hospital stay. It reads:
Delivery of Twins, breach presentation.
First baby—$100; Second baby—$5
(Sara is the five-dollar baby.)

In her June 25 letter to Margaret, Helen marvels at her good fortune.

The babies will be six weeks old tomorrow. We are due for a final check-up, so will drive to Amery on Monday. I had them weighed last Sunday at my neighbor's house. Sara weighs 9 pounds, 6 ounces and Susan weighs 9 pounds, 1 ounce, so they have made good gains. I am so glad they're both strong healthy babies. It's almost more than I dared hope for. I can't seem to realize yet that they are both ours. Dr. Cornwall says we're too greedy. He has only one—a daughter at the U of Minn.—and he would just as soon have kept these babies. He's one swell fellow and a good doctor. He's proud of the twins and has a right to be. All credit for their getting born safely goes to him. I was no help whatsoever. I had no labor pains that did any good so he had to dilate and take them with instruments. They gave me lots of shots to encourage the labor but I sat two days in the hospital waiting. The only contractions I had were up too high to help. Dr. Cornwall said I was so stretched that my muscles had lost all power of contraction. I could never have delivered those babies by myself in a hundred years. Susan, the smaller one, was lower down and he snared her out by one foot. Sara came nine minutes later. She had her hands wrapped around the back of her neck and was the tough one but both were without a scratch.

The little shoes you sent for the twins are so nice and are certainly appreciated. Adele sent the babies two little pink wool knit wrappers and bonnets to match. This twin business is hard on relatives and friends who have to make or buy double.

Sat., 6:15 a.m.—By the time I had finished breakfast dishes, baby baths, fixing bottles and washing 8 dozen diapers, yesterday afternoon was shot and I missed the mailman. I will try to finish your letter this morning before the day gets away from me. Susan has eaten already but Sara hasn't wakened yet. I suppose they will be eating in shifts all day. I have to make up a new batch of formula this morning. I add Karo syrup to the milk and pressure-cook it like Mama used to do.

Harvey hopes to make hay today if the weather holds, and I want to weed my garden. It's hard to get much done out there because I have to keep running in to check on the babies. My garden is out behind the granary. I wish it were closer so I could hear the babies cry. Peggy loves working outdoors with me and I hope she always will. Harvey will need a helper and we don't seem to have any luck getting boys. But he says if we raise them right and let them help outside from the time they are little, he might get some good help out of these gals. If they inherit my liking for milking and digging in the dirt, he will.

I am sorry my letters have been so few and brief lately. And there is so much more I would like to write. Next time I get into town I will get a batch of penny postcards and try to drop one to you regularly. At least that way I can keep you posted on the babies' progress.

Love, Helen, Harvey and Girls

Some excerpts from Helen's postcards to Margaret:

OCTOBER 26, 1943: Peggy is thrilled over the nursery rhyme book you sent her. Twins are sleeping through the night, until 7 every morning. Weighed them at the doctor's office last week. Sara is 14 lbs. 13 oz., Susan is 14 lbs., 9 oz. Sara continues to be the easy-going little fatty and Susan the dainty, fidgety one. But that could change. Don't you feel sorry for the fathers overseas? Kids can change so fast that in a couple of months they could become almost perfect strangers.

NOVEMBER 2, 1943: Twins are growing fast. Still in their baskets, scratching at the wicker sides, so we'll have to get beds soon. Washed 8 doz. diapers again today and got 'em dry by this evening. Last two diapers were on the kids, so if it had rained I'd have been in a pretty pickle! Harvey wants to move in the spring if we can unload this place and find something better. He says the only crop he can count on here is ROCKS. The plow keeps turning up more. They must go all the way to China.

JANUARY 22, 1944: Thanks a million for the many nice Christmas gifts. Peggy's pajamas are perfect and she is so pleased with them. Twins have worn their adorable new bonnets. They're sitting up in highchairs now, eating like little horses. Each has 6 teeth. Sara 17# 4 oz, Susan 17# 1 oz. at last check-up. I now think Sara has the best disposition. Susan is the rascal.

Good news! Our neighbor wants to buy this place so we'll move early this spring. Papa has bought back the old Bateman place and we will rent that for now.

*

That move, in the spring of 1944, makes four moves in five years of marriage for Harvey and Helen. Now they will be just down the road from the Williamsons, sharing and trading machinery, equipment, and labor with Helen's father and brothers. Her mother will be glad to help with the little ones.

A note on some rural nomenclature: The rural free delivery (RFD) mail carrier cannot rely on road names or house numbers, since few have been designated. Most farms have no addresses, other than the family name and rural route number, which is usually sufficient. (No ZIP codes, of course, until 1963.)

An informal naming system has evolved for conversational purposes. Members of an extended family refer to the farm where they grew up as "the homeplace," no matter how many places they have occupied since leaving it. Surrounding farms are usually named for the original settlers, sometimes for their current owner, occasionally for an interim owner, if circumstances dictate. This is all based on common knowledge. The Bateman place Helen refers to in her postcard was originally Willie Williamson's farm, and now, in 1944, he owns it again. But this farm will remain the Bateman place because Fred Bateman owned it for the longest period. And since the Williamsons own another farm on this stretch of road, it's best to leave things well enough alone.

The current Williamson farm is, however, known as the Rolf place, after its original settler. As long as the mailman knows the Williamsons live there now, the old name serves just fine.

Many rural roads (not yet paved or named or numbered) are also labeled according to shared knowledge or history. For example, all the locals know the Donkey Corner. A stranger might have trouble finding it; there have been no donkeys in that pasture for twenty years, but they did graze there once upon a time. When a name sticks like that there is no call to change it.

Wilmar shares his memories of the Bateman place.

I married a neighbor girl, Gladys Larson, in 1943, and we moved up to the Bateman Place, as we called it. Pop said he paid $800 for that 80 acre farm in 1898, when it was thick hardwood forest.

He had to take out every tree and grub every stump himself. Sold it to Batemen in 1918, for $9,500, and bought it back for $3,000 after land prices went bust during the Depression. Damned good farm and Pop had put some good buildings up there, but water was always a problem. It took about 400 gallons of water a day to supply a herd of thirty cows. I used to make two trips to town every day with a 200 gallon tank. And I got extra water on Saturday so everyone could bathe. Well, all that water hauling meant I was spending time and energy I didn't have to spare.

I recall getting a fellow who was supposed to be a genius at witching for water and I told him I would pay top dollar if he could locate it for me. That fellow walked around with a forked stick in his hands like a goddamn magician and when that stick started bobbing up and down he told me RIGHT THERE! *That's where you gotta drill! He wanted $50 for his magic. I told him I would pay all right, after we struck a good supply of water.*

Well, we got only a trickle and it didn't last long. Later on, I had Ingorf Monson come out to drill a deep well, down through the trap rock, but that one petered out within a year or so. Gladys and I and our three boys lived in that Bateman house for thirty years. We used the cropland but moved all the livestock up to the Rolf place. As a result, I spent a lot of my time up there, working with Pop.

Sometime in 1944—the year after Gladys and I were married— Pop put in an electric milk cooler. We started selling our milk to Land O'Lakes that year. There were lots of expenses involved in getting certified with Land O'Lakes, but we got a better price for the milk. I recall that grade B milk got about three dollars per hundredweight, and Land O' Lakes was paying four dollars for grade A, so Pop figured it would pay off.

You had to have a proper cooling tank with regulated temperatures in order to get certified. Couldn't use the stock tank anymore. And we had to keep the barn whitewashed and the walks limed. Sweep the cobwebs down, clip the cows, especially the rear quarters, and hang those milk stools up on hooks. The inspectors were sticklers about that. They'd come every six months or so, unan-

nounced, and you'd better have everything in shape. Sometimes the Land O'Lakes field man would alert you so you could get ready for them. Water cups had to be non-siphoning, no water getting back into the well. Same with the pipe going down into the water tank. And you had to have a certain number of light bulbs in the barn, a certain wattage, and specified ventilation. We dreaded the inspections—those fellows could always find something that wasn't right—but for the most part the regulations made sense. And we formed some better habits, knowing what would be required.

Spring 1944. Much sacrifice has been required of all Americans since the war began. Shoe rationing has been in effect for more than a year; Americans are allowed three pairs per year. No rubber soles. Shortages are wearing on many citizens. Meat is limited to twenty-eight ounces per person per week, for those who can find it. Weekly butter limit is four ounces. Fresh food, however, is not restricted, and people are gardening wherever they can find a patch of dirt. The "victory gardens" are producing 40 percent of all vegetables consumed in the United States.

Community salvage drives have produced millions of tons of tin cans, newspaper, iron, and scrap steel for use in essential industries.

June 1944: the G.I. Bill of Rights is passed in Congress and signed into law by President Roosevelt.

On June 6 (D-Day), the Allies invade Europe at Normandy Beach in the largest amphibious landing ever attempted. In one thunderous day the Allies suffer an estimated ten thousand casualties but gain a foothold along sixty miles of the French coastline. It looks as if the end of Hitler's empire is near.

The *Polk County Ledger,* out of Balsam Lake, Wisconsin, is reporting news closer to home. On June 29, 1944, a notice appears: twenty pounds of canning sugar is now allowed per individual family member. Applications can be made by mail; ration coupons will be mailed to the head of family. A separate item states that new tires will be issued to essential workers only, with the War Price and Rationing Board issuing purchase certificates.

Willie Williamson with milk cans, about 1945

In this same edition, we read: "Ray Williamson Drowns at Amery."

Raymond Williamson, general manager of the Amery (Wis.) Equity Cooperative since June 1, 1943, was drowned in the Apple River on Monday, June 19. He had been suffering from a nervous condition. With his wife, he had driven to the co-op store that morning. A short time later he drove away alone. When he failed to return, a search was started and early in the morning Irvin Loock found the car, keys in the ignition, and Williamson's hat in the seat, in North Park near the river. The river was dragged and boats joined the search but it was not until 2:30 the next afternoon that the body was found.

Raymond Williamson, who was 41 years old, had spent much of his life in the cooperative movement. He was for several years in charge of Midland Cooperative's bookkeeping office at Sauk Center, Minn., and later at Jackson, Minn. He did some commodity field work for the wholesale market and later was employed by Cooperative Auditing Service before going to Amery. He was active in civic affairs, being a director of the Amery Community Club and manager of the Amery Flyers city baseball team.

He leaves, besides his widow Ethel, two sons, Robert (16) and John (12), his parents, Mr. and Mrs. William Williamson of Milltown and the following brothers and sisters: Clarence, Wilmar, Leland, Donald, Adele (Mrs. M. S. Fleming), Margaret (Mrs. M. J. Gorder), Helen (Mrs. H. Hellerud) and Alice (Mrs. E. J. Rostad). He also leaves many nieces, nephews and friends. Funeral services were held at the Milltown Lutheran Church on June 23 and burial was also at Milltown.

Olava writes to Margaret on July 4, 1944.

Dear Margaret,

I haven't been able to pick up the courage to write until now so I hope I can be forgiven and hope Adele has written as she promised to. You may have heard from Ethel by now, although I know it is hard for her to get all her letters written. She has a stack of cards and letters a foot high. I can't believe it yet, although we know it is all too true.

Papa and I were in Amery visiting Sunday night until 11:30 before it happened and we were satisfied that Ray was okay. Then when he said "I am going to resign Tuesday night"—that's when the board would meet—we thought he would take time off and get rested. He has been so tired and couldn't sleep and if we had known more about his mental condition we surely would have taken him away somewhere, but Ethel didn't say anything until the last days. We should have taken him home that Sunday night when we were there. That was the last time we saw him alive. The next morning he went down to the river when he left Ethel at the store about 8:00 o'clock. He didn't come to the store that morning and a search was started and later that evening his car was found, his hat in the seat, and that was all. The river was dragged and not until Tuesday afternoon was he found by two little boys.

We knew he had a nervous condition but he has been despondent before too—poor fellow never could get ahead as he would like to. You know it hasn't been his fault. God knows he has worked and tried all these years. We feel so crushed. I always had such hopes for Ray. He was so brilliant. Well it is all over and we must try to help those that are left. I feel I am no good—I'm still trying to understand that Ray is gone. It haunts me night and day. And the heart is taken out of Papa.

We are trying to help Helen and Harvey get established here on the old Bateman homestead. I have been helping take care of Helen's little twins while Helen gets the house in shape. They are dear little girlies and so smart. They are walking some now. Right now I don't know what I would do without them here this summer. They keep a person so busy that we don't get much time to think about our troubles. And I can't see how poor Helen could take care of the little ones and get anything else done so I guess that is the best arrangement for everyone. Little Peggy is three years old now and she is spending a lot of time with her Grandma Hellerud in Milltown. Helen has the old place in shape inside pretty well now, but of course the buildings need a lot of repair and paint outside.

Haying is in full swing and we have had so much rain all spring that some of the fields have been under water. Last winter we had so little snow that the hay—some of the new inseedings—froze out.

Sometimes we may wonder why we try to do so much—much more than one can stand. Those that take the easy way live too.

Ray had so many friends wherever he had worked. They came from all over for the funeral and the church was banked with flowers and donations to missions. Some gave money to the family. I think Ethel will keep the money you sent and it can go toward the vault she bought. She wanted a good one you know, which was $100. It was a great consolation to have people express their sympathy, which was so sincere. So many said it was not a suicide but that Ray was sick mentally and we should feel he died from natural causes. Try to think that Ray is better off because he has not been happy for some time and his work was getting him down. You have had some taste of what it is like to get so completely tired out and discouraged that you wish you could sleep and sleep, haven't you Margaret?

Perhaps you should still try to make a trip this summer. We

will hope for that. There is so much more that I would like to write, but I can hardly think of what to say. There are so many people I should write to, but I dread to sit down and do it. You are the only one I want to write to for now.

Love to you and Mel and little Charles and please try to be calm and take care of yourselves.

Lots of love, Mother

Near the end of his life, Willie speaks of this terrible time.

There was some land came up for sale over there in Amery in the spring of '44. It was a beautiful flat stretch—240 acres— that's where the school sits now. They wanted $12,000 for it and I wasn't sure I could swing it at the time. Ray was so burdened by that job. Getting him set up in farming might have saved his life. But I hesitated and a couple months later he was gone. If there is anything in my life I wish I could do over, that would be it.

Donald Williamson is hospitalized in Minneapolis, receiving insulin shock treatments for a mental collapse, at the time of his brother's suicide. (The shock therapies commonly used for schizophrenic patients at this time include electroconvulsive therapy and doses of insulin large enough to produce convulsions or coma, the goal being to jolt patients out of their mental illness.)

Adele is struggling with a handicapped child, her own ill health, and a failing marriage. After traveling from Detroit to Wisconsin for Raymond's funeral, she stays on to comfort her parents. Now, on July 12, she has undergone emergency surgery at the Amery hospital.

Sitting at Adele's bedside, Olava writes to Margaret.

JULY 12, 1944
Dear Margaret,
Adele had her operation this morning, which lasted two hours. They removed her uterus, one ovary and cords, a big job, but I guess it is best to do these things and avoid worse later on. She

has been suffering a lot today, although she has been dopey from the ether. Ethel and I have been with her and Ethel will stay in the hospital with her tonight. There are no special nurses to get. Don't worry, I'm sure she will feel better in a couple of days.

Adele is expecting Maurice to come, maybe tonight. He did come back from Detroit for Ray's funeral but has been gone again and now he is hoping that this new company (U.S. Rubber) will send him to Mass. to finish his training. After that he expects to be transferred to the new plant in Eau Claire. I hope he and Adele can get settled somewhere before long, if they can only find something to rent. Right now they have their household things in storage. I guess Adele is willing to keep trying with him, but she is pretty tired of moving around so much and living out of suitcases. At least we can help her out for now by keeping Bobby. He is a dear little fellow. I will send you a post card in a day or two so you will know how she is coming along.

I didn't say anything about Donny when I wrote you last but Adele said she has written so you should know something by now. There has been so much trouble lately—it is just about more than one can take. Donny, however, should be coming home soon. He was taken to St. Joseph's Hospital in St. Paul on the 16th of May to a brain specialist. Our Dr. Bergstrom was there himself and he gives the insulin treatments. Donny didn't exactly have a breakdown like Ray did. It worked different on him. He had sort of wild ideas or imaginings, and heard voices, thought the birds were talking to him and that everyone was making fun of him. We don't know how the farm will look to him when he gets back. Alice and Pud are up there on Donny's farm and Wilmar is helping them when he can.

Now don't worry about Donny. He has gained some weight and says he is feeling much better. He wrote a letter last week and wants to come home now, so I feel he will soon be okay.

I am sitting here in the hospital beside Adele. I will add a little in the morning and get this letter into the mail.

NEXT MORNING, JULY 13, 1944—

Adele is feeling terribly sore, worse today because the dope has left her, but they have given her a hypo so she can sleep. Still no word from Maurice. The rest of us are okay, busy haying, etc. Write to Adele at the Amery Hospital. And try to make a trip home sometime this summer if you can.

Love to you from all of us, Mother

Adele writes her own account of the surgery and other family news.

AUGUST 1, 1944

CENTURIA, WISCONSIN

Dear Margaret, Mel and Charles,

Thanks so much for your letter and card when I was in the hospital. I had so much mail and oodles of company and the 2½ weeks sped by fast. I got out of "hock" Saturday and spent a day and night with Ethel, then came up home Sunday with the folks. I will be at Helen's this week, at least. I have to go back down to Amery on Friday for a change of dressings. Bobby has had a flare up with his glands and tonsils so the doctor wants him there Friday too, to see if he needs to have the tonsils out before school starts. He has always had quite a lot of trouble with them, so it would be just as well to get it done this summer, I think.

My days in the hospital weren't too bad. The first several days, when one would feel really tough, I was so full of dope that I can hardly remember it. My only criticism is that I didn't get enough to eat. Of course I have an appetite like an old lumberjack anyway, so perhaps it is no reflection on the hospital. Right now I am miserable from my corset of adhesive tape. Since I've gotten up I have bloated a lot and something had to give, so the tape tore away from my hips and has taken generous patches of hide with it. I am supposed to hang tough until Friday.

Papa brought Donny home last night. He and Gladys went to St. Paul yesterday morning to get him. Donny looks good, weighs close to 190#. He is calm, settled, and in a better frame of mind than he has been for years. It would do your heart good to see him. So far nothing has been said to him about Ray and I have been delegated to tell him as easily as I can. He knows that Ray passed away suddenly but hasn't asked for more. That makes me think he understands something about it.

I plan to stay here and teach one semester in Milltown this year. Doctor said I could go to work if I would take it easy. Maurice has been sent from Detroit to Chicopee Falls, Mass., to complete training for U.S. Rubber before the plant starts rolling in Eau Claire. "Training program" is a misnomer—they should call it a hoarding of labor scheme. He will probably be there until the end of this year and I may as well work because Bobby has to be in school somewhere. I could make the trip east, but living quarters are so hard to get. People here don't realize that, like those of us who have pounded the asphalt, house-hunting. We have had our furniture sent from the east coast to Eau Claire, where we have it in storage, but haven't been able to get a house or apartment yet and I am expecting to have the devil's own time when it's time to get settled.

The men are harvesting grain right on top of the hay because of so much rain that delayed everything. It has been a delightfully cool summer and crops look pretty good here. The men have all worked hard because they have been short-handed with Donny gone, and then too, they are farming a thousand acres of land, you know.

Papa came home with a brand new gray suit (beautiful!) and a new straw hat last night and actually looked wonderful. It did me lots of good to see that he is interested in himself and his appearance. He seems to mourn the most deeply because he feels he could have avoided Ray's tragic death. But I think we have helped straighten out his thinking on that.

Did anyone tell you that I made the Medical Journal last July 12, when the doctors found me to be an anatomical freak? I'm not kidding. They removed my uterus, both tubes and left ovary, all of which were quite fibrous and tumorous. No cancer, thank God. In the 2½ hours I was on the table, these astounding discoveries were made:

(1) I had a double uterus—two organs grown together with no neck. Doctors said how I carried a baby full term and gave birth was a miracle. I have the specimen here now, so I can brag about my operation, but Friday it goes to Rochester Clinic. (2) I have NO GALL BLADDER. (3) I have only two lobes to my liver, when every normal person has three. (4) Appendix is just a vestige. (5) One kidney is where it properly belongs, but the right kidney is so low in the pelvic cavity that the doctor said if it were any lower it would be outside the body. So you see, you have been living pretty close to Barnum and Bailey material . . .

I surely hope you can come and see us all before the cold weather sets in.

All our love, Adele

Much as she wishes to visit her suffering family, Margaret will not make the trip. Travel has become more difficult; the trains are needed for moving troops and equipment.

Years later, she tears up as she recalls it.

I tried so hard to get home for Ray's funeral. As soon as I got the news, I packed a bag and Mel drove me from North Hollywood to L.A., which was quite a trip, and we stood in line at the train depot. I got up close to the ticket window, third in line, when they pulled it down and said "That's all!" It was war time, of course, and the troops had priority. I cried all the way home in the car. Little Charles kept saying, "Mama, don't cry. I'll be good." I suppose he thought he had done something wrong.

The next day I went to a church meeting and didn't say a word about what had happened. I knew I couldn't talk about it without losing control. Later my neighbor said, "Sometime circumstances save you. You would go home if you could and add your grief to theirs and they would add to yours and you would go through a very bad stretch. From here you can write and give some comfort to your folks."

Mama wrote me a long letter soon after that. She sounded sensi-

ble and brave. *I suppose she stood it because she had to. Donny was still in the psychiatric ward in the city and they didn't dare to tell him right away about Ray's death. Later when they did tell him, he didn't say anything, just turned his face to the wall.*

Sara and Susie were one year old then, just starting to walk, and Helen was so busy trying to get that old Bateman house fit to live in, scraping wallpaper, varnishing and painting walls and floors. She remembers falling asleep with the paintbrush in her hand. She depended on Mama to take the toddlers for her and Mama said later that having them around helped her pull through the worst of it.

I always found that work was such a blessing. And that was something our family always had in abundance.

Helen's letter to Margaret, dated July 5, 1944, is posted from Centuria, Wisconsin.

Dear Margaret,

We spent a safe and sane Fourth of July at home working and except for a lot of traffic going past us on Highway 35, we would not have known it was a holiday. Harvey cultivated corn and I scrubbed and polished the car. Mom watched our twin wildcats so I could stay on the job, and believe me they take some watching now. Mama enjoys the babies so much and I believe they are a godsend right now.

I spent all of April and May getting this house in shape—a huge job—and I never could have done it with the little ones around. This is a solid old house, but badly neglected. I have scraped and scrubbed and plastered walls in six rooms—three up, three down—then wallpapered or painted everything. Painted the woodwork too, three coats. I spent several days sanding floors, then put on three coats of varnish. Got most of the big work done before we moved in . . .

I am so glad to be living close to the folks again, especially after our recent tragedy. I always knew that Mom had a lot of spunk but her courage through these past two weeks just amazes me. She helps to buck Papa up too and they are bearing up remarkably well. All the neighbors have been wonderful and that helps.

It would have been good to have you here with us, but I understand the difficulties you are facing. Mama says she dreamed you were on the way.

Ray's death is a terrible shock and we can hardly believe it yet. We will probably never know what immediate thing prompted him to take his life but I feel sure that his work was not entirely to blame. I believe that the things that were bothering him most were so close to his heart that he couldn't even talk about them.

We all wish we could turn back the calendar and help Ray somehow but we can only move forward. I know one thing— I will always be proud that he was my brother.

Love to you and Mel and little Charles from all of us, Helen

Olava's letter to Margaret, dated October 2, 1944:

Dear Margaret,
I sure hope you had a nice birthday. We were wishing you could have been here celebrating with Papa. His birthday was Saturday, you know. Sixty-five years old. Helen arranged for the whole family to come here and we served an easy supper with ice cream that we made ourselves. Everyone came except Ethel and the boys. Ethel called and said she couldn't come when everyone would have been here except Ray . . .

This has been such a nightmare season for all of us. We are just getting through with corn cutting. Silos are filled, but Wilmar is threshing for a few farmers that stacked their grain. Papa and the boys bought a second-hand threshing rig real cheap and it works fine. I have been so busy helping here and there in threshing, corn picking, silo filling and canning that I haven't had a free day. Alice has plenty to do too, and I spend one day a week up there helping on that farm. We even picked wild raspberries and blackberries. I've got to be busy. That is the only thing that keeps me from losing my mind.

Donny seems to be okay but he doesn't talk much. I expect it bothers him about Ray . . . He would enjoy a letter from you more than anything, Margaret. You and Donny were always such pals and he thinks so much of you. Just write a jolly letter as you used to, it would do him good.

Adele and little Bobby are still here with us. Adele is looking for Maurice to return from Massachusetts in the middle of October, and they are hoping to get located in Eau Claire, but you know it is so hard to rent rooms now. Meantime, she is teaching in Milltown again this semester.

You would hardly believe that these little twins of Helen's can dance and sing tunes, at 16 months. They sing Red Bird clear through. And play Peek-a-Boo too . . .

The second page of this letter is missing, so we leave Olava here, glad that she is taking some comfort from her youngest grandchildren, who are singing and dancing in the parlor.

The final months of 1944 spend themselves at the usual measured pace, without regard for private agonies or global, world-changing events.

Willie Williamson riding a binder pulled by a jerry-rigged tractor, late 1930s

— V-2 rockets continue to strike Britain, averaging eight per day.

— On November 6, Franklin Delano Roosevelt wins a fourth consecutive presidential term.

— The Battle of the Bulge begins on December 16 as Germans penetrate the Allied front in Belgium.

— Band leader Glenn Miller is killed in an air crash over the English Channel on December 15.

— An antibiotic called penicillin is proving effective in the treatment of many infectious diseases, yet the elusive poliovirus continues to kill or cripple thousands of children each year.

War casualties mount with every passing day. Before it is over, the United States will count close to 417,000 military dead. An estimated six million European Jews will be exterminated. Total deaths from all nations, including victims of the Holocaust, war-related famine, and disease, will reach an estimated eighty million.

The Beautiful Country

1945–46

It began in mystery, and it will end in mystery,
but what a savage and beautiful country lies in between.
DIANE ACKERMAN

LETTER FROM HELEN to her sister Margaret, February 1, 1945, mailed from Centuria, Wisconsin:

Dear Margaret,
I have just finished washing dishes after putting the last of my brood to bed. I spent a half hour with Peggy and a teakettle under a blanket, trying to steam loose a head cold that has been bothering her for several days, so that slowed me up.

Harvey is doing his January bookkeeping tonight. He has already filed the income tax so that is done for another year. He says next year he is going to turn the job over to me. I bought a record book from the Watkins salesman when he stopped by and that should simplify our record keeping. We need to get a better handle on our expenses and net profits. I'm glad now for that bookkeeping experience I got in Minneapolis, though it seems like a lifetime ago.

There is never a dull moment in this house and most of the time it looks like a cyclone just passed through, thanks to the twins. Peggy does her bit too, with paper cutting and general hell-raising. You should hear these little girlies sing. Peggy has been teaching them nursery rhymes. The twins' favorite is ring-around-the rosy. Sara holds Susie's wrists and round and round they go, singing at the top of their lungs. Then they'll sit down and catch their breath and balance and start all over again. I drop my work to watch when they start that game. I wish I had a movie of it.

The twins rocked in their beds until just fifteen minutes ago. They are surely a wild pair—especially Susan. We are going to fence the yard as soon as the frost goes out so we don't have to keep the kids in sight every minute. This house is close to the highway and it isn't safe for the kids to play the way cars go rushing past here now. We are also going to have to install a furnace or get an extra heater before another winter rolls around. We burned nearly two tons of coal during January.

Spring will soon be here and I'd better hurry up and start some spring housecleaning. I don't get much extra done in a day, with four dozen diapers still in circulation. I hope to have the twins fully trained by their second birthday.

Harvey is about worn out from all this water-hauling. Our well dried up completely a few months ago and we will try digging for a new one in the spring. The last driller told us the entire acreage sits over a thick vein of trap rock, so we are not feeling too optimistic. We would like to buy this place from Pop, but if the water problem can't be solved we will have to start looking elsewhere.

Past my bedtime. Goodbye for now and lots of love, Helen, Harvey and kids

The Watkins salesman, mentioned in this letter, is a monthly visitor to many homes in the area. Like her neighbors, Helen looks forward to a little adult conversation as well as the convenience of shopping for household products right at home.

By the 1940s the Watkins Company, headquartered in Winona, Minnesota, is the largest direct sales company in the world, taking its health remedies, baking products, and other household items door-to-door. Watkins has competition from the Raleigh and

Fuller Brush companies, but the homeless peddlers of the Depression years have all but disappeared.

A sampling of news events from this tumultuous year:

— A dimout is ordered from January 15 through May 8, to help conserve the nation's dwindling fuel supplies.

— April 12: President Roosevelt dies of a cerebral hemorrhage in Warm Springs, Georgia. Vice President Harry Truman is sworn into office, bringing his plainspoken style and an oft-quoted slogan: "The buck stops here."

— V-E Day is declared on May 8, ending the war in Europe.

— August 6: A massive atomic bomb called Little Boy is dropped on Hiroshima, Japan. More than eighty thousand perish. On August 9, another bomb—Fat Man—is dropped on Nagasaki, killing forty thousand in a single day.

— V-J Day is declared on August 15, when Japan surrenders.

Polk County, Wisconsin, counts sixty-eight war casualties. Surviving soldiers are returning home. So are 325 remaining German prisoners from Milltown's seasonal POW camp, which has bivouacked more than four hundred men during peak census, putting them to work in the Stokely canning plant and surrounding harvest fields.

Thirty-eight POW camps located throughout the state have held up to twenty thousand German, Italian, and Japanese prisoners, supplying labor to fill the shortage created by war. Friendships have been forged, despite some strong community resentments. Courtships, and even a few marriages, have resulted from this ironic exchange of labor and lives.

Shoe rationing ends on October 30, 1945; most rationing will continue into 1946, and sugar supplies will not return to normal until 1947.

Before the year has ended, Helen and Harvey will decide to give up on the Bateman farm. They are making plans to purchase a farm of their own four miles to the south, near the village of Balsam Lake.

JANUARY 31, 1946
Dear Margaret,
Just a short note to bring you up to date on the latest news here. Harvey and I will soon be closing a deal on a farm of our own, located a mile east of Balsam Lake. Purchase price is $8,000, which we should be able to manage. Nearly half of the 120 acres is hilly or swampy, some forested, but that appeals to Harvey. There is a small pond fed by a good-sized creek, plenty of pasture for sheep and cattle and enough cropland to support a small dairy herd. There is a deep well, but the water is very rusty and not good for drinking or laundry. It should be all right for the livestock. Harvey will have to haul our drinking and wash water from town.

There is a long shed that Harvey plans to repair and use for his sheep. The barn is in fair shape but Harvey will have to build a milk house to comply with the new state regulations. And the house needs work. It's wired for electric but there is no plumbing or central heating. The floors are bare wood or cracked linoleum and the walls and ceiling will need a lot of patching and painting. I'll have to putty all the leaky windows. With time and elbow grease we'll make it livable. We know we have to have a place of our own if we want to get ahead. We'll move before spring plowing.

I have another piece of news. Our family will be expanding again, sometime in August! It would be mighty fine to get a boy this time, but of course we will be happy either way.

Love to all three of you, Helen, Harvey and Girls

Fast forward now, to the summer of 1946 and some news headlines.

— On June 3, the U.S. Supreme Court rules race separation on buses is unconstitutional.
— On July 26, President Truman orders desegregation of U.S. armed forces.
— President Truman establishes the Atomic Energy Commission; the U.S. starts atomic testing on Bikini Atoll.

— Servicemen who have returned from war are marrying and starting families.

— Dr. Benjamin Spock publishes his *Common Sense Book of Baby and Child Care.* Many rural parents who are not accustomed to Dr. Spock's child-centered philosophies will question how much common sense is involved.

Helen is not writing letters to her sister during the summer of '46 since Margaret has come home to Wisconsin for an extended family visit, bringing seven-year-old Charles (now called Chuck) along with her.

Sister Adele and her almost-twelve-year-old son, Bobby, are also visiting the home folks. Maurice and Adele Fleming have reconciled again, and the family has moved to North Hollywood, California, where they are renting a small home not far from Margaret, Mel, and Chuck. Adele has been teaching English and history at a private school called Pinecrest Academy, which enrolls several children of well-known movie stars. The country nieces and nephews enjoy hearing Aunt Adele insist, "These wealthy kids are no brighter, no better looking, than you. And they are not nearly as well behaved."

Margaret writes frequent reports to her husband, Mel, throughout the trip. Her letters begin with the long journey on an express train, across the southern California and Arizona deserts, through the sands of New Mexico and Texas, wheat-covered Kansas, corn-and-pig-rich Iowa, and on past lakes and rivers and a lush green countryside.

Margaret's travelogue includes some observations by her wide-eyed son.

As they pass a tumbledown adobe house in the Arizona desert, Margaret remarks, "Boy, what a wreck of a place!"

Chuck says patiently, "This is cowboy country, Mother. You must expect it to be wrecked." But he is disappointed that he sees no cowboys and Indians on horseback, no blazing guns.

"This sure is a long strip of country!" Chuck exclaims, his nose pressed against the window. The band of scenery sliding past him makes the entire continent appear less than a mile wide. Margaret reflects that when she was a child the country seemed to be circular in shape, with Polk County positioned dead center. Whatever lay beyond that circle was so distant, so foreign, she could not picture it.

Margaret realizes that her Wisconsin girlhood has shaped her vision of the world, for all time. She knows the sights, the smells and sounds, the inner workings of this place. She is drawn to the center of this circle time and again. It is too soon to know that a way of life she feels in her very bones will crumble before the end of the century, as surely as the country schools, the barns and silos and corncribs, and the tidy fences that contain them will all but disappear.

Margaret writes a final letter aboard the train as it leaves Milwaukee on June 27.

Dear Mel,

We have just left Milwaukee station, after a stop in Chicago. Now we are heading for Minneapolis. This is the ultimate in travel. I have never been in a parlor car before and I sure have had a thrill out of riding in such style. We have roomy seats that lean back for napping and our own small table too. This is more expensive than coach seating, but well worth it. I feel like such a LADY!

I have had to spank Chuck only once. I used a wooden coat hanger on his bottom last night because he wouldn't stop teasing Bobby and settle down. He has been good as gold ever since.

The first cornfields we saw looked awfully good to us after a day and a half of sand and nothing much worthwhile. We are going through beautiful farming country now. You can't beat these states of Wisconsin, Minnesota, and Iowa for beauty during the growing season. Lot of nice herds of cattle here too. Early this morning Chuck saw pigs near the tracks and he got really excited.

This train travels so fast I can't write very well. I'll do better when I get home to the farm and it won't be many hours now. I just saw a hay loader at work near the tracks. The crops look good.

Love and goodbye for now, Margaret

On June 28, Margaret describes the greeting and unpacking process at the Williamson farm. Already Chuck is following Grandpa Willie around the barn and outbuildings, "trotting like a little dog at his side."

Alice and Helen are visiting the homeplace with their kids. Alice has three rowdy boys and a baby girl. Helen has three girls and is eight months pregnant with a fourth child. Margaret, Helen, and Alice share adventures and misadventures from the past year, laugh at their kids, at themselves. They laugh until they cry.

Chuck comes running in, screaming that a "yellow coat" has been chasing him. They guess he means a yellow jacket. His seventh birthday will be celebrated soon. Margaret intends to give her mother a Toni Home Permanent in time for the big family gathering. Olava and her daughters plan the menu, expressing their hopes for sunny weather.

All the commotion is overwhelming to young Chuck—a city boy and an only child who is not accustomed to a boisterous extended family.

Chuck dictates a letter to his dad on June 29; Margaret writes down his impressions, word for word.

Dear Daddy, I have a lot of cousins here, about a hundred I guess. Wisconsin kids are really loud. Also there are thousands of mosquitoes here and I have bites all over me. Flies have been crawling on me all day too. I think I am going to get a black eye from being hit by the pump handle. When I went down to the barn tonight I let a calf suck my hand and he sucked it until I thought I would die and I had to tug and pull and pull and tug to get my hand back. But I am okay Daddy and tomorrow I am going to ride on the tractor with Grandpa. Good-bye, Daddy. I have got to go to bed now. I love you, Daddy. Good-bye now. Period.

Enclosed note from Margaret:

It's almost seven years ago that I had my first look at our little guy. He is awfully nice. He gets along well with most of these kids (Alice's boys are an exception—not Chuck's fault!) and the folks are very proud of him. He has nice manners and thanks Grandma for his meals and gives enough hugs to keep everyone happy. When he dictated this letter last night they were all highly entertained. But when he got tired, he was really through. PERIOD, he said. That's all I am going to do. That is just plain all I am going to do.

He loves the little black bulldog, Tippy—the only creature who will sit still and listen. He is a little tired already of flies and mosquitoes and fist-fights and banging doors. He doesn't mind mud or manure. He loves the farm machinery and the exciting work, and MOST of his country relatives. You are probably going to get several more entertaining letters from your son. And of course I will keep you posted as well as I can.

We miss you! Love, Margaret

JULY 2, 1946

Dear Mel,

Well, our little guy is officially seven years old. We had a birthday party for Chuck on Sunday at the home place, and I counted forty people, no less. We were grateful for a dry sunny day so the kids could play outdoors, but of course they ran in and out and brought a hundred or so barn flies with them every time they sailed through the screen door. Mama hung a strip of Tanglefoot over the table and it was black with insects before the meal was over. We served fried chicken, mashed potatoes, gravy, fresh tomatoes and green beans, and red Jello with bananas. Also watermelon, Kool-Aid and chocolate cake.

Chuck claims he liked his party, but toward the end he had enough of the noise and fuss. His description (enclosed) is pretty accurate, I have to say. He was more than ready to have some of those rowdy cousins go home.

Chuck loves the barn. He follows Papa and Wilmar around

like a puppy, begging for chores that he can help with. More news tomorrow.

Love, Margaret

DICTATED BY CHUCK, 9:30 P.M., JULY 2, 1946:

Dear Daddy, I had my birthday on Sunday and I didn't get as much toys as I thought I would. And the kids wrangled and bangled with the toys I did get and when I collected my toys I could not find my army tank and I could not find my ball either. I hope my ball and tank will show up. I had two cakes and they were delicious, but I got a stomach ache. One cake was brown and one was pink. There were 36 people here and they wrangled and bangled until I was sick of it—sicker than I wish to be. I don't know if I will ever get over it. After a while night came, and the cousins finally went home and then I had a good time. I laid on the davenport and talked to the little dog, Tippy, and told him all about it. And Aunty Plump Lump [his nickname for Adele] sat on the davenport with me and laughed at all the things I said to the dog and all the things I said in this letter. Mother just sat at the table, writing and writing and writing. I think she is writing another letter to you. Dear Daddy, good-bye. I love you. Charles

JULY 3, 1946

Dear Mel,

Today we went to Helen and Harvey's place near Balsam Lake and spent the entire day with them. I did some sewing for Helen on her Singer and Chuck kept the little girls entertained.

Harvey has made three swings for the kids, using pine boards and ropes suspended from a high oak branch. Chuck went from one twin to the other, swinging them. In the afternoon they all put on bathing suits and took a swim in the creek. The twins squatted in the water and announced that they were going to the bathroom and Chuck told me later, "They don't have any manners. They go anywhere!" He splashed and played with them in the water and had a heck of a good time.

The pet lamb was the biggest attraction. Chuck carried the

lamb into the house and the kids put clothes on him and treated him like a toy. He is a size that Chuck can carry him and the lamb licks Chuck's face.

Chuck "helped" Harvey in the barn this evening, scraping the barn floor and pouring milk into the cans. I let him try a squirt or two on a cow they were stripping by hand. I showed him how to work his fingers and he got a full sized squirt on the very first try. He was really pleased about that.

When all the barn chores were finished we relaxed awhile in the parlor. Helen sat at the piano and played old tunes from the '20s with the twins sitting spellbound on either side. They show signs of being musical.

We plan to drive down to Helen's again soon so I can give her a Toni Home Permanent. So far I have permed Adele, Mom and Alice. All very successful, too.

Speaking of hair—Chuck's hair smells strongly of manure. (I probably won't notice it four weeks from now.) I'll enclose Chuck's account of his day. Hope it gives you a laugh. We miss you—Love, Margaret

DICTATED BY CHUCK:

Dear Daddy, I saw a lamb and he was cute. His name is Lambie and he is furry and small as can be. There are baby kittens too. And there are three girls in this house. Their names are Susan, Sara and Peggy. But really, I like Lambie the best.

Today I ran into some barbed wire and my neck is bleeding. I hope it isn't broken. And Daddy, there are mosquitoes on this farm and they are big and they make holes. I am all bit up. I hate mosquitoes. Love, Chuck

JULY 6, 1946
Dear Mel,
Yesterday Adele and I and Chuck and Bobby spent another day at Helen's. Adele did her ironing and I finished sewing a dress for Adele on Helen's singer. I cut it out the day before

and it is already finished so I am proud of myself. It fits the Plump Lump too.

Chuck watched Harvey put hay into the haymow with a fork. Chuck says, "Uncle Harvey pulled a rope with the tractor and a bale of hay went up!"

Chuck put Helen's three-year-old twins into a fast spin on their swings and they loved it.

After we got home, we watched Pop and Wilmar finishing the milking. Then we helped let the cows out of their stanchions, chased them out into the barn yard. Then it was time to scrape and lime the gutters and walks. Chuck loves the barn, and especially the haymow. "Show me, Mother, where you used to climb in this barn when you were a little girl." He also asked me to explain how old I was "when all these uncles were your brothers and lived in this little house." He still has some confusion over so many people in one family and how it all fits together. I guess you could tell that from the birthday letter!

Chuck has a few comments for you before I close. He says: "Tell Daddy that I have trouble. I think my neck is broken. And tell him I hate barbed wire!"

Don't worry. His neck is not badly hurt. That broken-neck business is probably from tussling last night with Uncle Wilmar. He will forget all of it tomorrow when we try fishing in the pond with some angleworms we dug today. I wish you could come with us.

Margaret reports in a letter dated July 9, 1946, that Harvey and Helen have purchased two Surge milking machines, so named for the surging action designed to duplicate the tug and pull of a nursing calf. The bucket is suspended below the udder by means of a steel spring rod attached to a leather strap over the cow's back. If the four teat cups should fall off, they will automatically shut off; the design of the machine prevents them from falling in the dirt. The four teat cups must be carefully attached, buckets manually emptied into cans, the cans hefted to a cooling tank. The machines must be carefully cleaned after each use, but they save considerable time and effort compared with pumping out a cow by hand. Many area farmers, including Willie Williamson and sons, have been milking with machines for several years. Only those cows needing special treatment due to illness or injury are "stripped" manually.

JULY 10, 1946
Dear Mel,
Here is something that might shock you. This afternoon I took a bath in the stock tank after the "bossies" were done drinking their fill. Not as sanitary as a city gal might like, but the water gets almost lukewarm in the sun and the fellows change it every day now so we can get the farm smell off us. Chuck says, "You shouldn't worry about it, Mother. Farmers are supposed to smell like that!" Maybe so, but unlike my son, I aim to do something about it if I can. Mama doesn't use the kitchen range except when she bakes, so we don't have warm water every day.

I caught rainwater yesterday and washed my hair. My hair was sticky last week when I washed it in this hard well water, but the rainwater made it feel really nice. I am going to sneak up on our boy's hair tonight and try to get down to the skin. Man, what a farmer he is turning out to be! When they unloaded pea vines for Uncle Donny's pigs today (a smelly job!) Chuck said happily, "Look at 'em come! There are MILLIONS of 'em!"

Continued July 11—Today I am an important person. I did the family banking and grocery buying, serviced the car, got frozen meat from the rented locker in town. Next time I get into town I am going to buy Mama a few items for her kitchen. She works with such poor equipment and never thinks of buying anything that would make her life easier. I've got a list started: new mop, pancake turner, ice cream scoop, sharp paring knife, fly-swatter. Small stuff like that. Every day I add something more.

Mama is baking bread now, making donuts, and washing clothes too, talking a blue streak all the while. I am having the best time I have ever had on a trip, partly I think because it's fun to see Chuck having such a great time.

We were up in Wilmar's hay barn earlier today, watching the men smooth out the mow after haying operations there. A mow full of good-smelling hay to jump in, ladders to climb, ropes to swing on—that is a boy's dream come true.

They'll be haying here on the home place tomorrow. Chuck and I will help in the hayfield, driving tractor ahead of the wagon and hay loader. I will try to quit the field in time to help Mama get dinner for this crew. There will be ten men at the table, counting the nephews and two hired men, and they will eat like twenty. Beef roast, mashed potatoes and gravy, peas and corn, fresh bread, apple pie—the works—all at 12 noon. And boy—the way these guys pile the butter on everything! I had forgotten how they use bread just as an excuse for lots of butter.

Pop and the boys seem well supplied with big, expensive machinery. Five tractors and five trucks between them, not to mention the plows, planters, cultivators, binders, loaders, baler, threshing machine, etc. It's an impressive operation, I tell you. As a kid growing up I could never have imagined anything like this . . .

In the eleven years that Margaret has been living in California, the farming life she left behind has been mightily altered. Since the end of World War II, American agriculture's thrust toward "bigness" has taken on new momentum. Expanding technology, new machinery, cheap gasoline—all serve to fuel the race for increased production and greater profit. The Depression of the "dirty thirties" seems like a dark and distant memory.

Yet few can predict the speed and scope of change yet to come. Who, in 1946, could imagine that the single-row corn harvester will be replaced by a combine that can handle four rows, then eight rows, simultaneously? Who would believe that the shiny new 130-horsepower John Deere tractor will give way to a towering 235-horsepower machine with an enclosed cab, costing forty thousand dollars? Who would predict that the size of the average

American farm will double by 1975, or, to put it another way, that half of the nation's six million farms will be consolidated out of existence?

JULY 12, 1946, 7:30 A.M.
Dear Mel,
I was a real farmer yesterday, driving tractor in the field ahead of the wagon and hay loader. After a few loads I was getting the corners pretty clean. Chuck rode atop the load part of the time, and with me on the tractor part of the time. (I couldn't let him stay up there when the load got too high.)

The fellows are unloading three wagons full of hay they hauled in last night, then out to the field we go again. I got my face pretty burned yesterday and have two owl eyes where my colored glasses protected me. I am not glamorous looking, that's for sure. I dug up the biggest old straw hat I could find today. I'll be driving Leland's new Farmall H today.

Continued at 10:00 a.m.—I am off the tractor for an hour now so I will talk to you. I just wiped the breakfast dishes for mom and right away it is time to get started fixing the noon meal.

We had trouble this morning. Lee tipped a load of hay crossing the railroad track and all hands came to the rescue. Also Pop ran over a skunk. Good thing Chuck wasn't right there because Pop had to kill the skunk with a fork. He had cut a leg off.

After that we got slowed down by a broken slat on the loader. Luckily the fellows are handy at fixing things, but it will be nip and tuck to get through this field today. They have 55 more acres of hay in addition to this, and rain is predicted in a couple more days.

Well, there is more I could tell you, but I want to get this letter out to the box before the mailman comes. I'll write again real soon.

Love, Margaret and Chuck

Haying is big work, and often urgent work, since the hay must be cut and dried, then gathered and loaded, hauled in and hoisted into the hayloft as quickly as possible. A rainfall can spoil the mown hay, which explains a saying that everyone understands: "Make hay while the sun shines." Loading hay requires a measure of skill. The goal is to pile on as much hay as possible without the load tipping before it reaches the barn.

JULY 14, 1946

Dear Mel,

We got some rain, as promised, and it has slowed things down for a little while. Mama and I had a good time today, with no menfolks around. I cleaned and ironed and she did other stuff. She really visited all day—didn't mumble to herself at all. I stopped my chores a couple of times to play some hymns on the piano and pretty soon she was hovering around, singing alto. She has a nice voice. If she isn't too busy she comes with her crocheting and sits in the rocking chair and sings. Then I play a little longer than I had planned to. It is so good to see her sit like that, forgetting her little frettings for a while.

In a couple of days I am planning to borrow Pop's car and take Chuck with me to Minneapolis to visit some of our old friends. We will stay two or three days, so you may have a little wait for your next letter, but I should have some city news for you.

Love, Margaret

The city trip includes visits with several old friends, as well as a ride to the top of the Foshay Tower to look out over the city. The observation deck on the thirty-first floor provides a dizzying view from the highest point in the Upper Midwest. Chuck dictates on July 18:

You could look for miles and miles! And Daddy, I saw where you used to take Mother ice skating in Loring Park. When I went up in the elevator it felt so funny in my stomach. And when we got back down I had a soda and got so full of ice cream I could hardly eat it. And we forgot where we parked Grandpa's car but we knew it was by a little gas station and then we had to go back up on the Tower so we could find it! I thought I was going to throw up but I didn't. I don't think I like ice cream anymore.

Margaret adds:

> Funny how one trip to the city can wear a person out more than a week of hard work on the farm. I feel fifty years old!
>
> Boy, the grain got ripe while we were gone. Wilmar has me lined up to run a tractor on a binder beginning Monday. There is a forty-acre field north of the house and tomorrow morning we will tear into it.
>
> I just learned that there is a case of polio in Milltown and there are over 200 cases in Minneapolis. I'm glad I came home with Chuck when I did. I'll have to keep him away from the water now, because he has a little cold. I am told it is wise to keep children from getting chilled while swimming and it's probably best if we avoid crowds of any kind for the rest of the summer.

The farm chores are changing with the season. Margaret is pressed into service for the grain harvest. "Forty acres looks awfully big," she writes, "when you have to travel around it on foot, throwing heavy bundles of grain as they come off the binder."

In order to produce quality grain, the crop must be cut before the kernels have ripened. It is too moist to be put in storage at this point, but will cure in bound bundles that are stacked in the field during the final hot, dry weeks of summer.

Next comes the shocking—standing six to eight twine-bound bundles on end for drying. The golden teepees will stand in tidy rows for days, or even weeks, depending upon the weather, until they are ready for threshing, a process that separates the nutritious grain from the chaff and stems, or straw. The straw will be blown into a huge stack in the barnyard and used for bedding the livestock throughout the winter.

Shocking grain is too much for Margaret. Building a shock that will repel the rain is a skill that requires strength and practice. She returns to kitchen duty, helping Olava feed the men. On July 20, she takes time to write a short letter to Mel, sharing the latest news.

> . . . Pop and the boys have a McCormick-Deering threshing machine and an elevator too, so they are getting very mechanized

all around. Once they finish their own fields they will get 4.5 cents per bushel threshing for the neighbors. They supply the equipment, including pickups for handling the grain. The activity around here leaves me breathless.

I need to start making plans for our return trip soon. I wish I could stay and help Helen with the baby, but she isn't due until at least the middle of August and I don't think we can stand to be away from you that long. And I am eager to get back to some of the comforts of home. (Yes, my home is out there with you!) Among other things, I miss good reading lights and comfortable mattresses. These folks are so tired when they roll into bed at night they could sleep on anything!

I miss the newspaper most of all, I think. I try to pick up the Minneapolis Tribune whenever I get into town but often they are sold out.

I'll make some calls tomorrow and try to figure all of this out, but you should be seeing us within a couple of weeks or so.

Love, Margaret

Margaret is sounding a little restless, ready to enjoy some of the comforts of her California home. She is also proud of her Wisconsin family and all they have accomplished. Willie and the boys have prospered in recent years. Now they will be doing "custom work" for their neighbors. As the owners and operators of a threshing rig, they enjoy not only added income but also a measure of prestige in their community.

The machine itself is impressive: massive and noisy, its body thirty feet long even before it is fully assembled. Two ten-foot wings jut out from the front on each side, with loose conveyor belts that carry bundles of grain into the mouth of the beast. Slashing blades and an array of belts and trays form the digestive tract that separates the grain from the stems. A fifteen-foot blower pipe at the rear spits the chopped straw high into the air. The operation of this machine and its power source (a large tractor connected by a fifty-foot drive belt) requires mechanical knowledge, especially when breakdowns occur.

The typical threshing crew consists of eight to ten men, in addition to the haulers and stackers who bring in the bundles. The owner, who has carefully positioned and leveled the machine, oversees the work, often standing atop where he has a high, wide view, making sure the straw blower doesn't clog, keeping a sharp eye on the flow of bundles into the blades. One man oversees the power source. By the 1940s, this is usually a gasoline tractor rather than the steam engine of previous decades. Two or more men unload the wagons and pitch the bundles in. One or two men sack the grain as it pours from the spout, and a couple more manage the straw. It is a complex operation.

The appearance of the threshing rig lumbering up the driveway signals an important day on any farm—a day that will fade away within a decade, with the invention of the modern combine that can harvest grain in the field much more efficiently.

JULY 24, 1946

Dear Mel,

You are probably going to hear about this from your son, so I will tell you first: Chuck got lost in the cornfield coming home from Wilmar's place yesterday and had a hard time finding his way out. He was really worried about it and cried when he told me. It would be as bad as getting lost in the woods, I suppose. Or worse, because he couldn't climb up anywhere to get his bearings. He guesses he will have to walk on the ELBOW of the road from now on (he means the SHOULDER!) instead of short-cutting through the corn, which is many feet higher than his head, and all tasseled out. I said yes, that sounds like the best plan.

Mama and I are home alone today. Chuck is at Lee's place, where some of the men are finishing up the second crop of hay and some are cutting grain.

Donny and Pop are at it again. An elevator burned at Moorhead, Minnesota. They have hauled home almost five tons of flax at $50 a ton. Donny plans to go up this evening for another load. Pop stayed up there to keep his place in line and sack

it up. Donny said fifty trucks were lined up for flax. What he
brought home hadn't even been wet, so he figured he made
$180 in two days.

Yesterday Chuck and I made a trip to town. I bought Mama a
new pancake turner and a new mop. I like to surprise her. I make
a mental note of her sputtering during the week and sometimes
it is a funny present that I bring her. One day it was a deodorizer
for the toilet bowl. Another day it was four cups (with handles
on 'em!) because she was short of just that many when she set
table for all the men. She is a worse handle-snapper-offer than
I am.

We are doctoring a sick pig today. I saved his life yesterday.
He had fallen down in the pigpen and the other hundred or so
pigs were rooting at him and biting and walking on him something terrible. I jumped into the pen with a shovel and drove
them off. Then Mama and I got him into his own private quarters in the chicken coop.

Tomorrow I will take Helen to the doctor at Amery. I hope
her baby will come along before August 16, because we plan to
leave that date. I also hope Adele and Bobby will get back from
Pepin soon. They have been spending some time with Maurice's family there, and I haven't heard a word about how that
is going . . .

AUGUST 1, 1946
Dear Mel,
Yesterday we drove down to Helen's and Harvey's place. Helen
still shows no sign of any serious labor . . . On the way back to
the homeplace, we stopped in Centuria and bought two watermelons and ate half a big watermelon as we rode. We stopped off
at Lee's farm and left half a melon there, then left another half at
Wilmar's. Mom will have the last half, and I expect she will give
a generous piece of it to anyone who happens to come by.

Adele and Bobby got back from Pepin a couple days ago.
Adele is up at Helen's today, helping with ironing and housekeeping. Bobby is helping Pop and Wilmar. The fellows threshed

until dark last night. They threshed for one of Donny's neighbors and started another . . .

Threshing season will soon be over. The noisy activity will cease, without tractors, pickups, wagons churning in and out of farmyards, without the pounding, grinding, whirring, chugging, clanking of machinery—all that commotion mixed with the bawling of cattle, the squealing of pigs, the shouting of sweaty men, the bustling of the harvest kitchen, the hearty noontime dinner full of jokes and laughter, sighs of satisfaction and relief.

Following a burst of activity when the corn is cut and shocked and harvested—after the silos have been blown full of chopped corn and the dried cobs have been stored in the cribs—winter preparations for the human residents will begin. Wood will be split and stacked; buildings will be banked with hay bales to hold back the cold. Vegetables and meats will be pressure-cooked and put by; potatoes will be dug and stored in the root cellar. Livestock will be housed in barns and sheds, and by Thanksgiving—surely by early December—a blanket of white will descend. After the Christmas celebrations, winter will begin to feel like an endless tunnel, deep and cold and dim. But life will expand again in the spring as it does every year, more or less on schedule.

Margaret and Chuck, Adele and Bobby leave from Minneapolis by train on August 16 for the return trip to California. The sisters are sorry to leave Helen, who is overdue with her fourth baby, at such a busy time.

Harvest is in full swing on the Hellerud farm near Balsam Lake, but on a smaller, less mechanized scale. Harvey is too proud and independent to crew with the hard-driving Williamsons. He does share labor and equipment with some neighbors. But his most reliable helper will not be in the harvest field this season.

Helen writes to Margaret on August 29, 1946, from the Amery hospital.

Dear Margaret, Mel and Charles,
I hope you have received Harvey's note by now announcing the arrival of our SON. I will add some details. He has lots of tan hair and is so fat that his eyes are just little slits in his head. His nose is small—like the Williamsons—and he has a dainty mouth with a darling little sideways slant, like Harvey. I think when he loses some of the fat he will be quite a small boy because he doesn't have a heavy frame at all. He has short feet and square hands.

This baby really took his time about coming, but when he decided on the date he made up for it. Luckily we got to the hospital in time. I was able to get a call through to Mama yesterday. She was pretty glad to get the news. She is keeping all three girls for me so probably they will have to wait to see our little Teddy until we get home. I expect that should be in three or four more days, if all goes well.

That fills you in on a few particulars. Harvey was too excited the other night to write much. He has already bought Teddy his first toy—a little farm tractor. He'll have his boy riding around on the real thing, plowing and planting, before you know it.

Love, Helen

Helen is right about that. Like most farm boys, Teddy will be working in the barn and fields—milking cows, driving tractors, running powerful machinery—by the time he is nine or ten years old. With any luck he will grow into his man-sized chores and take over the farm someday.

The girls will be thoroughly trained in housework—cooking, cleaning, gardening, canning, sewing, and laundry. When their chores are done they will enjoy marvelous freedom, climbing on roofs and ladders, roaming the woods, and swimming in the ponds, with little supervision from busy parents. There will be many close calls.

Helen's letters grow shorter and less frequent once she is back to the bottle-and-diaper routine. She writes that Peggy has started school at Balsam Lake and is doing well so far. The school bus picks her up at the end of the driveway, and the ride is not too long.

She reports on Teddy's progress. He is finally sleeping through the night. Now he is smiling, cooing, sitting up, playing with his hands.

Helen has ordered fourteen yards of flannel from Sears, Roebuck and Co. and plans to make warm night clothes for all the family. She has managed to get her garden harvested; the cellar shelves are full of tomatoes, pickles, corn, peas, beets, and apple butter, sealed in mason jars.

If only she could be more help to Harvey. But she doesn't dare leave the baby long. Too bad the girls aren't old enough to watch him. Things should be easier next year.

Back Where I Belong

1947–49

I have come back again to where I belong;
not an enchanted place, but the walls are strong.
DOROTHY H. RATH

NEWS FROM the wider world of 1947:

— The Marshall Plan is proposed with the goal of helping European nations recover from the economic devastation of World War II.

— In a speech on March 12, 1947, President Truman proposes containment of communist expansion.

— The House Un-American Activities Committee (HUAC) begins its investigation into domestic communism. A Hollywood blacklist has been created for the purpose of eliminating communist influence from the mass media culture. The list is expanding to include respected athletes and scholars.

— Congress passes the Taft-Hartley Act in June 1947, restricting the activities and powers of U.S. labor unions.

— Captain Chuck Yeager, U.S.A.F., breaks the sound barrier in an X-1 rocket-powered research plane.

— On July 11, the *Exodus* leaves France for Palestine with 4,500 Jewish survivors of the Holocaust on board. Later this year the United Nations General Assembly votes to partition

Palestine between Arab and Jewish regions, resulting in the creation of Israel.

— Princess Elizabeth (later to become Queen Elizabeth II) marries the Duke of Edinburgh at Westminster Abbey in London on November 20, 1947.

— The U.S. population exceeds 144 million; life expectancy has reached 66.8 years.

Major changes are occurring in the U.S. dairy industry, with the invention of improved milking machines, tanks, pumps, and pipes that will soon make it possible to transfer milk directly from the cow into refrigerated containers. Mechanization will bring an end to the old "armstrong" methods. The three-legged stools, open buckets, milk cans, and cream separators will become antiques. Breeding and feeding technologies will increase the amount of milk each cow can produce. Production per cow (about 4,800 pounds per year in 1947) will more than triple by the end of the century. The number of dairy cows will decline accordingly.

In July 1947, Margaret Gorder makes another summer trip to Wisconsin, bringing her eight-year-old son, Chuck, and thirteen-year-old nephew, Bobby Fleming, with her. She has a mission this year, in addition to her visits with family. Thirteen years in California have shown Margaret that life can be more than mere subsistence; spirits can be lifted by bright colors, touches of beauty, small luxuries. She intends to lighten and brighten the farmhouse on the homeplace.

Writing to Mel on July 14, Margaret describes her redecorating efforts and asks him to share the letter with sister Adele, who has been unable to make the trip.

... The enclosed smears of paint represent the bathroom in its new dress. When I put the yellow on the wall behind the tub, everyone who saw it very politely said, "Yes, that's nice." They didn't have to say so to make it plain that they thought I had gotten a little carried away with my tube of chrome yellow. But now that it is in balance with the blue trim, they use a different tone of voice and say, "By golly, now that sure is pretty!" Wilmar was upstairs just now and said, "Now that's a pretty shade of blue you got there!" Adele, you would love the curtains. I'm enclosing a sample of the material.

Chuck has been busy catching turtles from the pond. He also collects large moths and keeps them in a glass jar. He lets the moths go every morning and catches a new batch come evening. He insisted on getting up at 5:30 with Grandpa yesterday, just to prove that he is equal to this farming schedule. He had to further establish himself with his country cousins by climbing up and jumping off the chicken house roof the past two days. I do hope they accept the city kid as a "regular" or I am going to be a nervous wreck. I don't know what he will think up next to prove himself. Today he is baling hay with Wilmar and Bobby. Mama and I washed many loads of clothes and put a second coat of blue on the bathroom so we had a busy day . . .

Helen's kids with "California cousin" Chuck Gorder

Raymond and Ethel Williamson's younger son, John, sixteen, is living with his grandparents, Willie and Olava, on the farm, and attending high school in Milltown. He is a big help with the chores and enjoys all his relatives, especially Clarence's son, Billy (fourteen), and the California cousins, Bobby and Chuck. Margaret's letter of July 19, 1947, includes a description of some creative entertainment the boys have devised. They are holding puppy races in the farmyard, each boy sponsoring a different collie pup, yelling encouragement.

The boys have rules. The winning dog MUST put his paws across the finish line. But yesterday the pups all stopped and sat down just about a foot from the line and all four boys were down on their hands and knees in the horse barn door coaxing and calling. Bobby finally won but what a struggle. John got called a cheat because he tried to keep Bobby's dog from winning by holding the mother dog where Bobby's pup would be tempted to drop out of the race to nurse. We laugh more over those darn dogs. The hired man announces every day that something is going to be done soon about so many dogs or he won't be responsible for keeping them out from under tractor wheels.

JULY 21, 1947

Dear Mel,

I took the whole family to a movie in Milltown last evening after chores, the hired man, too. (That outing took some fast talking on my part—the folks almost never take time for any "foolishness.") Mama really enjoyed it. We could hear her laughing there in the dark. The show was Fred MacMurray and Paulette Goddard in "Suddenly It's Spring." Mama was impressed when I told her I have seen Fred M. many times on the street in North Hollywood and have talked with Paulette Goddard on the phone when I was working for Jimmie Fidler. She thinks it is a glamorous life I live out there.

The hay baling goes apace. Pop and the boys are doing a whale of a business with their new baling machine. Their own hay is baled and in the mow, which is bulging, and now they are working for cash or on shares at neighboring farms. They have built extensions on the rears of their trucks so they can haul 100 or more bales at a time. Pop says by spring the best hay should be worth a dollar a bale. Man these guys really know how to farm! The thing that keeps Pop going so strong is the complete success they are all enjoying. He and Wilmar had milk checks last winter of nearly $2,000 per month.

Advantages of baling, as explained by Pop and Wilmar: (1) Easier to handle from field; (2) Easier to get into the barn—the hook lifts 8 bales at a time; (3) Easier to feed—knock a definite number of bales down through the chute, snip the twine, and it falls apart in nice layers; (4) Get more into the barns; (5) In selling hay, they usually bale it from the barns in order to measure and haul it easier.

Continued July 22, 1947—103 bales loaded on one truck last night. The fellows drove in with three truckloads after 6 p.m. All went home to do their milking and came back at 9 p.m. to unload. Chuck wouldn't go to bed with all that activity so I went down to the barn to pull back the hay rope and keep an eye on Chuck and his cousins. Chuck has been driving trucks in the field and driving tractor on the hay-line! What would our California neighbors say about letting an eight year old handle that kind of equipment?

A full-blown haying operation requires a sizeable crew. Once the baling is completed, two or three men drive tractors with empty hayracks into the fields, with two more per rack to load and stack the bales. Once the load is positioned below the hayloft door, a crewman sets the tines of the hayfork—resembling a giant iron spider—that lifts eight or more rectangular bales on a rope and pulley system to the hay-hood and through the gaping door. (Sometimes the fork lets go and the eighty-pound bales tumble back onto the wagon, bouncing everywhere.) Someone drives a tractor or pickup attached to the rope that lifts the load. A kid is usually assigned to pull back the rope, or "hayline." One man is stationed in the loft to yell "Whoa! Trip 'er!" when the load has reached a good position on the metal track. Someone below pulls the release. The man in the loft tosses the heavy bales around to achieve an even distribution after the landing.

Of course there is a crew of women and girls in the kitchen, keeping the crew fed and watered. Everyone is exhausted at day's end. If things have gone well, they are also feeling very satisfied.

JULY 23, 1947

I'm patching overalls today. I finished sewing one apron for Mama, and started another. The pants have preference over the aprons, though, so I have set them aside for the moment.

Alice is here washing clothes today. She doesn't have a washing machine up where they are living, so she comes down here with several baskets of laundry and all four kids in tow. Right now she is also cooking and baking and folding up clothes between loads. I think I am going to have to leave my sewing and patching (and letter-writing!) in favor of laundry and kid-watching, the way this day is going.

You would be amazed to see the way Alice manages those kids of hers. She never puts underpants or pajamas on them. They wear a shirt and overalls—that's all—and go to bed raw. Cuts down on the laundry, I guess. Little Dean and Donny Rostad have been eating too many raspberries lately so when we see them standing real quiet somewhere we just unsnap the suspender buckles and lift them out of their drippy pants. If the toilet was six feet away they couldn't make it. They wouldn't have it running all the way to their heels if they had underpants on. Alice says never mind, they will soon have their fill of raspberries, so until then . . . She never worries. She drops the dirty pants down the cellar stairs in the general direction of the washing machine and says, very nonchalantly, "Wash these next time you do a load." She will live a long and merry life, diarrhea being no great concern.

Chuck and Bobby are with the men today, hauling bales from Frederic. They finished unloading last night at 11 p.m. and all the trucks left again this morning. If the men and trucks hold out, there will be plenty of hay to feed all the livestock and some to sell besides. They can do 1,000 bales a day if everything goes according to plan.

SUNDAY EVE, JULY 26, 1947, 7 P.M.

If they have any more of these gatherings of the clan, I'm just gonna take to the woods till it's over. I came back from a party at Clarence and Louise's place an absolute wreck. We had cousin John's birthday in mind when we planned the get-together and Louise offered to have it there, thinking it would be too much for Mama. It would have been. Imagine 18 kids, most of them under 8, and 16 adults, everyone talking at once. All crammed into that little house, because it was raining cats and dogs. Speaking of cats and dogs—there were several of those in the house too.

Today I have been at Helen and Harvey's place most of the day. These little kids get so worn out from parties that you can't live with them. Helen's kids get crabby when they are just a little tired, and they were impossible today. Susie has a temper and she wouldn't take a nap so Helen took her bodily and laid her on the couch. When I looked in to see what the racket was, I found Helen SITTING on Susie. Susie was face-down and kicking like a steer. It was a funny sight but Helen was too mad at the time to laugh about it. She said—by way of defending herself—"Well, sometimes I can't handle her any other way so I just sit on her until she gives up and goes to sleep."

Sara never needs that kind of discipline. I think Pop was right about those twins. When they were born he noticed that Susie was narrower between the eyes than Sara. He said that in a horse, narrow-between-the-eyes means stubborn as a mule! Helen laughed, remembering that. "Look at her eyes! It's true!"

Hot today, 90 degrees at least, and the humidity was terrific. We sweated like everything. Helen and I divided up the housework and sweated our way through it. Not a fan in the house either. I dusted and mopped all the floors and ironed a pair of curtains and washed all the dishes. Helen fed baby Teddy, and bathed all the kids in her galvanized washtub, cooked and baked, and sat on Susie.

9:30 p.m. Now I am back at Mom and Pop's. Pop and Bobby and the hired man came in about 8:30 wanting something to eat and I scurried around trying to find some supper to warm for them. We had thunder and lightning all evening, and now it's finally raining—big, steady drops—so the fellows worked late to get the last of the hay in at Donny's farm. Mama gets mad when the men come in so late. Just when she thinks she can finally rest a little, she has to get all that food out again.

Olava has taken on an almost comfortable grumpiness, talking mostly to herself, seldom directing it at her loved ones. She mutters, "Uff-da!" (a Norwegian epithet). Or when things are really bad, "Fy-da!" Or "Ish-ta!" Sometimes she uses the American version: "Oh, shit!" Her feet hurt and her ankles are swollen. Her shoulders are rounded, her head bent forward as she shuffles around the kitchen, peeling potatoes for the noonday meal as soon as breakfast has been cleared away. Hungry men need hearty meals three times a day.

Summer brings many extra chores to the farmhouse. One of them is battling flies.

"He built that barn too damn close to the house! I told him that, but does he ever listen to me?" she mutters, making her rounds with the swatter or a spray pump filled with strong insecticide. She hangs long strips of yellow, sweet-smelling Tanglefoot over the kitchen table and within minutes it is black and wriggling with insects.

It's only July. The fly wars will continue until the first hard freeze.

JULY 31, 1947

The twins and Teddy stayed overnight with me last night and I took them back home today, then stayed to have dinner with Helen and Harvey. Helen got some good sewing done on her rare, quiet day. The twins and I had a good make-believe visit to California, complete with phone calls to Wisconsin to report about picking oranges, seeing movie stars, etc. They folded up little pieces of paper to use as train tickets and make believe money. Pretty exciting stuff. They want to visit California someday, worse than anything. I hope we can somehow arrange that when they are a little older.

These kids don't need any toys! They have each other and their imaginations. Also their swings and a hammock in the back yard. Most of their play is make-believe.

Peggy didn't come along on this adventure with me because she is taking swimming lessons this week at Balsam Lake. She walks a mile and a half to town, all alone, for her lessons. That is good for such a little kid, just seven. She goes after the cows alone too.

It has cooled off again and feels almost fall-like. I think I may swing a paintbrush in the west bedroom upstairs. Maybe tomorrow. I'm pretty tired out right now, from having the kids here. I don't know how Helen keeps up the schedule she does, day after day. She is a marvel.

AUGUST 6, 1947—WEDNESDAY, 12:45 P.M.
I am certainly in super-high gear again. I got up early and helped with the laundry, carrying all the water DOWN and the clothes UP and hanging the wash OUT on the line. Then I washed my hair and planned my next painting job. I did the second and final coat on Mama's bedroom yesterday, and Mama is thrilled with the results. She is talking about a neighborhood coffee party to show off her home improvements.

It is beastly hot again, but there is a little breeze. The clothes are already dry.

Forgot to tell you—I painted the toilet seat yesterday, but when Helen brought the kids for a visit, Susan sat on the toilet before it was fully dry and got a white ring on her bottom, so I'll have to do it over. She FORGOT what I told her about the fresh paint, she said. Oh well, at least I will be able to tell them apart now. Susan is the one with the painted bottom.

*

Margaret's 1947 "vacation" is coming to a close. On August 8 she writes about more scorching heat, the grain harvest, and the Polk County Fair, complete with barns full of prizewinning livestock, roller coaster rides, and horse-pulling contests. She reports that she has re-sanded and brushed another coat of enamel on the toilet seat. She has helped Olava feed twenty-two threshers—counting the kids—on threshing day. Olava has been talked into trying out a new electric stove but is not much impressed with it, since it has no warming ovens overhead and no water reservoir, either.

Margaret's last letter to Mel from this Wisconsin trip is dated September 3, 1947. Margaret, Chuck, and Bobby are preparing for their return to California. The final coats of paint have been applied to bedroom walls. Decorative floral decals have been glued into place. The result is tasteful and elegant, the women agree. Even the men are nodding their approval.

The hired man, Lawrence, has gone off on a drinking binge. There are two fields of corn ready for harvest, and his timing is terrible. Margaret writes:

Mama would like to wear his scalp on her belt. She is furious! On top of that, Pop has just bought fourteen more cows and a bunch of equipment from a farmer who had them do his baling. Mama's hair stood on end when she found out. The equipment was a great buy, Pop said, but that didn't impress her. Pop is a horse-trader at heart. Mama has hoped all the time that he would cut down on the work, but this sure doesn't sound like cutting down to her. He is going to die on his tractor and Mama will be feeding harvest crews until she is ninety years old. There isn't much anyone can do about that.

No, there isn't. That is pretty much the way it is going to happen. Margaret can see it coming. When we live with a story long enough, we know the final scenes before they are written.

On November 24, 1947, Olava writes a short letter to her daughter Adele, addressing it to 6222 Elmer Avenue, North Hollywood, California. She begins with thank-yous for a birthday gift and photos of Adele's ranch-style house, which "looks like a swell place."

Olava is seventy-two now, tired and ready for a change of pace. It doesn't look like that will happen any time soon.

. . . There won't be much chance this winter for us to make any change. We finally have a decent hired man. And the barn is so full of stock and plenty of feed and prices are good. It is all quite a strain on Pop but he looks better and feels better than he has in years and wants to keep going. And of course we have John here and would like to keep him on the farm through high school. He likes the Milltown school and is getting all A's on his report cards. He is a swell kid, so nice to have around, and so good with the cattle too . . .

Olava and Willie would be proud if they could look into the future and see their grandson John with a large-animal veterinary practice in central Wisconsin. The veterinarian is an essential and respected member of society, often called more readily than the family doctor.

Helen writes from the Amery hospital on April 14, 1948.

Dear Margaret,
Susie and I have been here in the Amery hospital since a week ago Monday when she broke her leg. She and Sara were riding on the low two-wheeled trailer behind the tractor when Harvey was hauling a heavy load of gravel to fill in some of the low spots in this muddy driveway. Susan took a notion to jump off—over the FRONT end of the trailer. As nearly as we can figure out, the corner of the trailer box knocked her down, because she had one cracked rib that caused her lung to hemorrhage. Sara was the only one who saw it happen so we are not sure how the wheel went over her, but her body seems okay other than the left leg and ribs.

The break is in the thigh bone, so Susie has to lie flat on her back with her leg straight in the air. They had traction on it, but it seems they haven't found the proper amount yet so nothing is being accomplished. They took x-rays yesterday but none of them were clear and good. I gathered that the bones are still too far spread out. As far as I'm concerned, these past eight days have been wasted. I pinned the doctors down this morning and they promised to take more pictures today so they can adjust the weights properly. They are busy here but my time is precious too, and it makes me boil to sit with no progress being made. And of course it is terribly hard on Susie.

Clarence and Louise have taken Teddy and Sara. Peggy is staying with the Dahlstrom family in Balsam Lake so she can go to school. Poor Harvey has the toughest row to hoe, with 17 cows to milk, lambs coming and field work to do, besides "batching it." I managed to get home for a couple afternoons and I cooked up a big kettle of beef stew so he gets along, but it's too much work for one person. Meantime I sit here and try to keep Susie contented so she won't tear her harness and bandage apart. The itching is almost as bad as the pain. The first two days and nights she just about tore the pulleys down with all her tossing. She misses Sara and feels so alone if I am not here. I don't dare leave her for long.

They have only one nurse on here at night for both floors of patients so anyone who fusses much is not very popular. The nurses have been cross with Susie and she has made up her mind that she doesn't like them. She tells me to shut the door and keep them out. She got mad at the doctors the first night when they had to cut off some of her clothes. She said "Don't you DARE cut my good flannel petticoat! Mama spent a long time making that! Don't you DARE cut my new garterwaist either!"

Talk about a spunky five-year-old. She always had enough sass for both twins. Sara would have been ever so much easier to handle in bed than Susie. It would have to be Susie. Such is life. I guess we will live through it. I try to remind myself that we are lucky to have just a broken leg and a cracked rib. It could have been so much worse.

Continued Thurs. a.m.—I spent three hours at home yesterday afternoon. Washed a sink full of dried up dishes and cooked some more food for Harvey to re-heat, so he will manage for a few more days. Saw the doctor this morning and he says now the pictures show the bones lapping. They have all the weight she can stand without being pulled off the bed. That means surgery and Susie will have a scarred-up leg but at least it should be straight and the proper length. They will open up the leg tomorrow and put in a metal plate. Susie will have to have a cast right away, over some serious tape burns, so we are in for several more days of misery. I expect Susie and I will be here for at least another week. I will be more than glad the day we can go home.

Harvey is hauling manure and will be ready to seed by the end of the week if the weather holds. He has a larger tractor now, so it goes faster. Lots of lambs are coming these days and we are grateful for mild temperatures.

It is dinnertime now so I must feed Susie, then walk downtown to find something to eat for myself. How I loathe eating out! I am no expert cook but I think I can do better than any of the restaurants I have tried so far. And the prices are ridiculous, nearly a dollar for a sandwich and a small cup of soup. A farmer's budget can't stand that for long.

My next letter will not be so full of complaints, I promise.

Love, Helen and Susie

Olava writes to Margaret on April 16, 1948.

Dear Margaret,

By now you have no doubt heard about little Susie's accident. I worry about it early and late, every day. You know how I love those twins. This is going to be hard on Helen and Harvey with such a long time in the hospital and I suppose the doctors want money now. No paying with eggs and butter like we used to do. But as Helen says, it could be so much worse. Write to Helen, won't you Margaret? Your letter will help, I know. Love, Mother

*

Five-year-old Susie wears a heavy plaster cast from hip to ankle all through the hottest summer months and gets around on crutches. She names her legs Fling and Bum. Poor Bum is healed by autumn and the cast is removed, revealing milky-white, wrinkled skin and a long purple scar on the outside of her right thigh. For years to come, relatives who want to tell the twins apart will hike up their skirts to find that scar—or lack of it. It's a dandy identifier.

In one year the twins will be starting first grade at Balsam Lake Elementary. They plan to keep the scar a secret.

— In July 1948, President Truman issues the second peacetime military draft in U.S. history, amid increasing tensions with the Soviet Union.
— Truman is reelected to a second term in November, defeating Republican candidate Thomas Dewey and Dixiecrat Strom Thurmond.
— In December, the United Nations General Assembly adopts the Universal Declaration of Human Rights.

Helen writes to Margaret soon after the New Year has arrived.

JANUARY 5, 1949
ROUTE 1, BALSAM LAKE, WISCONSIN
Dear Margaret,
Happy New Year to you and Mel and Chuck! Harvey and I spent a quiet New Years Day at home with the kids, celebrating the fact that we are all in good health here. After our close call with Susie last year, we can't take that for granted.

The kids were thrilled with the Christmas package from California. The girls love their little baking set and I wish you could see how much Teddy loves his Tinker Tom. Mom and Pop gave me money for the kids and I have ordered sweaters and jerseys from the Monkey Wards after-Christmas sale book.

We went to Mom and Pop's on Christmas Day and everyone was there except you California folks. We surely missed you. Pop was in his glory tossing the little kids up in the air and treating them with candy.

Harvey and I will soon be celebrating our tenth wedding anniversary and we decided that instead of exchanging Christmas gifts we should save the money for a photograph. We didn't have wedding pictures made ten years ago, so it's high time we did this. Someday our kids may want to remember what we looked like.

I am back at my sewing machine this week, making blouses and skirts for the girls, shirts and pants for Teddy. I sew at night, after everyone is in bed. With help from you and others who have handed down clothes for makeovers, we save a lot on dressing the kids. Our dentist gives me his frayed white shirts and I make them over into the prettiest blouses.

Speaking of the dentist—the twins pulled a little stunt when Harvey was getting ready to take them for a check-up last week. Peggy had warned them it would be painful if they had to get cavities filled, so they prepared for the worst. They actually smuggled a splitting maul into the back seat of the car. Sara had instructions from Susie to attack the dentist with the maul if things got too tough in there! (Fortunately all went well.) Harvey didn't discover the weapon until they got to town. He doubles up laughing every time he tells it.

Lots of love and thanks again for the swell Christmas gifts– –
Helen and family

Helen and Harvey's tenth wedding anniversary—March 29, 1949—comes and goes, and there is no portrait. Chances are that another, more pressing need has arisen.

Helen has new worries on her mind on July 14, 1949.

Dear Margaret,
I apologize for the long gap between letters but you will understand when I explain that I am managing this farm alone right now. Harvey is working for a few weeks with his uncle Theodore in Halstad, Minnesota. He's been very restless about our situation and feels we should be getting ahead faster. As

you know, Harvey has never been crazy about milking cows. He thinks that sheep or beef cattle—like his uncle has out there— might be the answer. I am hoping he will see that the grass is greener HERE, and get his mind settled. If that happens, the trip will be worthwhile.

If only Harvey had been raised on a farm like we were, he might have the necessary patience for this kind of life. He feels as if the whole big world is passing him by while he is tied down 365 days a year. I look on it differently. To me, farming means independence and security. Even in the hardest times we have never gone hungry . . .

Well, I have to keep a positive frame of mind about all this. We are expecting another baby about mid-January. Not something we had planned for, I'll admit.

It has been hot and dry this month and the pasture is pretty sparse. The sheep have been breaking through their woven wire fences but I'm getting good at making repairs. This morning I straightened fence posts and plugged holes for a couple of hours and rounded up all the escapees. Two ewes and their lambs were way down in the swamp by the creekbed. I had to put on my high boots to get them out of there. I hope they will all stay put now.

I'm also doctoring a couple of cows for mastitis. The girls have been a real help in the house and garden and also pretty well take charge of Teddy.

Have to make a quick trip to town now and pick up a few groceries. I hate buying bread at the store, but have no time to bake these days. Will mail this letter from the Balsam Lake post office and hope I get a chance to write again soon.

Love, Helen and family

Harvey saves the letters Helen writes to him during his weeks at Halstad, Minnesota. They are full of farming details, news about weather, kids and sheep and cattle. Helen's tone is optimistic, encouraging, supportive. And tender.

JULY 14, 1949, THURSDAY NOON

Dearest Harvey,

Your card came yesterday and I'm glad you had a good trip. I'm taking time to drop you a quick note before the mailman comes.

It's another hot and sunny day here with no sign of rain. It sure beats everything how some places get too much rain and others go dry all season.

I'm ironing today and catching up on housework. May run to town to get some bread since I can't fit baking into the schedule and it's too hot to turn on the oven anyway. Everything is going all right outside, so far. Erla had a swollen hind quarter this morning so I gave her a tablespoon of Sulfa in her feed. How much do you give? I wasn't sure and didn't want to overdo it.

The kids are fine. There is a nest of new kittens in the haymow and the girls climb up there several times a day to check on them.

A half dozen sheep broke through the fence and got into Hank Jensen's grain, but the kids helped me round them up and I got the fence wired back together. It should hold for a while anyway until you can make a better repair.

Well, time to get dinner for the kids.

We all love you and miss you. Helen

Erla had a swollen hind quarter this morning . . . All the cows have names, of course. Like humans, they have personalities, physical and temperamental differences that suggest likely names—like High Rump (unusually high hip bones) and Beauty (a sweet face and expressive eyes). Helen names some of them after women in the Lutheran Church choir—Erla, Doris, Maude, Carrie, Henrietta. Some cows are stubborn, some are compliant, some walk head high like aristocrats, some are shy, some can be downright mean—just like those choir gals.

Udders are very individual, too. Helen can identify a cow by her udder, even at a distance, even from the rear. Milking machines do not work equally well for every animal. One size does not fit all. In the days when farmers milked manually, they could adjust for this by altering the squeeze-and-pull motion of their hands to fit the cow's anatomy. Machines treat everyone the same.

Helen washes and grooms the cows when she can find the time. She scrubs mud and manure off their hocks and brushes their necks and backs, talking gently as she works. They turn their heads and look at her with big, wet eyes. She knows they like it.

JULY 30, 1949
Dearest Harvey,
Little Adele* has come for a few days to help me. She is amazing for a girl of thirteen, worth more than a hired man to me. She gets up with me in the morning, waters calves and sheep while I feed hay, tends to the salt for all the livestock, helps dump milk and lifts cans into the cooler. She sees what needs to be done all by herself. Peggy helps too, with dishes and water and lambs, but she is not as observing and not nearly as husky as Adele. I am going to pay Adele $5 a week if I can get her to stay longer. She is worth that and more.

Yesterday we cleaned the barn. We took care of that flooded manger and scraped down the feed alley too. Adele limed the stalls and walks and the barn looks good except for a few cobwebs. The Land O'Lakes inspector came today so I am mighty glad it was all cleaned up.

I plugged holes in the sheep pen for a couple of hours this morning and chased the hole-hunters in. I haven't seen any sheep out this afternoon so maybe they'll stay now. There were two ewes and their lambs that ran through the swamp by the creek bed and into the pasture so I put on some high boots and rolled out the rest of the woven wire and tied it with twine to the brush along the way. It was pretty wet in there since the rain and I can't see why they would go to all that trouble to get out.

This afternoon I weeded cucumbers and picked a half bushel.

*Harvey's niece Adele Ostrom, from Lindstrom, Minnesota, is called "Little Adele" to distinguish her from Helen's sister, Adele Fleming.

That must have been quite a rain we got Sunday night because the garden is still pretty wet and difficult to hoe. This afternoon I'll go to Centuria to do the banking and also get rid of the pickles.

Susan came down with a fever and sore throat tonight. She vomited a while ago and is complaining of a crampy stomach. I hope we don't all catch it.

Peggy wrote you a note and is enclosing it along with a stick of gum for you. The calves she writes about got their heads into the same slot and couldn't get out without my help. Good thing it didn't happen at night. They could have strangled by morning.

The kids loved your little note and I loved the whole letter. The only nice thing about having you away—if there could be anything nice about it—is the cute letters you write. I always did like them you know and I guess ten years haven't changed that at all.

Good night, dear. I will write again in a couple of days.

Love from all of us, Helen

Enclosed note from nine-year-old Peggy:

Dear Daddy, You should have been here Monday night and seen what happened to the two biggest calves. Hannah was eating feed in one of those holes where she could get her head out. Bully put his head in the same hole where Hannah was eating. Hannah tried to pull her head out and both heads got stuck. Bully's little horns are so sharp. They kept sticking Hannah in the neck and she was really bawling. Then Mama took a saw and a hammer and a chisel. She sawed the board and then got the board up with the hammer and chisel. Then Hannah pulled her head out and Bully pulled his head out and that was the end of that.

I miss you Daddy. When are you coming home? Love, Peggy

JULY 24, 1949, 9:30 P.M.

My Dear Harvey,

It is too hot and sticky to sleep so I guess this is a good time to talk to you.

It rained again last night—just poured in fact—and was hot

and humid all day. Three downpours in one week! The corn is really popping now.

Adele and I had to bail water for an hour before milking this morning. The manger was full to the top and the gutters were overflowing. I think most of the water comes in through the silo chute. We cleaned the calf pens out too. This was the day of the church picnic up at Wood Lake but with all those extra chores we couldn't think of going.

This afternoon we drove up to the home place. Pop had bought a big truck load of hay—13 tons—and he and the boys were unloading it. It is second crop alfalfa from Fergus Falls—$28 a ton. Wilmar and Pop trucked 43 bales of it down here for me this evening. It will be wonderful for the sheep. I wheeled a couple bales into the sheep pen tonight and they really went after it. There is no waste on those fine stems. It should help to put a little weight on the lambs and keep the ewes from getting too thin.

Jug Johnson brought me a load of wash water again tonight. If I had put tubs out last night I could have caught all the rainwater I needed but I didn't want to get soaked at 3 a.m.

Susan is feeling much better. The kids and I roasted some marshmallows in the back yard last night to make up for missing the picnic.

I guess I have exhausted my news for this time. I hope it is a nice breezy washday tomorrow. The laundry is piled high around here.

Love from all of us, especially your honey Helen

Harvey will be home by mid-August. Wisconsin is moist and green; the crops are thriving. The plains of western Minnesota look less appealing now. But Harvey will continue to struggle with work he feels ill suited for. "A square peg in a round hole"—that's how he will see himself for years to come. How can a fellow extricate himself from something as all-consuming as dairy farming? He has no other vocational training. He also has a wife who loves the farm, four children to raise, and another on the way.

Helen is thirty-four years old at midcentury; Harvey is thirty-six. They are moving into an era of sweeping social, political, economic, and technological change.

Life expectancy in the United States has risen to sixty-five years for males, seventy-one for females. The family is shrinking. Average household size is 3.37 persons.

Thirty-one percent of American women are working outside the home.

An article titled "What's Wrong with American Women?" by Leland Stowe, published in the October 1949 issue of *Reader's Digest* (condensed from *Esquire*), has much to say about women's increasing assertiveness and independence.

> The American woman is the most spoiled and self-centered woman in the world; the most aggressive; the most unhappy and dissatisfied. She is less feminine and less interested in men, in husband, home and family than are women of other lands; she is the world's most expensive woman; she is more restless and bored, and in general is less spiritual and possesses less individuality than other women.
>
> These are the conclusions of a distinguished array of psychologists, psychoanalysts, and sociologists, as well as most foreigners who have spent much time in the United States, and of an increasing number of traveled Americans.
>
> Our service men discovered overseas what traveled observers have long known: that, on the average, the women of other continents are considerably more interested in (1) pleasing men as men; (2) in their own personal lifetime jobs of being successful as women, wives, and homemakers.

Mr. Stowe has apparently not spent much time in rural America. He most certainly has not met Helen Hellerud. While he might find farm women looking less than feminine, he would be hard pressed to label them selfish and spoiled.

By midcentury, the annual salary for U.S. nonfarm workers has risen to three thousand dollars. Average net farm income is about the same, but farm expenses are inflating considerably faster than income. Electric power is one of the few costs that is actually shrinking. Rates in Polk County, Wisconsin, have dropped 50 percent since 1933; similar reductions are seen all across the country.

The census shows that the number of farmers has declined to 15 percent of the American population. The 1950 census will register only 23 million people living on farms; that trend is likely to continue with the increasing mechanization of food production. Yet the family farm can still provide a livelihood for people willing to work seven days a week. In the Upper Midwest, 120 acres, a herd of twenty-five or thirty cows, and maybe some pigs or sheep or chickens can still sustain the average dairy farming family.

While farms are becoming fewer and larger, the world itself seems to be growing smaller, spinning faster. Pan American Airways is now flying passengers from New York to London in a mere nine hours.

— Television is bringing news and entertainment to American families, coast to coast.
— World War II victory has thrust the United States into a position of world leadership.
— NATO has been formed as a defensive alliance of western nations.

The Soviet Union has torn up its wartime agreement with the Allies and gobbled up half of Europe. Military experts suspect that Russia has three times as many combat airplanes as the United States, four times as many troops. Russia has exploded its first atomic bomb. Americans are increasingly worried about the dangers of atomic weapons. Communism seems poised to conquer the world. If this is peace, it is a nervous peace indeed.

Yet the American view at midcentury is also proud and confident. The past five decades have been a time of dazzling achievement. Cities have expanded outward and upward. Modern inventions have altered life in rural America most of all. The family farm system—long idealized as the essence of the American spirit—is being utterly transformed into something modern and complex, now referred to as "agribusiness."

In the words of historian Allan Nevins, "All the farm legislation of the New Deal did little for rural America compared with the revolution brought by electricity, radio, tractors, the village movie, the telephone, the truck and automobile, the township high school. These city-based innovations have given rural America the means to change its own way of life."

Love Made Visible

1950–55

Work is love made visible.

KAHLIL GIBRAN

ON JANUARY 2, 1950, *Life* magazine publishes a special midcentury issue, reflecting on "American Life and Times, 1900–1950." In an essay titled "The Audacious Americans," Allan Nevins writes, "Bold experimentalism gave us five decades of dazzling achievement. That was our adolescence; now we have come to responsible maturity."

An article on "The Acceleration of Science" in the same issue states that the past fifty years brought more progress than was made in the previous five thousand. The writer concludes,

The accumulation of technical knowledge has brought in the past ten years a breakdown of barriers that had once seemed to be impassable. Planes have been built which fly faster than sound, breaking through the sonic barrier which was thought to set an absolute limit on air speed. Gigantic computing machines have been developed which for the first time free mathematicians from the drudgery of time-consuming calculations. The release of atomic energy, most formidable of physical problems until a few years ago, has at last been exploited to set new records for destruction. The span of human life, determined for hundreds of years by factors that man could not control, has been dramatically extended by the discovery of cures for diseases which could never be cured before. Now, at the century's midpoint, there is little that can be imagined which is too fantastic to become reality before the year 2000.

Helen and Harvey's fifth child—a sturdy daughter named Priscilla Elaine—is born at the Amery hospital on January 23, 1950. Harvey brings Helen home with her newborn three days later, shortly before Polk County residents experience record-breaking temperatures.

The weather is reported in a typically understated manner by the *Polk County Ledger:* "The temperature on Monday, January 29, was -52 degrees in the Polk County icebox of Lykens [near Balsam Lake] with enough breeze to make it downright miserable. Many have experienced broken water pipes. Schools in the area were closed for two days. Business has been hurt. There has been a lot of talking, and little spending."

Since the Hellerud farmhouse lacks central heating and tight windows, Harvey and Helen work hard at keeping the family comfortable. Before tucking the older children in for the night, Helen warms their beds with bricks heated in the oven. Baby Priscilla sleeps between her parents under heavy quilts.

Spring is slow in coming. Helen writes to Margaret on March 14.

Dear Margaret,
We are getting one of those long, late winters and wish we could be out there in California with you, enjoying sunshine and flowers.

Your letter came last Saturday and the box arrived today. What a welcome surprise! The girls are thrilled with the dresses. The little yellow frock for Priscilla is beautiful. We are going to have her baptized in it after the weather moderates. If you can come home this summer, we will wait until then.

Harvey says we should really scold you for spending so much on us, but of course we greatly appreciate it. I don't have time to sew as much as I should since Priscilla came, and this round of clothes will really give me a lift for the summer . . .

The girls are good about changing into denims when they come home from school so they can wear a dress for two days, sometimes three, which saves on laundry. And of course everything lasts longer that way.

The jersey you sent for Teddy is heavy and nice. I will have to get busy and make him some new pants now. I have 3 or 4 pairs already cut from the backs of old suit pants legs—nice and warm and dressy looking.

I meant to write to you when I got home from the hospital, but kept too busy to sit down with pencil and paper. I thought the doctor was kidding when he said I could go home on the fourth day, as long as I was careful. Apparently it didn't hurt me any and it saved on the hospital bill. Total cost was $108. Not bad, considering what we have to show for it.

Our baby just finished her bottle and is off to dreamland. Already she sleeps through the night and I am so grateful because it is hard to get up on these cold nights to warm bottles. She seldom fusses. Harvey thinks she is extra special and doesn't mind her not being a boy. He calls her "Precious" or "Princess."

Peggy is a good help now—almost ten years old!—and she will be able to watch Priscilla this summer when I am out in the garden or giving Harvey a lift with chores when he is in the field. Susan and Sara do need some minding. Susan, especially, is a wildcat and can get into so much mischief. The twins bring home identical report cards, but not because their work is identical. The teacher doesn't dare make any difference in them, probably because she is never sure which-is-which. They realize it too, and keep her in a state of confusion by switching desks and signing each other's names. Susan is a whiz with arithmetic. Sara reads better and is more careful with her written work.

This has been a tough winter and we still have over three feet of snow on the level. It's still zero degrees, with no sign of a thaw coming any day soon. Makes the chores twice as hard. When the snow finally goes we will be wearing hip boots because it will surely go all at once after hanging around so long. Harvey had wanted to work in the woods to get up next winter's fuel supply but had to give up because of the deep snow. We have a month's supply of corn shocks and cane in the field yet too, beside a mountain of manure that had to be piled up. Such is the life of a farmer!

Love to the three of you from all seven of us, and thanks a million for everything,

Helen and family

As usual, Helen's concerns during the long, cold winter of 1950 revolve around the needs of her family. If she worries about the events creating national and global headlines, she makes no mention of them.

America's fear of communism is escalating. The mainstream press is running feature articles with ominous titles such as RUSSIAN SPIES—TRAINED TO RAISE HELL IN AMERICA! and REDS ARE AFTER YOUR CHILD!

President Truman declares that Soviet Russia's attack on North Korea makes it plain that communism has passed beyond the use of subversion to conquer independent nations and will now use armed invasion and war. By June 1950, the president has ordered American GIs to the Korean battlefield.

Air raid drills will soon become routine in American schools. Citizens will begin building bomb shelters filled with food, books, and supplies. Information—and misinformation—supplied by radio and television will contribute to anxieties.

There is no television set in the Hellerud farmhouse. Harvey and Helen will resist that purchase for another decade. But the influence of this remarkable invention is felt everywhere. Americans are fascinated by the miniature movie screen that occupies a central place in their very own parlors.

Editorials begin to denounce the "one-eyed monster," declaring it a dangerous "opiate of the masses." Some alarmists predict a decline in reading, cultural pursuits, and independent thought. One writer warns, "By the dawn of the twenty-first century our people will be squint-eyed, hunchbacked and fond of the dark!"

Americans will continue to buy television sets. Before this decade is over, "TV" will be found in 86 percent of American homes. The average family will be watching forty-two black-and-white hours per week.

Life itself may seem largely a matter of black and white at mid-century, with manners and morals clearly defined. This is a time of conservative politics and social conformity, a time for focusing on the time-honored virtues of home, church, and neighborhood, a time to pursue economic growth and security. In spite of the specter of communism, most Americans are feeling optimistic about the future.

Helen writes to Margaret on August 18, 1950.

Dear Margaret,
Time has just flown since your visit. Priscilla has grown so much in the past month. She sits in a high chair now, has one tooth, patty-cakes, and eats to beat the band. I don't think she is going to be as dainty as her older sisters . . .

School will begin next Monday, August 28. Peggy will be starting fifth grade and the twins will start second. It hardly seems that we had any summer with spring coming so late. Now threshing is nearly finished. The grain didn't do well this year because it has been so dry, and the corn suffered too. Then last Wednesday when we finally got a good rain, it hailed for about half an hour and shredded the leaves terribly. My cucumbers got a terrible beating so there won't be many to pick this year. I was counting on that crop to help me buy school clothes for the kids this fall. If I had known the cukes would get hailed out just when they were beginning to bear, I would have spent my time sewing this summer. As you know, we are dependent on the weather, and when the elements won't cooperate, there isn't much you can do about it . . .

That's one thing that hasn't changed over the years: a farmer's reliance on the natural elements. Everything revolves around the weather.

OCTOBER 12, 1950, 10 A.M.

Dear Margaret,

This is one of those beautiful Indian summer days that makes one glad to be alive. The kids are busy making leaf houses in the woods and front yard. I have my boiler boiling and will wash woolens and coats. They should dry well in the sun with this good breeze.

Thank you for the birthday card and enclosed five-spot. I am going to get a new cardigan sweater and some new kitchen curtains with it.

The home permanents you sent arrived last week, all intact. I permed the twins last Saturday (my birthday) and kept so busy I didn't even make a birthday cake. I followed directions to the letter and have we got curls! The first two nights the kids were afraid to lie down and sleep for fear their hair would straighten out. That always happened with the Toni's, but these curls seem to be lasting better. I'm going to do my own hair and Peggy's hair soon.

I made $115 off my cucumbers this year—took them to the pickle factory in Centuria every two or three days while they were producing. The pickles paid for school clothes and shoes for kids plus 16 crates of fruit for canning. Yesterday I picked a milk pail full of wild grapes in the woods and made twenty pints of nice jam.

All the kids were disappointed that we didn't get to the County Fair this year. We decided to stay home and spend the $10 on polio insurance instead. Two neighbor children came down with it and that really gave us a scare. I heard those two little ones are home again and should recover completely but some have not been that lucky.

Time to get to work washing clothes, so this letter will be brief.

Thanks again and love from all of us, Helen

Employer-based health insurance benefits are becoming more common by the 1950s, with companies competing for labor and unions negotiating benefit packages for their members. Most self-employed workers, including farmers, have no health insurance, trusting to luck and extended payment plans in case of unforeseen medical bills. Some are purchasing low-cost coverage for a specific disease, such as polio.

A health report contained in the July 16, 1951, issue of *Time* magazine states, "So far this year, cases are running close behind those for 1950, an epidemic year. The National Foundation for Infantile Paralysis: the U.S. must raise its idea of 'normal' polio incidence from about 10,000 cases a year to perhaps 30,000."

In fact, the United States will report a peak of 68,000 cases annually before the Salk polio vaccine is introduced in 1954, sharply reducing the incidence of this crippling disease.

By 1951, U.S. unemployment has dipped to 3.3 percent. The annual inflation rate has risen to nearly eight percent. The average family income of $3,700 is rising along with inflation. A new house can be purchased for $9,000, a new car for $1,500, a loaf of bread for sixteen cents. American families pay an average of 19 percent of their incomes for food, compared with 23 percent during the previous decade. Many people have a little extra money to spend. Cars are becoming more luxurious and powerful, with many options, including two-tone paint. Television sales continue to expand. A new comedy show called *I Love Lucy* has made its debut.

More news from 1951:

— The new United Nations headquarters officially opens in New York City on January 10. The Korean War is escalating; Chinese and North Korean forces capture Seoul on January 17.
— On March 31, Remington Rand delivers the first UNIVAC 1 computer to the U.S. Census Bureau.
— On September 8, a peace treaty with Japan is signed by forty-eight nations, formally ending the Pacific War.
— On October 24, President Harry Truman declares an official end to the war with Germany.

— By year's end, the Marshall Plan has expired after distributing more than \$13.3 billion in foreign aid to rebuild Europe.

And now the United States is heavily involved in the "Korean Conflict." Young men are being drafted into military service from every region of the country. The *Polk County Ledger*, on December 21, 1950, reports that nineteen local men have been called for the January draft. They will report for induction on January 4, to leave by bus from Centuria at 8:30 AM.

People are talking on street corners, at the feed stores and barber shops and church suppers. Why are we sending soldiers to Korea? Will this conflict escalate into another global war? What losses will be suffered? Will the sacrifice prove necessary in the end?

On March 1, 1951, Willie and Olava Williamson lose one of their twenty-five precious grandchildren. Leland and Violet Williamson's eight-year-old daughter, LeeAnn, dies at home from a sudden illness, thought to be encephalitis, following a severe case of measles. The extended family mourns; the loss of a child is the hardest thing to bear.

When Helen writes to Margaret six months later, she focuses, as she must, on her own family and how to keep them clothed for the coming season.

SEPTEMBER 12, 1951

Dear Margaret,
It's a bright, breezy day, perfect for hanging out laundry, so I'm going to tackle that as soon as I get this letter into the mailbox. It will be a short one, but I figure that a few lines are better than none at all.

Peggy started sixth grade a couple of weeks ago, and the twins are in third.

I just sent an order in to the Monkey Wards catalog—sweaters, socks and underwear for the school kids, and some warm jerseys for Teddy and Priscilla. I'm still sewing skirts and blouses for the girls, but don't find time to knit. Once I make over some hand-me-down coats for the kids we should be all set for winter clothing this season. I am so thankful for this sewing machine. It would break our budget if we had to buy everything like some of the town folks do.

Harvey is harvesting corn this week, crewing with a couple of neighbors. They should be filling silo here in a day or two. Good timing. The kernels are fully formed and the stalks and leaves are still moist. That should mean some first rate silage.

We hope things are going well for you and Mel and Charles and that we will hear from you soon. Love, Helen and family

Margaret, Mel, and Chuck Gorder and Adele Fleming return to Wisconsin in the summer of 1952. This time they fly in a large plane called a Stratocruiser, making the entire trip in one day. Wilmar drives to the Minneapolis/St. Paul airport to pick them up. All the home folks are mightily impressed by such speedy and costly travel.

Willie and Olava celebrate their fiftieth wedding anniversary on Sunday, August 3, with over one hundred relatives, friends, and neighbors attending an open house at the farm. If the social connections of this rural community are beginning to weaken, it is not evident on this grand day.

There are no more letters from Helen to Margaret until the end of 1952.

Surely Helen is writing at least a postcard now and then. It is the only way to stay in touch. The Helleruds still have no telephone in the farmhouse. And long-distance calls would be too expensive if they did.

While news of world events remains limited in the Hellerud home, Harvey tries to buy the *Minneapolis Tribune* whenever the family drives to Balsam Lake for church on Sunday. They also listen to the noontime news on WCCO radio from the Twin Cities—farm reports, weather news, national and world headlines, and commercial messages. ("Are you cooking with Crisco and sudsing

Willie and Olava's golden wedding celebration, 1952. Front: Willie and Olava.
Back: Alice, Donald, Margaret, Wilmar, Adele, Leland, Helen, Clarence.

with Dreft? This is Cedric Adams with your noontime news . . .")
Harvey keeps the radio on a shelf near the kitchen table. Dinner,
the main meal of the day, is timed for twelve noon, and when the
kids are at the table they know enough to keep quiet during Cedric
Adams's broadcast.

They learn that Adlai Stevenson has been chosen as the Democratic candidate in the upcoming presidential race. He will soon
be campaigning in the Upper Midwest. The Republican candidate,
Dwight D. Eisenhower, and his running mate, Richard Nixon, will
also be stumping in the area. Harvey hopes for a Republican victory. He has seen enough failed farm policies from the Democrats.

Wisconsin's Republican senator, Joseph McCarthy, is the subject of much debate. Many believe he is fighting a courageous and
important battle to expose the "Communist menace," including
all spies and sympathizers. Others see him as a radical, trampling
on civil rights, exploiting fears of communism to further his own

career. Harvey and Helen—who usually vote Republican—are hoping for McCarthy's defeat.

On November 6, 1952, Eisenhower wins by the greatest landslide since FDR's victory over Herbert Hoover in 1932. Joseph McCarthy is reelected to the U.S. Senate.

DECEMBER 2, 1952
Dear Margaret,
We had Thanksgiving here at home and I can tell you we felt mighty thankful. We are ready for winter with a mow full of hay and plenty of corn silage for the cows, not to mention rows of canned goods in the cellar and five healthy kids around the table.

I am thankful, too, that all this political wrangling is over. Some of the boys up home are pretty staunch Democrats but Pop likes Ike, and there have been some heated arguments. Harvey and I have been careful to stay out of that. Truth is, we have had our fill of Truman and all those farm bills that have done more harm than good.

Toward the end of this long letter, Helen reports that nine of Polk County's rural school districts are being dissolved. Beginning next fall, most of the Polk County farm kids will be bused into town. South Milltown School, where all the "Willie kids" got their elementary education, is not yet on the closure list, but Helen doubts it can survive much longer. That's the direction everything is moving these days. Bigger and better.

Margaret, Chuck, and Adele fly to Wisconsin again in the summer of '53. Mel has advanced to an executive position at Buzza-Cardozo in Los Angeles and cannot make the trip, but he is able to finance expensive plane tickets. Margaret writes to him on August 1, describing a driving adventure in Eureka Township, near St. Croix Falls, Wisconsin.

Yesterday forenoon, Papa and I and four of Helen's kids toured the countryside where Papa grew up. We walked into the fields where the original log cabin stood and even got inside a vacant country schoolhouse. We managed to leave seven-year-old

Teddy in the schoolhouse and drove away before we missed him. (With so many kids jammed into the back seat, no one noticed his absence!) We went back and found him climbing the rafters, not at all worried. We visited three different grave-yards and planted grass seed on eight family graves and every-one helped to fix and weed as we remembered the folks buried there. Little Priscilla left her dolly on a tombstone and realized it after we were a mile or so down the road, so we went back a second time and retrieved it.

Papa got real sentimental about the whole thing and talked all day about his childhood. He remembered drawing little farms in the dirt, with all the buildings and field and fences when he was just a tot. He said he used his mother's yarn to make har-nesses for the kittens and hitched them up to miniature hay-racks that he made from match boxes. He used empty spools of thread for wheels. I always knew he was a born farmer!

Adele and I agreed we should be writing his memories down and put it all into a book someday . . .

Helen's daughter Sara, who is along on that excursion, listens care-fully to the adult conversation. At the age of ten, she has devel-oped a keen interest in the family's history. She also guesses that her aunties are never going to sit still long enough to write a book. The job will probably fall to her, so she had better start paying at-tention, start asking questions and collecting stories. She doesn't know that it will take her sixty years to get down to business, but she feels sure she will get it done.

The national news is full of hopeful stories and predictions by the summer of '53. The highly unpopular Korean War seems to have ended. President Eisenhower is promising an era of peace and prosperity.

Cold War fears of advancing communism and annihilation by a Soviet H-bomb continue to simmer, but Americans are gradually abandoning their bomb shelters, building barbecue pits instead. Suburbia is flourishing. Farmland is receding near the nation's major cities, making way for row upon row of low-slung housing, shops and schools and playgrounds, and the highways that are needed to tie it all together. Between 1950 and 1960 more than forty thousand miles of highway will be constructed.

During the "nifty fifties," the majority of high school graduates are not going to college; those who do are likely to remain conservative in their social and political views. Many young women talk of education as "something to fall back on," in case of divorce or unforeseen disaster. In any case, college is a great place to go shopping for a mate.

By 1950, young women are marrying at an average age of twenty. Forty percent of American families are living in suburbs by the early fifties, raising 3.8 children, owning two cars and two televisions.

In the popular *Coronet* magazine we read, "The smart woman will downplay her abilities and focus on keeping herself desirable. It is her duty to be feminine at all times in the eyes of the opposite sex."

According to such criteria, Helen Hellerud is seriously neglecting her feminine duties. She is dressed in sturdy denims and barn boots as she spends more and more time in the barn, tending the livestock. Her home-styled hair smells strongly of manure.

At thirteen and ten years of age, Peggy and the twins are responsible for much of the housework and childcare. Helen has become more than a helpmate to Harvey. She has gradually assumed the leading role, directing the dairy operation, buying and selling cattle, managing as diplomatically as possible with a mixture of fierce purpose and gentle persuasion.

Helen's new assertiveness is not the norm for farm women of the fifties. Many have been freed from barn and field by new laborsaving machinery and are returning happily to traditional work within the home.

Not Helen. She is a skilled homemaker—especially when it comes to scrimping and saving and making do—but she knows how to produce income, too.

Seeing no future for her family on the hilly, sandy Balsam Lake acreage, Helen goes shopping—not for feminine fashions, but for fields and pastures, barns and silos and corncribs. Again, the house will have to be her last concern.

OCTOBER 20, 1953
MILLTOWN, WISCONSIN
Dear Margaret,
Thanks a million for your letters and the photos you took when you visited this summer.

It is already 22 days since we moved the cows to this farm—the old Ulrich place, a mile south of Milltown. We have just the lambs left down at the Balsam Lake place, plus the piano and canned goods and a few odds and ends to move. Harvey drives the 7 miles down there twice a day to feed lambs—about 150 left. After we sell off half of those (providing we can get a decent price) we will move the rest of them. We have 12 acres of corn to pick down there yet too.

Harvey has been less than enthusiastic about this move because he loved those woods and hills and hollows at Balsam Lake. But this farm has so much more potential. It is only slightly more than 100 acres, but most of that is tillable and it lies nice and flat. Some clay, but almost no sand and no rocks to wreck our equipment. Pop helped us with a down payment of $1,000, which will tide us over until we can sell the old farm. Purchase price for the Ulrich farm was $12,000. I don't see how we can go wrong with a deal like that.

We have had to go from Grade A to Grade B milk with this move, at least until we can get this barn and milk house into better shape and meet Grade A criteria. That means a smaller milk check, but some of the loss will be recouped when Harvey starts hauling our milk to the Stella Cheese receiving station in Milltown, just a mile away. Up to now we have been selling to Land O'Lakes in Turtle Lake, but it's not sensible to keep paying those trucking fees.

We are fairly well settled in the house, except for curtains. The kids are mightily impressed by the telephone, and the bathroom with a flush toilet, bathtub, and hot running water. All that will make my life easier too. Once again I will have painting and plastering to do and that will take time. I scraped down to the plaster in one corner of the dining room and counted seventeen layers of wallpaper! That will mean many days of steaming and scraping and peeling. I have already replaced a broken window, which took me all afternoon. There are many leaky windows needing putty, and I only hope the warm weather holds until I finish my repairs.

Funny how fast kids adjust to big changes. They like the Milltown school and come home talking about their new friends. It will take Harvey and me a little longer. We feel pretty uprooted, and sometimes wake up in the morning thinking we are still at Balsam Lake. We worked hard there and don't forget so easily.

You will get a kick out of the enclosed list of rules that Peggy wrote out for the twins, who can be careless with their clothing, especially Susan. Peggy is so conscientious. She may have better luck training them than I have! (I swiped the list—but since it is several weeks old, they probably won't miss it. Now you are my partner in crime.) I plan to tackle some laundry today. If it weren't for Peggy, I would have twice as many loads.

Love, Helen

The enclosed list is written in pencil on lined tablet paper.
NEW RULES FOR THE NEW SCHOOL:

1. Clothes must be placed as follows: Small top dresser drawer—scarves and accessories. Large top drawer—underwear. Middle drawer—School clothes. Bottom drawer—Nightwear, summer wear and everyday.

2. When clothes are half dirty put them in the bottom drawer.

3. Change clothes IMMEDIATELY after school or church.

4. Hang up all dressy clothes—don't let them lay around.

5. Mend all rips and replace missing buttons. Mama is TOO BUSY to do this for you!

6. Wear one outfit for everyday ALL WEEK.

7. Put clothes in hamper when they are dirty.
THESE RULES MUST BE FOLLOWED!

MAY 3, 1954

Dear Margaret,

We are having another late spring and Harvey has been in bed for several days with a bad sinus cold. This damp weather is hard on him and I think he will start feeling better both mentally and physically when things dry out and he can start working these good flat fields. A long, hard winter like the one we just had really wears a guy out. Harvey is talking about giving up on this whole enterprise, but he can't figure out a good alternative either. I think we need to give this place at least a good trial year before we make any big decisions. I talked with Pop about it one day and I know he feels that is the sensible thing to do. I need to put my worrying aside so I can concentrate on keeping Harvey encouraged and lightening his load in the barn. He never liked working with cattle the way I do. If we can get through this tough spell I feel sure we can succeed in the long run.

You will be surprised to learn that Mom and Pop have bought a television set—a big 21-inch tabletop Philco—that sits on the library table in the living room. They eat their supper in front of it with plates on their laps and their heads just inches from the screen. My girls are begging for a TV too, of course, but Harvey and I are dead-set against it. I don't know how anyone gets youngsters to work with that contraption in the house. And it surely must be hard on the eyes. I let the kids watch TV at Mom and Pop's on Sunday afternoons and they come home so dizzy they can hardly see straight. From what I've seen, the programs are pretty much a waste of time—silly comedies or cowboys and Indians chasing each other around the desert. I can't see anything educational about that.

I don't know what Mom and Pop paid for the TV—they aren't saying, so I know it had to be a lot. I hear they can run up to $200 or more.

It seems that history is repeating, as it has a tendency to do. Helen and Harvey are stubbornly resisting the temptations of TV, just as Willie and Olava resisted the radio some thirty years earlier.

It is natural that Helen, who has always measured the worth of a day by the work accomplished, should disapprove of this new distraction. She guesses it's all right for her parents to take a break in front of the television screen now and then. After all, Pop is seventy-five and Mom is nearly eighty. They deserve a little rest and relaxation. But younger folks have no business sitting around when there is work to be done.

Popular television entertainment from the early fifties includes a favorite of Olava's: *GE Theatre,* with Ronald Reagan as the handsome host.

The first color television sets, marketed by RCA in the mid-fifties for a thousand dollars, are well out of reach for most American families. Minimum wage is seventy-five cents per hour. Gasoline has risen to the painful price of twenty-nine cents per gallon. A new Chevy Bel Air can be purchased for $1,095.

Senator McCarthy is still dominating headlines with his allegations of communist infiltration in high places. However, televised images of McCarthy's crude and irresponsible rantings will soon help to bring him down.

Dr. Jonas Salk's polio vaccine is administered to schoolchildren in a mass inoculation program that will eradicate this dreaded disease.

A groundswell of dissatisfaction and turmoil is developing among America's growing black minority. A 1954 landmark decision by the U.S. Supreme Court—*Brown v. Board of Education*—ushers in the long and bitter process of desegregating the nation's public classrooms.

A rebellious subculture that calls itself the Beat Generation bewilders the nation's elders. The wild rhythms of rock 'n' roll have parents shaking their heads, wondering how things could have gone so terribly awry.

Teenagers are developing a colorful vocabulary all their own, with words like *cool, neat, hip, chick, dig, hang loose.* Cars are called *wheels;* tires are *skins;* snow tires are *snowballs. Square* is the shape of their parents, or anyone too old fashioned to dig the slang. *Square* is something no teen can afford to be.

Old fashioned is what no farmer can afford to be—not any longer, not if he wants to keep pace in a changing world. The change from horse to tractor has been gradual, but by 1954 the U.S. Census of Agriculture has stopped recording the number of horses per farm. Tractors are supplying the power, pulling manure spreaders, plows and cultivators, balers, choppers and blowers, combines and corn pickers. All this laborsaving technology is not doing much to shorten the farmer's work day, but it does enable him to expand his herds and barns and silos and plant more crops so he can pay for more machines.

Modern dairy farms are using artificial insemination to improve their herds; bulls are disappearing from the barns and pastures. Cows are being bred to produce large volumes of milk, with Holsteins averaging about five thousand pounds per year by 1950. Substandard producers are culled from the herd and sent to slaughter.

No one can yet imagine that milk production per animal will increase so dramatically—more than three-fold—by the end of the century, the result of improved genetic selection, nutrition, health care, and management techniques. Cows' lives, however, will be much shorter; instead of ten or more lactations, they will last for three or four.

While farm productivity is rising sharply during the fifties, indebtedness is rising, too. The farmers' margin of profit is shrinking. In 1954, farmers are retaining only 36 percent of their gross income, the smallest percentage for any year since 1932.

The editor of *Country Gentleman, The Magazine for Better Farming,* offers these words of caution: "Keep debts below half of what you own. Keep INCOME above OUTGO so UPKEEP and OVERHEAD don't become your DOWNFALL."

Harvey Hellerud does his best to follow this advice, yet he knows he can't keep up without some modernizing. He has never wanted to farm on a large scale, preferring to keep his operation small and manageable. He loves nature and wants some quiet time for walking in the woods, admiring a sunset. He craves travel. It's a big world out there, and he wants to see more of it. At the very least, he'd like a little time for rest and recreation now and then. Helen and the kids deserve that, too.

Since Harvey is not mechanically inclined, farming suited him much better when he worked with horses and simple machinery. This race for expansion, bigger investment, higher productivity, faster pacing goes against Harvey's nature.

He will talk about it many times in years to come.

When I had to get rid of the horses, and start buying all that machinery, I was just finished. Too bad I didn't understand that sooner. I spent so many years feeling helpless and depressed and Helen had to carry the extra load.

Helen's letter to Margaret, August 12, 1955:

Dear Margaret,
You will be glad to know I have taken your advice and started making time for my music again. It's amazing what a lift it gives me to sit down at the piano with some of the old sheet music or a hymnbook. Just fifteen or twenty minutes a day helps like everything. I'm still pretty rusty but with practice I should be able to help with some music at Milltown Lutheran—maybe even try for the organ job . . .

We have had a busy couple of weeks here. The kids made a good showing at the Polk County Fair with their lambs as well as their baking and sewing entries. Harvey showed his prize Shropshire ram (Gus, short for Caesar Augustus!) and brought home a blue ribbon.

I felt his outlook was improving this summer, but right after the Fair was over Harvey announced that he had to get away from this grind for a while. He took a Greyhound bus to the Black Hills and from there will continue to Kaycee, Wyoming, where his cousin has a ranching operation, mainly sheep. I don't think Harvey is going to see any land that will be more attractive or affordable than what we have right here. I know he would like to escape from the dairy routine, but we simply can't start all over again in a strange location and a way of farming that we know so little about.

Harvey said he felt guilty about leaving me with all this work, as well as spending the money for travel, so I know his heart is in the right place. I encouraged the trip because I think he needs a rest and a change of scenery. If he gains a fresh perspective, it will be money well spent.

We have done some remodeling in the barn and installed five more stanchions so we can milk 27 this winter. The five extra cows should boost our monthly check from the creamery. I don't see how we can miss if Harvey can just get straightened out in his thinking. Once he starts getting ahead financially, this terrible inferiority he feels when he is around Pop and the boys should be eliminated.

Don't worry about us, Margaret—we are getting along all right. Pop's old hired man, Lawrence E., is working here temporarily and we will get by all right for a few weeks if he will just stay sober. Trouble is, I can't let him stay here overnight with Harvey gone, because you know how some people will talk. Every time Lawrence leaves the property I worry he will wind up at the tavern. But so far, so good. If I can just hold things together until Harvey gets back here with his mind settled, I think I will feel equal to most anything.

Peggy and the twins are a big help in the house and garden and you would be surprised how Teddy pitches in with barn chores. He'll be nine years old in a couple of weeks and works almost like a man. I'm pretty proud of all of them.

I must say the girls do have some big ideas. Peggy wants to be a nurse and keeps a scrapbook of photos from magazines— nurses and doctors in action, plus every scab or bloody bandage she can collect from the rest of us. Susie plans to become a concert pianist and Sara can't decide—it's either a ballerina or a famous writer—maybe both. We'll see. It's a pretty good bet that these girls aren't going to be content to stay at home and farm like their mother.

Well, I'd better be off to bed, since the alarm is set for 5:30 a.m. We're doing fine, remember that. Next time I write to you, Harvey should be home again.

Love, Helen

If "work is love made visible," as the poet Kahlil Gibran wrote, Helen's love for her husband and children and the home they share is visible to all of them during the summer of 1955.

Harvey returns to his family within a few weeks. "It looks desolate out west," he says. "Big open sky, but the soil is so dry and bare. No lakes and ponds, hardly anything you could call a real tree. How could anyone adjust to that, after living in Wisconsin?"

Yet he will continue to suffer bouts of depression, craving a broader experience than this way of life can offer.

Helen has been shaped and defined since childhood by the dairy farming culture. She feels grounded by the daily chores, the seasonal rhythm of plowing and planting and harvest. She is taprooted here. There will be no dislodging her. She and Harvey both know it.

Following the worrisome summer of 1955, Helen's letters to her sister grow shorter and fewer.

Long-distance telephone rates are declining, and the sisters are sharing some of their news over the wire. The Helleruds will soon be free of their thirteen-family party line. A person will soon be able to dial friends and relatives in the Twin Cities—even California—without having their conversations heard by all the neighbors, and without doing serious harm to the budget.

Life seems to be accelerating. There is no longer any energy for letter writing during the hour between barn chores and bedtime, no time for a few paragraphs while the bread dough is rising on a Monday morning.

Harvey and Helen have recently installed an electric barn cleaner with a chain conveyer that moves through the gutters and dumps the fresh manure atop a growing mountain in the barnyard. They have increased the dairy herd to pay for it.

Where, they wonder, is the extra time they hoped to gain from this laborsaving device? It has evaporated like a summer rain.

It seems that everyone is moving faster now, in ever-widening circles. Who will take time to write the detailed letters and thoughtful diaries that have so long provided our first-person, bottom-up history? Who will record the plainspoken narratives, reminding us that human nature remains remarkably constant across continents and cultures and centuries? Who will provide the bare story, the personal telling? *This is how I spent my days. This is how I felt about my life in the time allotted to me, in the place I called home.*

Helen writes to Margaret on December 16, 1955. The airmail stamp costs six cents. A postcard can be mailed for two cents. Ground delivery for a letter up to one ounce is still three cents; the rate has not increased since 1932.

Dear Margaret,

I have quite some excitement to report to you. Susan and Sara and I spent Saturday in Minneapolis. Our trip all came about because of Susan's piano teacher, Ebba Launsby, who lives close by, in Luck. She claims to be a Danish Countess, with some impressive connections in the city, and the twins were invited to perform at a wealthy home on Lake Harriet. Actually, they went down on the train last Thursday with Susan's teacher, a couple of days ahead of me. They stayed at a grand old home out on Pleasant Avenue (another friend of Ebba's.) Friday morning I got their excited phone call with descriptions of the elegant furnishings and twenty Persian rugs. (They counted!) I went down Saturday morning by bus and we came home together on the bus that evening, after the performance. It got bitterly cold that night and Harvey and I thawed frozen water pipes till 3 a.m. I am still so pleased that I hardly feel tired from all the extra work and lost sleep.

Susan and Sara looked so nice in the nylon dresses and ruffled petticoats you bought them last summer at Dayton's. Good thing you bought the dresses a size too large, because the girls have grown quite a lot since that shopping spree and they fit fine now.

The lady who hosted the tea was duly impressed with the girls' abilities and so were all of her friends. Susan played three piano pieces, including one of her own compositions, and Sara read two original poems. Then they danced a little routine they had put together, with Ebba providing the piano background. Best of all, they acted very natural and unspoiled, yet seemed so comfortable among those fine-feathered women that I was just amazed. To tell the truth, I didn't feel uncomfortable either, in spite of wearing that faded blue suit that I've had for years. (There simply wasn't time to do any sewing or shopping.) I came away with the feeling that I am richer by far than most of those women. I envy them not one bit of their fine Persian rugs and Cadillacs. It was a grand experience and one the kids— and I—will never forget.

Love to all three of you, Helen and family

Helen and Harvey are both proud of their five children, who now range in age from five to fifteen. Both parents are careful about doling out too much praise, but the older girls have overheard them referring to their kids as "the best crop ever." The girls feel annoyed to hear themselves discussed like a stand of oats or a field of ripening corn. They are also secretly pleased.

This family is living in a time and place that values modesty and reticence. Parents do not express affection casually, with their children or with each other. They seldom say "I love you," at least not where anyone can hear it. Everyone understands that actions are more telling than words.

Maybe the young ones, who do not get many hugs or compliments once they have reached school age, crave a little more attention now and then.

Maybe, in later years, letters like the one Helen wrote on December 16, 1955, will help to fill some empty spaces. But those aging children should understand by now that they were deeply loved.

Epilogue

It is the writer's privilege to help man endure
by lifting his heart, by reminding him
of the courage and honor and hope and pride
and compassion and pity and sacrifice
which have been the glory of his past.
WILLIAM FAULKNER

MY PARENTS, Helen and Harvey Hellerud, auctioned off their dairy herd in 1974 and moved to the Minnesota border town of Taylors Falls. Theirs was a surprisingly early retirement for dairy farmers. But, at the age of sixty-one, my father had had enough. He wanted to be free to explore the world beyond his own fence line, which he did, by bicycle, making several coast-to-coast trips, marveling at the varied scenery and culture, the rich and diverse ways of spending a life. My mother, on the other hand, grieved for many months, missing the rhythms she had been born to, the work that she had always loved.

When they retired, Margaret and Mel Gorder traveled the United States for many years in an Airstream trailer, making friends wherever they went. They spent their final years in Mesa, Arizona, returning as often as possible to their beloved Upper Midwest.

Adele Fleming moved from Los Angeles back to Polk County, Wisconsin, in 1957, teaching English, speech, and drama in the Milltown High School until her retirement. My twin and I were privileged to be students in her classroom. We watched her work her sorcery, turning the most reluctant scholars into lovers of well-crafted words.

My uncles—Clarence, Leland, Wilmar, and Donald—continued to farm throughout their long working lives, expanding their herds and fields, acquiring complex machinery, adapting as well as they could to the changes and challenges of agribusiness.

None of my siblings or cousins, or their descendants, are farming today. My generation is scattered across the continent. Several of our children have lived abroad or are routinely traveling the world, doing work that the futurists of the fifties could not have envisioned.

Much has been written to explain the disappearance of family dairy farms and the society that supported them. Simply put: mechanization demanded increased income to support it. That meant expanded acreage, bigger herds of cattle, bigger barns and taller silos, more expenses, more workers than one family could supply. Improved production called for chemical fertilizers, pesticides, herbicides, milking parlors, bovine growth hormone. Everything bigger, better, more efficient, until the day of corporate farming had fully dawned.

We couldn't see it coming. Certainly not in the 1950s. Not when we were standing right in the middle of it all.

Now, in 2014, my elders are all gone. Their brief flicker of time has been spent, all their struggles and frustrations, all their gladness laid to rest.

My mother was the last of her siblings to die, on December 20, 2010, at the age of ninety-five. She spent her final years in a nursing home in Amery, Wisconsin. Some days she saw the long green corridors as grassy country lanes, the handrails as fence lines.

"These flimsy fences will never hold a herd of cows," she fussed. "We're going to need some woven wire reinforcement."

Some mornings she worried about preparing the noonday meal.

"What are we going to feed the crew today? They'll be in from the hayfield soon, hungry as hounds."

"How about beef stew and mashed potatoes, Mama?"

"Okay. But will you help me peel the spuds?"

"Yes, Mama, right after you take your morning nap."

When she woke from her nap, the farm, the cattle, the hayfield, and the pressing work would have disappeared.

As much as we might try to hold on to them, memories have a way of shifting and fading, becoming unreliable. Finally, our stories die with us, unless they have been written down.

Before my mother's sense of time and purpose slipped away, I showed her a bundle of letters she had written to her sister Margaret during the 1940s. Mama read through several letters, amazed at the level of detail she recorded. "My goodness! How did I ever find time to write all that trivia?" she exclaimed.

I told her it was the small particulars that mattered most to me. After all, we live in details, not in generalities. She shook her head and laughed.

I like to picture my mother, my grandparents, my aunts and uncles sitting around the kitchen table at the homeplace, talking over all they have achieved and endured, marveling at the changes they have witnessed in their time.

"We should write a book!" Helen exclaims.

"Yes, yes, we should," Margaret agrees.

I wish I could tell them that they did.

Sara Hellerud in hayloft door, 1949

Acknowledgments

WRITING, SHAPING, and publishing a book often requires a village. This one is no exception.

The writers of all the honest and articulate letters that appear in this work have passed beyond my ability to thank them. But their words remain, revealing a way of life that has served as a foundation of American society.

I owe much to several other contributors, including my sisters, Susan Hellerud, Margaret Behling, and Priscilla Fjorden; my brother, Ted Hellerud; my cousin Joyce Williamson and her friend Joyce VanHaren. They have spent countless hours documenting family genealogy and history, keeping the facts straight and the stories alive. Minnesota poet John Caddy has mentored and inspired my writing efforts over many years.

Kate Sweeney prompted me to return to this project after I had long abandoned it.

The *Polk County Ledger Press* generously allowed me access to newspaper archives, where I spent many happy hours researching local history.

Rebecca Watts and the writing group at the Peachtree City, Georgia, Public Library provided valuable encouragement and critique. Manuscript readers Janet Laughlin and Paul Lentz generously gave of their time and expertise. Karin Adams assisted with research details. My husband, Michael DeLuca, who has been so supportive of this work, deserves extra credit for keeping my computer operational and for eating many dinners alone without complaint. My sons, William and Michael Drury, and their beautiful families, have been a constant source of pride and motivation.

Thank you all.

Minnesota Historical Society Press editor Shannon Pennefeather encouraged and guided the manuscript from rough draft to final form. To her, and to her dedicated colleagues at MNHS Press, I express heartfelt gratitude.

Source Notes

pages 17–18, 67–70, 160
Interview with Willie Williamson, August 12, 1975.

pages 22–23, 42–44, 65, 164–65
Interview with Margaret Williamson Gorder, March 4, 1996.

page 30
Mary Neth, *Preserving the Family Farm* (Baltimore: Johns Hopkins University Press, 1995), 130, 131.

pages 51–53
Alice Williamson Rostad, "Does Life Begin at Forty?" unpublished essay, 1956.

pages 53–55
Interview with Donald Williamson, April 26, 1995.

page 66
Interview with Margaret Williamson Gorder, August 12, 1983.

pages 70–71
Interview with Wilmar Williamson, April 26, 1995.

pages 76–77
Interview with Adele Williamson Fleming, June 18, 1981.

pages 90–91
Interview with Margaret Williamson Gorder, March 6, 1996.

page 122
Interview with Adele Williamson Fleming, August 5, 1981.

pages 127–28
William Fletcher Thompson, *The History of Wisconsin: Continuity and Change 1940–1965* (Madison: The State Historical Society of Wisconsin, 1988), 77.

pages 128–29

Interview with Willie Williamson, August 10, 1975.

pages 132–34

Interview with Donald Williamson, October 4, 1995.

page 150

Conversation with Helen Hellerud, October 6, 2006.

pages 154–56

Interview with Wilmar Williamson, July 17, 1995.

page 171

David J. Butler, *History of Half Moon Lake: A Story of Trust,* Kindle edition (Half Moon Lake Conservancy, 2013); Betty Crowley, *Stalag Wisconsin: Inside the WWII Prisoner of War Camps* (San Francisco: Badger Books, 2002).

page 213

Allan Nevins, "The Audacious Americans," *Life,* January 2, 1950.

page 217

Mary Scott Welch, "Temptation!" *Look,* April 24, 1951.

Index

Page numbers for photographs are shown in *italics*.

helping out on the farm, 119; marital problems, 89–90, 100–1; marital reconciliation, 148–49; place in Williamson family tree, viii; relocation to California, 173; temper and mood swings, 77, 95, 100; training for new job, 161, 163, 167; working for the post office, 75

Fleming, Robert ("Bobby") (son of Maurice and Adele): birth, 81–83; growing up on the farm, 121; hand and arm disability, 89, 93, 95; kidney and bowel problems, 104, 121–22, 147–48; removal of tonsils, 162; visits to Wisconsin farm, 173–88, 192–200; Williamson family tree, viii

Fond du Lac, WI, 45, 48–51

Ford, Henry, 55

Ford Motor Company, 60, 63

genealogy, family tree, viii

Germany: Adolf Hitler rise to power, 72; invasion of Poland, 124; Jewish Holocaust, 107; war ends, 171, 220

Gibran, Kahil, 234

Goddard, Paulette (actress), 194

Gorder, Charles ("Chuck"), *193*; birth, 116–17, 119; birthday, 176–77; train trip to Wisconsin, 173–74; visit to Wisconsin farm, 134–43, 175–88, 192–200, 222, 224; Williamson family tree, viii

Gorder, Margaret Williamson. *See* Williamson, Margaret (Aunt Margaret)

Gorder, Melvin: courtship and marriage to Margaret, 65–67; death of mother, 90–91; job loss and relocation to California, 81; return visit to Wisconsin, 222; Williamson family tree, viii

grasshopper plagues, 102–3, 106–7

Great Depression: 1929 stock market crash, 64; bank closures, 67; dairy farming during, 67–71; Dust Bowl period, 78; employment, wages, and trade, 70, 73–74, 108; Farm Holiday, 102–3; "making do" and doing without, 145; New Deal pro-

grams, 71–72, 93–94, 98, 213; Willie Williamson recollections, 67–70; Wilmar Williamson recollections, 70–71

The Great Gatsby (Fitzgerald), 41

Great Mississippi Flood of 1927, 60

Harding, Warren G. (president), 15

health and medical issues: advances in treatment, 40; antibiotics, 168; at-home treatment, 122; blood poisoning, 119–20; insurance coverage, 219–20; mental illness, 157–59, 161; polio, 168, 184, 219–20, 230; predictions of the future, 114; prevalence of disease, 14–15; rheumatism and arthritis, 18, 120; rumors of radio causing cancer, 45; scarlet fever siege of 1929, 65; strychnine poisoning, 143; tuberculosis, 14, 16, 19, 24–25; U.S. life expectancy, 14, 192, 211; vaccines, 14

Hellerud (Grandma), 159

Hellerud, Harvey, *110*; children, 126–27, 236; courtship and marriage, 106, 108–12; dissatisfaction with farming, 205–6, 210, 231–34; farming at Center City, 112, 126; farming the Bateman place, 154, 159; purchase of Cylon farm, 130–32; purchase of the Ulrich place, 227–28; purchase/sale of Balsam Lake farm, 171–72, 226–28; retirement from farming, 237; wedding anniversary, 205; Williamson family tree, viii

Hellerud, Helen Williamson (wife of Harvey). *See* Williamson, Helen

Hellerud, Margaret Ann ("Peggy"), *193*; birth, 125–27; character and personality, 169–70; going to school, 189–90, 202, 218, 221; help with chores, 152, 199, 208, 216, 226, 228, 233; strychnine poisoning, 143; three years of age, 159; two years of age, 135; Williamson family tree, viii

Hellerud, Priscilla Elaine, viii, 215–16, 218

Hellerud, Susan and Sara, *193, 239*;

The Crops Look Good was designed and set in type by Judy Gilats in St. Paul, Minnesota. The text face is Arno Pro Caption and the display face is Apres. The book was printed by Versa Press in East Peoria, Illinois.